Sylvia Pankhurst

Sylvia Pankhurst

A Crusading Life · 1882–1960

Shirley Harrison

AURUM PRESS

First published in Great Britain
2003 by Aurum Press Ltd
25 Bedford Avenue, London WC1B 3AT

Design by James Campus

A catalogue record for this book
is available from the British Library.

ISBN 1 85410 905 7

1 3 5 7 9 10 8 6 4 2
2003 2005 2007 2006 2004

Typeset by M Rules
Printed in Great Britain by MPG Books Ltd, Bodmin

The author and publishers are grateful to the following for permission to reproduce illustrations used in this book:

International Instituut voor Sociale Geschiednis, Amsterdam: Dr Richard Pankhurst; Sylvia, Emmeline and Adela in 1890; Sylvia in 1896; Sylvia in 1904; Sylvia with Norah Smyth and Zelie Emerson; poster 'Aren't they worth defending?'; Sylvia with baby Richard; Campaigning for Ethiopian independence; Sylvia with Emperor Haile Selassie; *New Times and Ethiopia News*. The Museum of London: Sylvia in 1910; making banners for the Women's Exhibition; force-feeding illustration from the *Daily Sketch*; Sylvia addressing East Enders: Emmeline Pankhurst; Christabel Pankhurst; the Cost Price Restaurant (all copyright © The Museum of London). Mary Evans Picture Library: Annie Kenney; Charlotte Despard; Elizabeth Wolstenholme; Flora Drummond; Teresa Billington-Grieg; Emmeline and Frederick Pethick-Lawrence; Harry Pankhurst; Sylvia's designs for the Skating Rink Exhibition. East Ayrshire Library Registration and Information Services: Keir Hardie with George Bernard Shaw; Nevill's Court. Marx Memorial Library: George Lansbury; Sylvia with Willie Gallacher. Tower Hamlets Local History Library and Archive: the Toy Factory. London Borough of Redbridge: the Red Cottage. Arcadiu Petrescu: Sylvia and Corio with the Petrescu family. Dr Richard Pankhurst: message on Romanian holiday snap; Sylvia in Ethiopia; the Pankhurst family.

Contents

Acknowledgements

To Doreen Montgomery, my 'special agent' for over thirty years. Without her confident encouragement, the story of Sylvia Pankhurst's courageous turbulent life would not have been told.

To friend and colleague Sally Evemy, whose good-humoured, patient 'nit-picking' attention to detail has kept me on course as we attempted to sift our way through sometimes unassailable paper mountains of Sylvia's own writings and an unusually rich archive of those who knew her.

The time and energy that so many people have shared with us is a reflection of their warmth for Sylvia's memory and their appreciation of her unique contribution to history. I hope we have forgotten no one, for we are grateful to them all.

The Pankhurst family – Dr Rita and Dr Richard Pankhurst, Dr Helen Pankhurst and Dr Alula Pankhurst. Mieke Izermans at the IISG, for help and accommodation during our stay. Susan Hogan, Adela Pankhurst's daughter. Sylvia Ayling for putting me on the right road. Josephine Boyle for her knowledge of Woodford. Leslie Powter for sharing his childhood memories. The archivists at St Aubyns, Chigwell and Bancroft's Schools. Sandie O'Connor of the Essex Art Club. Billie Figg for acting as a link in the chain. Tudor Allen and the staff of the Redbridge Library Local Studies. Basil Taylor for lending us his diary. John Lawenson fo help with Keir Hardie. Dr Arcadiu Petrescu for his memories.

The National Federation of Women's Institutes. The Museum of Labour History, Manchester. The Ethiopian Embassy. The Novosti Press Agency. The Pankhurst Centre, Manchester. Tish Collins and the staff at Marx Memorial Library, London. Historical Manuscripts Commission. Gail Cameron of the Women's Library. The staff at the Museum of London.

The Rt Hon. Tony Benn. The Rt Hon. Michael Foot. The late Baroness Castle. C.T. Isolani CBE LVO, Norah Smyth's nephew. Maureen Nield for her knowledge of Norah Smyth. Molly Cook for her enthusiastic introduction to

Sylvia's paintings. Professor Ullendorff, Professor Emeritus of Semitic languages at the School of Oriental and African Studies, London, and Dr Catherine Hamlin of the Fistula Hospital, Addis Ababa, for time on the telephone. Geoffrey and Jill Last, Sir Dennis and Lady Wright and John Gardner, for their hospitality and memories of Sylvia in Ethiopia. Barbara Winslow, Assistant Professor History, Medgar Evans College, City University, London. Joanna Durham, Amy Browning's niece. Simon Houfe for sending excerpts from Sir Alfred Richardson's memoirs. Ingleby Kernahan for his enthusiastic help on the life of Richard Pankhurst. Eric Pankhurst for his work on the family tree. Richard Hardy Smith, bookseller in Wadhurst, Sussex, for his introduction to the Anglo-Ethiopian Society. Adrienne Hack of the Anglo-Ethiopian Society. Mr J.A. Flower of Penshurst. Marie Bird, President of the Woodford Bridge Townswomen's Guild. Professor Joe White, University of Pittsburgh. Nancy Buckland, Jackson Library, Michigan, USA. Giles Peppiatt, Bonhams Auctioneers. The Staff at Fairfield House, Bristol. Irene Cockcroft, Soroptomist International of Greater London. Megan Dobney of the Pankhurst Memorial Committee. The Random House Group Ltd for permission to quote from Caroline Benn's *Keir Hardie*, originally published by Hutchinson.

Introduction: Who is Sylvia?

'When I muse alone under the old trees of Epping Forest, or watch my young hopeful playing in the short grass, finding the new-old treasures that we as children loved; as I pass through the sad, seer streets, the dreary wastes of crowded little houses, same in their ugliness, and among the pale and shabby throngs of the East End . . . as I view the great shops and the flashing equipages of Piccadilly, or tread the stately, ordered precincts of Parliament Square, memories, vivid and turgid, crowd upon me . . . imparting their influences to the experiences of today . . .'

Sylvia Pankhurst, 1931[1]

On a hot summer day in July 1956[2] an elderly lady sat, with her white Persian cat comfortably secure in his travelling basket, waiting for a taxi. At her Edwardian home in Woodford Green, Essex, she was surrounded by tea chests stuffed to overflowing with the records of a turbulent, courageous life, telling not only the story of her part in women's struggle for the vote and of her suffering in prison, but also of the rise of Communism and her fight against Fascism. There were parliamentary papers and intimate poetry, packed between the paintings and letters of her youth.

The furniture was ready for auction and the house echoed with the voices of famous ghosts from the twentieth century: the Labour party icon and her long-time love Keir Hardie, Lenin, Winston Churchill, George Bernard Shaw, Herbert Asquith and David Lloyd George were a part of her world. She had tangled with them all.

Few of those shopping in Puddicombe's old-fashioned drapery store, across the road in The Broadway, were aware that they were about to lose their most notorious resident. The local newspaper, the *Woodford Times*, headlined

1. Sylvia Pankhurst, *The Suffragette Movement*, Longman, 1931. Republished Virago, 1977.
2. *Woodford Times*, 10 July 1956.

instead an outbreak of dysentery and the last 'old timers' dance of the season – Danny Kaye was showing at the local cinema. This was Winston Churchill's constituency: respectable, reactionary Woodford, the archetypal suburb, headquarters of one of the oldest cricket clubs and the largest Young Conservative Association in Britain.

For over thirty years Woodford Green had also been the unlikely home of someone whose name remains, even today, synonymous with shocking images of women chained to railings, suffering the torture of force-feeding, burning buildings and hurling bricks through windows.

The name is Pankhurst.

She was Sylvia, second daughter of Emmeline, in 1903 founder of the Women's Social and Political Union (known later as the Suffragettes). Yet when the vote was finally won, while her mother and beautiful elder sister Christabel vanished from the public eye, Sylvia's fight had only just begun. For her the franchise was only the first of many, passionate worldwide campaigns to help the oppressed and under-privileged, regardless of race, class or gender.

Sylvia had arrived in Woodford in 1924 with an Italian socialist revolutionary, Silvio Corio. Scandalously, they lived together in a ramshackle cottage on Woodford Green, where they ran a teashop for bus drivers and trippers from the East End of London. In 1927, when she was 45, news of the birth of their son, Richard, was splashed in newspapers around the world.

During most of her time in Woodford, Sylvia was seldom involved with local affairs. Residents grumbling mildly about the jungle growth of her garden were sometimes hissed at by the white Persian cat. They were mostly unaware of her role as an *enfant terrible* on the world stage, a renegade, a rebel, a woman who had relentlessly handbagged the leaders and governments of many countries. They did not know what an extraordinarily rich archive of twentieth-century history had been crammed into the cupboards, drawers and shelves of her home in Charteris Road.

Former Labour MP the late Baroness (Barbara) Castle (1910–2002), said of her:

> Sylvia was one of the great influences of my life. Sylvia . . . never allowed the
> issue of 'Votes for Women' to dominate her. She believed, passionately, in the
> context of the current politics, that all citizens, including women, should be
> included in the international fight for justice – and that you should not isolate
> one little section of that fight. She had enormous physical and political

courage … Unlike Christabel, Sylvia experienced the gamut of normal feminine emotions and her writing reflects real understanding of all the people who were part of her world.'[3]

George Bernard Shaw once compared Sylvia to Joan of Arc: 'She lectured, talked, won and over-ruled statesmen and prelates. She pooh-poohed the plans of generals leading their troops to victory . . . she had unbounded and quite unconcealed contempt for official opinion, judgement and authority . . . there were only two opinions about her. One was that she was miraculous. The other that she was unbearable.'

Wherever she saw injustice she was there, hotfoot, sometimes travelling rough in cargo boats or walking alone across the Alps; she visited Italy, Scandinavia and later Romania, the United States and Russia. Her literary energy was phenomenal, covering amongst other subjects nutrition for children, the value of goats' milk, caring for mothers, prison conditions, vegetarianism, Indian Independence and social deprivation in America.

And now Sylvia was leaving Woodford. The 'sold' board in the garden confirmed the fact. Silvio had died and Richard, soon to be a University professor in Ethiopia, was helping her to pack. There was nothing to hold her. The Emperor Haile Selassie, Elect of God, Conquering Lion of the Tribes of Judah, King of Zion, King of Kings, Emperor of Ethiopia, Chevalier sans Peur et Sans Reproche and Epitome of True Nobility, had offered Sylvia a home in Addis Ababa in gratitude for her long, dedicated contribution to Ethiopian Liberation from Italy.

'Wherever there is a need, there is my country' had always been her philosophy, and she was eager for the new challenge. It was time to pack away the memories. Time to move on.

3. Barbara Castle to the author.

1

The Pankhursts

'Englishwomen have always held a prominent place in English life. Without direct political power they have unbounded personal influence and by that influence they have greatly helped to form the national character. A breath of the strong, old Norse life, still lingers about them and makes them emphatically the fit companions and worthy mothers of men.'

Woman Magazine, 3 January 1890

On 18 December 1879 the beautiful, wayward 21-year-old Emmeline Goulden walked down the aisle of St Luke's Church in Eccles, Lancashire, to marry her 44-year-old sweetheart. The erudite, radical Dr Richard Marsden Pankhurst's courtship of his bride had been a passionate, whirlwind affair, and she was even accused by her mother of throwing herself at her suitor.

Richard Pankhurst had had an impressive start to his professional life. Born, it is believed, in 1835, to a Liberal, Baptist family, he moved with his parents from Stoke-on-Trent to radical Manchester in 1847. He was a brilliant scholar, graduating at Manchester University, a Gold Medallist and Doctor of Laws at London University. He was called to the Bar at Lincoln's Inn, London, in 1867.

The Gouldens were a spirited, politically lively family. Emmeline's father, Robert, was a self-made manufacturer; her mother, Jane Quine, came from the Isle of Man. Emmeline was the first of the Gouldens' ten children. At the impressionable age of fourteen she had been sent to the Normal École in Paris and developed a love affair with France that was to last throughout her life. There she became best friends with Noemie, daughter of Henri Rochefort, who had been instrumental in the establishment of the Paris Commune in 1871 after the overthrow of Napoleon III. Emmeline had returned to England in 1878, politically eager and youthfully restless but, like many middle-class women, frustrated by the lack of career openings. Marriage to such a successful man offered the opportunity she longed for.

The wedding itself was, necessarily, a low-key affair. Dr Pankhurst's parents, with whom he had lived, had recently died, and a full-scale white wedding was inappropriate. Neither was it wanted. Instead, Emmeline wore a brown velvet gown from Kendall Milne's department store. Even at this stage she had showed signs of a rebellious streak by shockingly suggesting that they should not get married at all but merely live together – she argued that this would demonstrate their own independent spirit. With uncharacteristic caution, Richard persuaded his bride-to-be that such unconventional behaviour would endanger her reputation and could jeopardize any chance they might have of achieving their goals. Through him she gained additional maturity and the self-assurance that was to stand her in good stead for the high profile life ahead.

Agitation was in full swing for a new, more radical Married Woman's Property Act, and Richard was drafting the Bill that would form the basis for the Act of 1882. Since the first Act in 1870, which had permitted a married woman to keep her earnings, Richard had supported the fight to win for her in addition rights of redress, against fraud, libel and assault, a right to property she had owned before or acquired after marriage and to the care and control of her children.

Emmeline's family hoped that she would steer her new husband sensibly towards the legal heights they felt he could accomplish. But no. Excited by the political cut and thrust, she longed to play her part by her husband's side, helping him to achieve what she felt was his deserved seat in Parliament. To the ambitious girl, Dr Pankhurst was a heroic figure, sacrificing himself for the greater good and, in particular, dedicating himself to the escalating demand for the rights of women.

In Britain there had always been a scattering of powerful women who exercised a certain political influence: the formidable Abbesses of the Middle Ages or wealthy landowning aristocrats like the Tudor Bess of Hardwick. In general, for centuries life for everyone, men and women, was based on a rural economy and organized locally. The concept of national democracy was unknown.

Gradually through the seventeenth and eighteenth centuries the spread of industry brought increased social and economic divisions. A new, educated, literate middle-class emerged, with professional ambitions. Alongside came the first flutterings of female protest for fair play – and with fair play, the vote.

A few lone voices had spoken out; the rebellious young Mary Wollstonecraft (1759–1797), energetic reformer and prolific writer, was mocked by Hugh Walpole as 'the hyena in petticoats'. Yet her writings influenced such great thinkers as John Stuart Mill, and her groundbreaking *Vindication of the Rights of Women* (1792) can be seen as a first blow in the struggle for change. But there was no orchestrated action.

Back in 1825 the first true statement of the case for female franchise had been made, ironically, by a man. The freethinking philosopher William Thompson (1775–1833) was spurred on by his friend, the equally unconventional Mrs Wheeler, great-grandmother of Lady Constance Lytton (who was herself to play a pivotal role in the twentieth-century heyday of the women's suffrage movement). With her help, Thompson published a book entitled *An appeal of one half of the human race, Women, against the pretensions of the other half, Men, to retain them in political, and thence in civil and domestic slavery.* It was rousing stuff: 'When will you, the most oppressed and degraded of the human race – for no vice, for no crime, degraded and oppressed – see your wrongs, commune about them, break in upon the leaden slumbers of your masters, and remonstrate and petition for their removal?' But it failed to rouse most women. Their time had not yet come.

As a result of the Great Reform Act in 1832, parliamentary seats were more fairly distributed, but although female suffrage was debated for the first time in Parliament and the right to vote was extended, it was still confined to male persons only. A protest petition, organized by wealthy Miss Mary Smith, who lived far away in the East Riding of Yorkshire, proposed that 'every unmarried female possessing the necessary pecuniary qualification, should be allowed to vote'. She argued that since she paid taxes, she should be allowed to choose her parliamentary representative. There were hundreds of Mary Smiths around the country: widows and spinsters who devoted much of their fortunes to good works, including, eventually in the time of the Pankhursts, to that of votes for women.

When Queen Victoria came to the throne in 1837, at the age of 18, married women could not own property, had no legal control of their children and middle-class women were not expected to work. The universities were not open to them and the only respectably acceptable professions were those of writing, or perhaps, like Charlotte Brontë's Jane Eyre, of governess. Women in the lower classes went into service or shopkeeping or laboured in factories while rearing enormous families. Many became prostitutes. None had any overt influence over the legislators in Parliament, nor for the most part did they demand it.

Sadly, the accession of a woman to the throne did nothing to help. Queen Victoria remained relentlessly opposed to female franchise throughout her life.

There is a letter dated 6 May 1870 in the Royal Archives at Windsor, to Mr Gladstone, in which she says:

> . . . The Queen is a woman herself and knows what an anomaly her own position is – but that can be reconciled with reason and propriety, tho' it is a terrible, difficult and trying one. But to tear away all the barriers which surround a woman and to propose that they should study with men – things which could not be named before them – certainly not . . . let women be what God intended – helpmates to man – but with totally different duties . . .[1]

The stimulus that was finally to awaken interest and curiosity and create the climate for change was brought about to a large extent by the development of the women's magazine and its means of distribution.

In 1848 bookseller W.H. Smith[2] had opened the first railway station bookshop, at Euston in London, so that 'all who ride may read', offering undreamed of access to knowledge and information for the middle-classes and facilitating the mass production of tailor-made ladies' magazines. At last they had a vehicle through which to explore and voice their wishes. The working-class woman, however, could not afford this luxury.

Mrs Isabella Beeton (1836–1865) is largely associated with her classic book *Household Management*. It is less well known that Isabella, eldest of twenty-two children, was married at the age of 19 to a young entrepreneur, Samuel Beeton. She was only 28 when she died. Sam Beeton launched the *Englishwoman's Domestic Magazine* in 1852. They were a powerful, professional partnership, commuting daily to Fleet Street from their home in Pinner, Middlesex. Together they ran what became the most successful and often controversial women's journal in Europe. It was at one time banned from the shelves of the British Museum Reading Room for its open championship of a lady's right to abandon the wearing of corsets: the equivalent of bra-burning in the 1960s!

Slowly, a few determined crusaders were beginning to blaze a quiet trail towards a better standard of life for all women. The work of Florence Nightingale in the Crimea in 1856 won the respect of the nation and transformed the status of nurses, although even she did not like the idea of

---

1. Royal Archives, Windsor, L13 A39 no.88.
2. W.H. Smith (1825–1891) was the grandson of Henry de William Smith who founded the company in 1792. William Henry II became MP for Westminster in 1868, First Lord of the Admiralty in 1877 and Lord Warden of the Cinq Ports in 1891.

women doctors. The Victorian period produced many remarkable women whose abilities focused on intellectual rather than electoral reform and who were all the more notable for their achievements against the odds.

The Victorians loved meetings, and women now began to band together in groups and societies. The Kensington Society in London was started in 1865 for ladies of 'above the average in thoughtfulness and intelligence'. Discussions did not deal exclusively with the franchise, but speakers on the subject were invited. Among its gifted members were Emily Davies, who founded Girton College for women only in 1869; Frances Buss, founder of the North London Collegiate School for Girls in 1850; and Elizabeth Garrett (later Dr Garrett Anderson). Together, the ladies of the Kensington Society were to provide a launching pad for the suffrage movement. They were peaceful, pioneer feminists, known as suffragists.

June 1866 brought the Conservatives to power, led by the Earl of Derby, with Disraeli as Chancellor. In April 1866, while in opposition, Disraeli had commented, 'where a woman may by law be a churchwarden or an overseer of the poor I do not see reasons, if you come to right, she has no right to vote'. The Ladies of the Kensington Society seized this opportunity to ask John Stuart Mill, MP for Westminster, converted to the cause by his late wife Harriet Taylor, 'a woman of force and genius', to take a petition signed by 1600 women before Parliament. They asked for the enfranchisement of 'all householders, without distinction of sex, who possess such property or rental qualification as your Honourable House may determine'. He presented it on 7 June but Parliament was prorogued on 10 August for the rest of 1866 and the matter was forgotten.

Among those who heard later about the petition was Lydia Ernestine Becker. Lydia Becker was the daughter of a German father and a Lancashire mother. With her hair scraped back and her steely eyes grimly peering over narrow spectacles, she became the first major figurehead for the suffrage movement and, according to historian Roger Fulford, author of *Votes for Women*,[3] she 'will receive the applauses of posterity'.

In October 1866 Lydia Becker attended the annual meeting of the National Association for the Advancement of Social Science, in the Assembly Room of the Free Trade Hall, Manchester. The talk, by a member of the Kensington Society, was on women's suffrage. Lydia was galvanized and in January 1867 she formed the Manchester Women's Suffrage Committee, the first of its kind in Britain. There she was joined by Elizabeth Wolstenholme-Elmy

---

3. Roger Fulford, *Votes for Women*, Faber and Faber, 1956.

(1834–1918), described later by Sylvia Pankhurst as a 'tiny Jenny wren of a woman'. Her 'bobbing ringlets' and youthful effervescence later became a feature of Suffragette photographs in the militant days of the early twentieth century, by which time she was elderly. She, too, deserves far greater recognition than she has been given.

On 20 May 1867 John Stuart Mill stood up in Parliament to move an amendment to The Representation of the People Bill (the Reform Act). He said, 'we do not sufficiently attend to the fact that there has taken place around us a silent and domestic revolution: women and men are, for the first time in history, really each other's companions . . . the two sexes must rise or sink together'. The amendment was defeated, but this Reform Act of 1867 extended the franchise to make a total electorate of 2 million men.

Undaunted by the defeat, Lydia Becker spotted that one of the names on the electoral register of those entitled to vote in a Manchester by-election at the end of 1867 was 'Maxwell', a kitchen crockery shopkeeper. But Maxwell was a woman – Lily – and her appearance on the register was a mistake. It was considered indecorous for 'ladies' to become involved in politics but, undeterred, Miss Becker walked Lily Maxwell into the history books when she took her to cast her vote for the Liberal candidate, Jacob Bright. He was to become a fervent supporter of female franchise.

It was then that Dr Richard Pankhurst erupted onto the political stage.

Prompted by Lydia Becker, a large number of women applied for inclusion in the Parliamentary register being prepared for the 1868 General Election. The majority were struck off. An appeal was launched in the High Court and young Richard Marsden Pankhurst was the junior counsel in the unsuccessful presentation of the case.

Over the next ten years many private members' bills were introduced and then talked out. Queen Victoria was determined in her opposition. In 1872 she wrote the now famous letter to Theodore Martin:

> The Queen is most anxious to enlist someone who can speak and write etc checking this mad wicked folly of women's rights . . . It is a subject which makes the Queen so furious that she can't contain herself. God created Man and Woman different – & let each remain on their position.[4]

Despite all the hard work, it seemed that very little visible progress had been made since Mary Wollstonecraft. The new partnership of the Pankhursts, and

---

4. Sir Theodore Martin, *Queen Victoria As I Knew Her*, William Blackwood, 1901.

eventually their children, was to provide the necessary and spectacular catalyst for change.

Estelle Sylvia Pankhurst was born in 1882. Her sister, Christabel Harriet, had been born in 1880. Their formative years were to be shaped not by childish toys or games, but by the growth of the socialist movement.

2

The First Pillar

'Our father, vilified and boycotted yet beloved by a multitude of people in many walks of life, was a standard bearer of every forlorn hope, every unpopular yet worthy cause then conceived for the uplifting of oppressed and suffering humanity . . . His struggle was the background of our lives and his influence, enduring long after his death, the strongest determining factor. "If you do not work for other people you will not have been worth the upbringing." Almost daily he exhorted us!'

Sylvia Pankhurst, *The Suffragette Movement*

Dr Richard Pankhurst's controversial and outspoken views were always in the news, and his reforming zeal had by now overtaken his work as a barrister. He was one of the best known personalities in Manchester. With his pointed red beard and high-pitched voice, he spoke out on art, science, education and politics at every civic function and was a vociferous member of the Manchester Liberal Party.

His legal knowledge was, at least according to Sylvia for whom he could do no wrong, 'unsurpassed'. He used it not in practice as a barrister, but for effecting change. The author of many important papers, he argued for a Court of Criminal Appeal and believed that the treatment of the law-breaker should be designed to reform rather than to punish. He stood for free, secular education and public control of schools, and was responsible for reform of the Patent Laws.

But his political and religious views brought him the greatest notoriety. He was a rebel, playing a prominent part in the growth of Socialism and the eventual birth of the Independent Labour Party. Sylvia said he was 'a communist . . . in the broad sense which would cover William Morris, Peter Kropotkin and Keir Hardie . . . not in the narrow sense of the word, after the Russian Revolution'. He urged the reform of the House of Lords, he labelled the clergy 'monstrous beadledum', and he warned his children, 'if you ever return to religion you will not have been worth the bringing up'.

A pacifist and a republican, he also supported nationalization of land. Worst of all for his own political prospects, he unwisely spoke at a meeting in Rhyll, attended by Liberal leader William Ewart Gladstone. Knowing that Gladstone was searching for bright young talent, Dr Pankhurst's choice of subject was unfortunate: he proposed universal suffrage and the reform of the Liberal party. This, combined with his agnosticism, was the end of any real hope of being adopted as a Liberal parliamentary candidate. In addition he found it increasingly difficult to practise at the bar, since every time he spoke out he lost clients. No wonder, as Sylvia said, 'office was always refused him; honour never'.

Politically the 1880s were an exciting yet a terrible time. The writings of Karl Marx, who had lived in London since 1849, were beginning to have influence. He and Friedrich Engels, whose Manchester family cotton mill supported the impoverished Marx, met regularly at Engels'[1] house in Regents' Park Road, which had become a focus for socialists the world over. The two friends collaborated on Marx's mammoth and best-known work *Das Kapital*, the first volume being published in 1867.

As Britain's manufacturing monopoly was being broken in the 1880s by foreign competition, the working classes faced more and more unemployment. It is hardly surprising that 'The Woman Question' remained unresolved. Only the Isle of Man broke free. The island is a Crown Dependency with its own Governor and equivalent to the Houses of Parliament. It imposes its own taxes and makes its own laws. On 5 January 1881 the hitherto implacable Queen Victoria had to give the Royal Assent for female franchise. The Isle of Man – home of Emmeline's mother – became, appropriately, the first part of Britain to give the vote to women.

In 1884 Dr Pankhurst joined the newly formed, somewhat eccentric, socialist Fabian Society,[2] which stood for gradual change rather than revolution. He was in his element, mingling and debating with such mighty, and sometimes capricious, minds as those of George Bernard Shaw and H.G. Wells; Sydney and Beatrice Webb were there, as was Annie Besant, daughter of a vicar, in her shocking short skirts and red beret, campaigning for the unemployed workers of the East End of London.

That year Dr Pankhurst decided to resign from the Liberal Party in order to stand as an Independent in a Manchester by-election. He supported Home Rule for Ireland and he forecast the eventual coming of a United States of

1. Frederich Engels, 1820–1895. In 1848 he wrote the *Communist Manifesto* with Marx.
2. The society was named after Fabius Maximus, a Roman general whose military successes were the result of cautious, patient tactics.

Europe. It was all too much for the electorate, and even the once-admiring Lydia Becker called him a 'firebrand'. He lost to a huge Conservative majority but was immediately in demand on the public speaking circuit.

In 1884 in the midst of all this political activity, the Pankhursts' son, Francis Henry (Frank), was born, followed in 1885 by another daughter, Adela Constantia.

In the 1885 campaign Dr Pankhurst stood as an Independent in Rotherhithe, in London's Docklands, campaigning with Emmeline at his side, from a soap box brought along for the occasion. It was here that he was met and encouraged by the East End champion George Lansbury,[3] future leader of the Labour Party and later to become a dedicated friend to Sylvia. Once again Dr Pankhurst lost, and his opponent sneered to his supporters, 'next time you bring out a candidate bring out a gentleman and not a slum politican'.

All this furore was still beyond the understanding of the Pankhurst toddlers, although by the time she was ten, Sylvia had precociously declared herself a republican and knew she was 'on the side of the People and the Poor'.

Times were financially difficult and losing elections was an expensive business, so the family moved, first to share the home of Emmeline's parents and then to Green Hayes, Old Trafford. Sylvia paints a picture of her earliest childhood in this house, 'from the pinnacle of adult wisdom' in her book *The Suffragette Movement*. Her admittedly hazy memories were characteristically but genuinely romantic. Rather like a sentimentally lace-framed Victorian birthday card, they are gently coloured, wide-eyed and innocent. She was, and continued to be, a mistress of the purple passage – often to great effect but sometimes exaggerated, especially in matters relating to her father. He could do no wrong, whereas Sylvia's longing for her mother's love and attention was never met and probably accounts for some of the emotional pain and loneliness she suffered and which are often reflected in the pages of her books. It is not anger she expresses but regret. 'Green Hayes: the very name seems caressing. In its garden were borders of London Pride, the starry little pink flowerets, wonderfully beautiful amid the black soot of Manchester; like fairy flowers I thought them.' From the nursery window the children watched their father leave for work in the morning: 'wonderful father; the lode star of our lives'. The man with the beautifully shaped head, soft silver hair and fingernails, 'like no others I have seen', curling splendidly over the tips of his fingers.

3. George Lansbury (1859–1940) was the editor of London's *Daily Herald* 1919–22 and an MP 1910–12 and 1922. As a pacifist and socialist in London's East End, he became Labour Party leader 1932–35.

Throughout their childhood, when he returned home in the evening he would bring a book to read aloud: it was serious stuff – simple science, history, travel, engineering – and all formed the diet of their early years. He also introduced the children to the works of Walter Crane, director of the Manchester School of Design, friend of William Morris and a pre-Raphaelite, who believed that art, politics and religion were intertwined. Sylvia was particularly influenced by both his books and his paintings.

From the cradle Sylvia felt a sense of destiny and duty that seemed to fire rather than frighten her. Not so Adela, who, like so many younger children, felt sidelined by her older sisters. Adela's childhood memories were revealed years later in an explosively bitter, angry attack on Sylvia after the publication of *The Suffragette Movement* in 1931. By then the sisters were living 4000 miles apart and had not seen each other for almost twenty years. Tragically, Adela carried throughout most of her life the deep, terrible, unresolved and festering jealousies of childhood, although in old age the pain seems to have softened.

It is hard to reconcile the two pictures of that Pankhurst childhood in the 1880s: it was largely to her father and Sylvia, rather than to her mother or Christabel, that Adela attributed her own childhood misery. Not for her the rose-tinted spectacles or sentimental nostalgia. 'I was the fourth child, and my coming resented. No proper care was taken nor preparation made. I was only a few weeks old when my mother went to London to assist in my father's election,' Adela recalled when grown up. She claimed that Sylvia,

> dominated the family because she had a supreme self-love and a tenacity of purpose greater than belongs to most people . . . My father treated his elder daughters as if they were grown up when they were only little children. He gave them an exaggerated idea of their own importance and made them intensely self-conscious . . . Sylvia with her long face and in the sharp shrill voice was a fearful 'tell-tale'.

Of her father she wrote:

> To what a treadmill he condemned us helpless, hopeless children and his poor wife with her gaiety, her beauty. 'Working for others' was interpreted to mean of course, adopting his political and religious views and sacrificing everything to them . . . the children counted for nothing at all beside the cause . . .
>
> We lived too much together and within ourselves to be healthy-minded and brooded over troubles that children in more healthy surroundings would have forgotten in five minutes.

That 'brooding' seems to have become a part of her grown-up personality. She blamed her 'autocratic and jealous' elder sister Sylvia for causing trouble between her and her mother, for neglecting her 'hapless' siblings and for sponging on family funds.

Sylvia acknowledged that Adela always seemed 'a child apart'. Slightly crippled as a baby, she had been cosseted by grown-up visitors and relatives but largely ignored by both parents and siblings. That isolation was not of Adela's making or desire, yet, unlike Sylvia, Adela absolved her mother of any blame. 'My mother was neglectful from a mistaken sense of public duty and not from mere indifference . . . she had to choose between private and public duty, between her natural instincts as a woman and a mother and the rigid ideal of duty imposed on her in her young and impressionable days by my father . . . I . . . was terrified of him.'

Adela became a solitary child, creating and acting out dramas, playing all the parts and, to the delight of visitors, entertaining them with her performances or reading them made-up stories, until her sisters teased her efforts and she took to wandering off lonely and miserable. Miserable she may have been, but the truth is that Adela was born with the Pankhursts' stubborn, wayward, independent spirit, and once they were grown up, the three girls abandoned all pretence of family unity.

Sylvia herself was at first apparently content in a private world of painting and drawing. When she was a little older she was taken, as a treat, by her parents to her first political meeting in a dingy hall – made more entertaining when her mother made a hurried exit, caused by the discovery of a bug on her glove.

After the debacle of the 1885 Rotherhithe election, Emmeline discovered, to her distress, that a settlement she had expected from her father was not to be forthcoming. There was a feud with the Gouldens that was never healed and so, anxious to escape from Manchester, Emmeline persuaded her husband that London would provide a better base for his political future.

In 1887 the children found themselves uprooted and living in the capital. Determined to play her part, Emmeline decided to open a shop in an effort to boost family funds. They rented premises and lived above the shop at 165 Hampstead Road, noisy with the clatter and clamour of market stalls and traders. The business was called Emerson and Company, selling artistic household items, William Morris fabrics, painted milking stools and enamelled plates and jugs.

The enterprise was a disaster. Despite the estate agent's assurance that this was a 'rising neighbourhood', it was certainly not ready for such a classy venture. Much of the stock had to be disposed of – sometimes to the children's nursery and, that Christmas of 1887, with cruel lack of understanding, into the girls' stockings. An oblong box covered in red plush lay on the end of each of the two elder girls' beds; Sylvia was convinced that hers contained the violin, 'that heart-disturbing, heart-enchanting voice' she had recently heard and longed to master. But the box was empty and she could not hold back her tears. It was, in fact, from Emerson surplus stock. How was a five-year-old to understand her parents' financial struggles or that her mother could not 'bring herself to spend money on mere Christmas presents'?

At this tender age the books that were read to Sylvia included Dickens, which gave her horrible dreams or sleepless nights; she was particularly distressed by the miseries described in *Oliver Twist*. As an adult she was unable to read such books: 'There is too much of suffering in the actual world appealing to me and all who will, for aid, too much of tragedy.' They bred in her a child-like and somewhat unrealistic longing for a Golden Age, which she never lost. She was constantly drawing but her pictures were escapist – to a dream world of happiness and beauty. This was when she was at her most content. 'Visions lovelier than any on land or sea passed before my eyes.'

Later, when she was eight, she and Christabel loved to read William Stead's *Review of Reviews* – a very grown-up journal, full of serious articles. One about the brain frightened the introspective Sylvia because it claimed that 'by the age of ten the brain is fully formed'. She thought that this meant she had only two years in which to learn everything she wanted to know. The confident Christabel was, by contrast, excited by the realization that since she was already ten, she knew all she needed and could therefore do anything she wanted!

There was music in the house and songs around the piano, and Sylvia still ached for that violin, which, when one was eventually bought for her, was tucked away in a cupboard: 'Mother, poor busy mother, would find me a teacher some day.' But she never did, and Sylvia, with almost unnatural understanding, hid her pain and returned to her drawing: 'it was under my control'.

In the autumn of 1887 the *Illustrated London News* had been reporting regular meetings in Trafalgar Square to focus public attention on the condition of the poor. Queen Victoria protested to Gladstone that 'the triumph of socialism' was 'a disgrace to the capital'.[4] The year of 1888 was traumatic and tragic. The East End was unrelentingly sordid, choked with the stench of rotting

4. Caroline Benn, *Keir Hardie*, Hutchinson, 1992.

vegetables, animal corpses and urine. At least 1200 'unfortunates' worked the area, and by the end of the year the newspapers were full of sensational photographs of the five butchered corpses – victims of the killer who came to be known as 'Jack the Ripper'. Those hideous pictures tortured Sylvia. She was not old enough to appreciate the truth of a comment by her father's friend George Bernard Shaw when he described the killer as, 'An independent genius who, by disemboweling five women, managed to rally the newspapers to the side of the oppressed.'[5] These terrible images remained with her and she eventually made the East End the base of her ceaseless efforts to improve life for the poor.

Sadly, the attentions of the Pankhurst family in 1888 were far from the troubles of the East End. In September four-year-old Frank caught diphtheria and died. Faulty drains behind the house were suspected. Dr Pankhurst was in Manchester and Emmeline was distraught. Sylvia overheard her mother confide in an uncle, 'he had much finer eyes than any of these children'. The little girl longed to die instead of her brother. After all, she reasoned, her parents had three girls and Frank was the only boy. They could manage without her. The children were told they must not forget their brother and so she tried to draw a picture of him for her Father, 'but the figure I made was ugly'. The fact that her father encouraged her was, she said, 'like sunshine on my grief frozen spirit'.

A new name now began to appear regularly in the newspapers as a potential political troublemaker. James Keir Hardie, the Scottish Trades Unionist and former miner, arrived in London and almost immediately became a national figure.

James Keir had been born on 15 August 1856 in a small one-roomed cottage in Lanarkshire, Scotland. His father was unknown and he was largely brought up by his grandmother, while for his first three years his mother, Mary Keir, laboured in the turnip fields. A courageous woman from a farming family with a long record of political agitation, she was a tireless worker – characteristics that Hardie himself inherited. In 1859 Mary married David Hardie. The boy assumed his stepfather's name and, by the age of eight, since David Hardie drank too much and was often out of work, James took on the role of breadwinner for the rapidly expanding family.

He became first a messenger and then a baker's boy. He was also expected to help at home. The memories were often painful to recall and later for Sylvia

5. *Star*, 24 September 1888.

to hear. Two days running, when his younger brother was dying and his mother about to give birth, he was late for work. He was summoned before his employer (ironically, a devout churchgoer) who was sitting with his family round a mahogany table laden with food and steaming coffee – and sacked. The baby was born that night, in a house with no fuel or food. Later the family was evicted, and Hardie never forgot standing beside their meagre possessions at the roadside, being told that they could return home only if David Hardie gave up his Trade Union membership, which Mary defiantly refused.

At the age of ten Hardie went down the pit – a three-mile walk away. It was the only work available and he became a 'trapper', operating the trap door that let air into the mine. It was a solitary, eerie job, alone amongst the flickering shadows from his miner's lamp. At the age of 12 he was put to 'drawing' the ponies and developed the passion for animals that lasted all his life. He was particularly fond of a pit pony called Donald and for much of his life carried a battered watch that Donald had chewed.

Hardie remained with the pit until he was 23, by which time he had become a union organizer. During this period his natural intelligence matured and his experience of the reality of working-class life – the self-help ethic, the community loyalties and the bitter injustices – developed the sense of mission that was to motivate his later work. The Trades Union Congress (TUC) had been formed in 1868. The Trades Union Act of 1871 gave unions legal status and enabled them to protect their funds by registering as friendly societies. Trades Unions, the Co-operative Society, Friendly Societies and Funeral Funds became the building blocks of Hardie's adolescence.

Writing on the role of the temperance movement, Caroline Benn says: 'Modern readers tend to regard temperance as quaint or puritanical. Yet it was here where many learned their first political lessons . . . strongly allied to the working class self-help ethic, the pledge brought many advantages . . . temperance societies were not merely campaigning bodies but, like friendly societies, organised sick clubs and funeral funds. Temperance action was socially advanced and gave equal status to children and women.' Hardie had driving ambition but not for himself: he was utterly uninterested in power. He believed that the advance of Socialism did not depend on the actions of a few great men, but on the international co-operation of people with common social and political ideals. He taught himself to read not politics, but history and poetry and, like Sylvia, was greatly influenced by the thoughts of John Ruskin and his philosophy: 'there is no wealth but life'. For a short time Hardie became a Christian and remained a lifelong supporter of the temperance movement – this was his first political cause.

On 3 August 1879 Hardie married Lillie Wilson, according to Kenneth Morgan, 'patient, devoted, endlessly brave, in the face of repeated personal struggles and near tragedies'. The day after their wedding, he went off to a miners' meeting – a foretaste of the future for his new bride. In 1882 Hardie was offered a job as a weekly correspondent for the Cumnock News section of the region's main Liberal newspaper, the *Ardrossan and Saltcoats Herald*. He wrote a somewhat evangelically moral column, 'Mining Notes Worth Minding', under the name of 'Trapper'. He spent the next few years, uneventfully, as an investigative journalist, at this stage showing much more interest in self-help and moral regeneration than in socialism.

Then at the end of 1885 his life was changed by the colourful and eccentric arrival of Don Roberto Bontine Cunninghame-Graham, believed by faithful followers to be the uncrowned King of Scotland and first truly socialist Member of Parliament. He rode into Cumnock on a fine black horse called Pampa, who always travelled with him, by train, to Westminster. (He mounted, without a block, by leaping directly into the saddle).

From the moment they met, he became Hardie's mentor and his firm friend. It was Cunninghame-Graham who inspired and furthered many of Hardie's ideologies: pacifism, environmental passions, anti-racism, the abolition of the House of Lords, capital punishment, dislike of the Liberal party and Lib-Lab pacts, the need for a national Labour Party and, naturally, women's emancipation. He was one of those magnificently unorthodox fringe characters who has, so far, found no place in any book telling the story of the Suffragettes. Yet for the Pankhursts, and for Sylvia in particular, his peripheral but extraordinary presence was immensely significant. It was Cunninghame-Graham who eased Hardie out of Scotland and established a national platform for him.

During 1887 Hardie had agreed to become agent for the Ayrshire Miners' Union, a post which in 1888 took him to London and to that crucial meeting with the Pankhursts.

By November 1888 the Pankhursts were in action again. At the International Workers' Congress, organized by the Trades' Union Congress, they met Keir Hardie for the first time. They met again the following year, during a heatwave, at the second Trades Union Congress in Paris. Emmeline and Dr Pankhurst were there fighting for an eight-hour day, and found they had a great deal in common with Hardie, including, on a personal level, the shared grief of bereavement, for he had recently lost his four-year-old daughter, Sarah.

By this time the family had moved yet again, to a house with larger rooms and more suitable for meetings; therefore, 8 Russell Square was eventually demolished to make way for the Hotel Russell. Emersons was re-opened, first in Berners Street and then in Regent Street, as a more reasonably priced version of Liberty, selling furniture and exotic goods from around the world, with which Emmeline also furnished the house. The first domestic electric light had just been installed in Kensington, but she felt it an extravagance they could not afford and she hated gas, so the house was lit by the rather old-fashioned flickering cosiness of oil.

Although she was a practical Victorian wife, well able to upholster, make curtains and clothe the girls (a talent she did not pass on to Sylvia), Emmeline did not enjoy domesticity and was never a particularly good manager. There were staff to take on such chores. Sylvia was very fond of their nurse, Susannah, who, as was the custom at the time, assumed many of the parenting roles that Emmeline found irksome.

This was an age of fashionable middle and upper class 'Groups', 'Societies' and 'Sets'. The Manchester Pankhursts did not fit comfortably into intellectual London society. In fact, the novelist Rebecca West later claimed that Emmeline was an 'arriviste'. Nevertheless, the house in Russell Square became a hub of radical discussion and debate. Free-thinkers, anarchists, Fabians, atheists and humanitarians gathered at the Pankhurst home, all seeking answers. People such as William Morris, the revolutionary artist and founder of the Socialist League, whose work was to be such an influence during Sylvia's art student years; Malatesta, the Italian anarchist refugee; Dadabhai Naoroji, the first Indian member of the British House of Commons; Tom Mann, the fiery trades unionist; Fabian Annie Besant; and Harriot Stanton Blatch, daughter of the veteran American suffragist Elizabeth Cady Stanton. She had married an Englishman and lived in Basingstoke. Perhaps most memorable of all to the young Sylvia was Louise Michel, a heroine of the Paris Commune, 'a tiny old woman with gleaming eyes' and 'the most wrinkled face you ever saw'. These guests, each in their own way, provided the models for Sylvia's crusading adult years, first as a Suffragette, then as a communist, as an anti-Fascist and a tireless worker for the oppressed worldwide.

In the turmoil of the 1880s conflicting ideas were competing to form the basis of British Socialism. There were splits and divisions, libels and intrigues, muddles and manoeuvres, and all the while the misery of industrial and agricultural workers was increasing.

In many ways, at least for Christabel and Sylvia, this was their happiest time. They were now precociously aware that their parents were involved in matters of great importance and they loved the excitement of entertaining. They arranged the chairs for meetings, printed the notices 'to the tea room', took the collection in little bags and then sat listening while the grown-ups entertained each other before the serious business of the day. They also ran a family newspaper, *Home News*. Their father contributed weighty letters, Christabel wrote reports: 'Mrs Pankhurst looked elegant in a trained velvet gown . . . the Misses Pankhurst wore white crepe dresses with worked yoke and the refreshments were delicious, the strawberries and cream being especially so.' On a different occasion *Home News* recorded:

> Dr Pankhurst said in his speech that if Suffrage was not given to women the result would be terrible. If a body was half of it bound, how was it to be expected it would grow and develop properly . . . Some opponents tried to prove that women were naturally inferior to men, but our girls won degrees and honours at the Universities. Mrs Pankhurst wore a black sort of grenadine with a train from the shoulders and looked very handsome indeed.

Sylvia also wrote a series entitled 'Walks in London', and Adela, then still only six years old, dictated a story about a poor widow with a large family, rescued by a rich benefactor. She was a lively and mischievous little girl who made the grown-ups laugh, a talent that seems to have escaped most of the Pankhursts.

The dynamics of the Pankhurst family were complex. On the surface they presented an apparently model Victorian family. Sylvia's recollection of their life probably is what the visitors saw and doubtless what she experienced at the time. But, in hindsight, beneath the surface, dormant, lay seeds of unbearable tension and conflict.

There was, as yet, no school for the children and so a governess was employed. She gave them no lessons but took them out to the British Museum and other places of educational importance or read them improving literature. They brought home books from the London Library – Sir Walter Scott, George Eliot or Alexandre Dumas. Games were seldom on the agenda; instead they played 'elections', occasionally escaping to enjoy romps in the Square and hiding in the small enclosures at each corner. Their favourite, called the 'Swerdiggy', seemed a place of 'perfect beauty' according to Sylvia, and 'The Froggety' was a hidey hole where she once found a toad.

There was a short-lived attempt to educate themselves when the girls, worried about their ignorance, tried to teach each other. They loved delivering lectures written out in sprawling handwriting, which in Sylvia's case never improved. Subjects were varied, including such topics as 'coal' and 'cats', their audiences patient, captive visitors and relatives. But the initiative came to a stop because they lost heart when Emmeline was critical of their efforts.

The children's diet seems to have been plain in the extreme and may account for Sylvia's total lack of interest in food or knowledge of cooking later. During the week they breakfasted on porridge, like most middle-class Victorian children, in the nursery. But on Sunday, when they joined their parents, bread and butter and milk were also allowed. Discipline was typically strict, although Emmeline once admitted to friends that she had abandoned the idea of beatings because Sylvia always made her afraid she would kill her daughter before she gave way.

Little Frank's death caused the two older girls a great deal of heart searching about God. Sylvia, in particular, was worried because she was sure her parents were good, yet they had not spoken of God to her. Once again, a word from Dr Pankhurst set the child's mind at rest – he reassured her that understanding religion was a question of detached scientific examination. There should be no guilt or moral failure in getting it wrong. 'I saw my father as a lofty embodiment of the human mind.'

On 7 July 1889 a 'new Frank', as Emmeline called him, was born: Henry Francis. Known as Harry, he was present in his cradle when a group of ladies gathered around his mother's bed to form the Women's Franchise League. An early foretaste of parental priorities!

Both the Pankhurst parents were suffering from strain and exhaustion, and when the lease of Russell Square expired in the winter of 1892/3, they agreed it was time to close the shop and return north – first, to the children's delight, to the seaside at Southport, Lancashire, where they were, at last, to go to school. For the first time there was no nursery. They lived and ate with their parents and there was neither compulsory porridge nor accompanied walks. They were free to explore at will and felt very grown up.

As a pupil at Manchester High School for Girls, Sylvia enjoyed her work, made friends for the first time and was a 'most promising pupil'.[6] Adela, it appears, bullied at home and desperately miserable at school, tried to run away wearing an old hand-me-down plaid dress of Sylvia's. But the spirited adventure failed, she was returned to her family and eventually was sent to stay with an aunt in Aberdeen.

From Southport they went for a short time to the bliss of a farm at Disley, near Manchester, where Dr Pankhurst bought them a donkey called Jack, which kicked and reared but provided much amusement. There, much to their

6. Pankhurst Papers.

Sylvia Pankhurst

delight, even their mother joined in blackberrying and haymaking. Back in Manchester their new home was at 4 Buckingham Crescent, Daisy Bank Road, Victoria Park, where the children were able to play in the excitingly wild gardens of some unoccupied houses nearby and Emmeline picked up the reins of her public life.

Dr Richard Pankhurst's lofty socialist principles and unrelenting passion for work would have been a heavy burden for most children to carry: 'Drudge and drill, drudge and drill' was one of his favourite maxims. For Sylvia, Dr Pankhurst was a hero and her guiding light; she responded to, rather than reacted against, his ideals, and dedicated her own life to achieving the same. When she died, the words of his 1884 election address were framed above her bed:

> This is the hour of the people and the poor . . . This is a time of hope for the life of Labour. Old society was based on war, new society rests on work. There must be for every man a man's share in life, through education free and universal, training for work through technical teaching; full citizenship . . . Over the production of wealth preside the laws of nature, but over the distribution of wealth presides the heart of man.

His proud boast was always that, 'my children are the four pillars of my house', and there is no doubt that for the second daughter, who he called affectionately 'Miss Woody Way', he was the first pillar of hers.

– 3 –

An End and a Beginning

'Seen through the intervening years, childhood presents itself as a period of great activity and keen interest, transfigured by high delights, guided by large enthusiasms; but torn at times by the anguish of ethical struggle, and depression descending into agony and despair for trivial failings, of longing for affection, and misery at being misunderstood . . . Yet everywhere was – beauty, light, colour, form . . .'

Sylvia Pankhurst

The winter of 1893 was bitter. In London the Thames froze over and 60,000 people were homeless. In Manchester, Sylvia would join her mother on Saturdays to help with the distribution of food to the poor. Unemployment was spiralling out of control. There was no state insurance, no unemployment benefit and the Boards of Guardians gave no relief to the able-bodied. Dr Pankhurst had organized a relief committee, which attempted to feed at first 1000 and then 2000 people a day. Mrs Pankhurst, who had been elected to the Chorlton Board of Guardians, visited the street markets to canvass stallholders for contributions, and daily she distributed soup and bread to all comers. She was also passionate about the disgraceful conditions of workhouse children, housed with adults in insanitary and totally unsuitable accommodation. But her dreams of rural cottage homes for them were never realized.

Since his return to Manchester, Dr Pankhurst had been a director of the Manchester Ship Canal Company. Despite the cold, to Sylvia's uncontainable pride and excitement, on 1 January 1894 the young Pankhursts were taken with their parents and the directors on board the *Snowdrop*, the first boat to navigate the 23-mile long canal. The *Manchester Guardian* reported on 2 January, 'Any ceremonial, no matter how stately, with which the opening of the Manchester Ship Canal may be celebrated a few months hence will fail to efface from the recollection of those who saw it, the great popular demonstration of yesterday.' Later that year when the weather was more agreeable, Queen Victoria herself attended the official opening ceremony, at which the republican Dr Pankhurst had, somewhat undiplomatically, been invited to give the address – a speech that was apparently translated into several languages.

Keir Hardie's first visit to the Pankhurst house in Manchester deeply affected the intensely serious and emotional adolescent Sylvia. Their home had now become a centre for socialist agitation – and then, one day, Keir Hardie himself came to visit:

> I hurried home from school . . . Seeing the library door ajar, I hastened upstairs to the angle where one could see who was sitting in the big armchair by the fire. There he was: his majestic head surrounded by ample curls going grey and shining with glints of silver and golden brown: his great forehead deeply lined: his eyes, two deep wells of kindness. Like mountain pools with the sun shining through them . . . Sunshine radiated from him. Kneeling on the stairs to watch him I felt that I could have rushed into his arms . . . Like a sturdy oak with its huge trunk seamed and gnarled . . . he seemed to carry with him the spirit of nature in the great open spaces.

He was to become her first love, and her friend.

Meanwhile, in 1891 work had begun in Scotland on the house at Cumnock, which was to become Lillie's pride and joy. Hardie called it Lochnorris. Overlooking the River Lugar, this house became his refuge in times of stress.

In 1892 when Keir Hardie was elected socialist MP for West Ham in East London, there was euphoria in the Pankhurst household. The *Daily Chronicle* reported that his win was 'the first curl of the wave which is issuing from the dim depths of popular life', and Engels wrote, 'the spell which the great Liberal party cast over the English workers for almost half a century, is broken'. Hardie himself was already speaking of an independent Labour Party.

Hardie took his seat in Parliament on 3 August 1892, arriving in a hired wagonette, with a trumpeter playing the 'Marseillaise', and outrageously wearing a check tweed suit, a red scarf around the neck and a deer-stalker hat. No MP had ever done such a thing before. Mr Gladstone himself wore the usual silk top hat and morning coat. At Hardie's side was Frank Smith, a former Salvation Army convert, who was to become his most loyal and devoted friend, always there when needed, with moral and financial support.

The following January, 1893, in Bradford, Hardie with a group of friends founded the Independent Labour Party (ILP), forerunner of the Labour Party, creating a new social fellowship. It was to be an umbrella organization, including women on the same terms as men and encouraging a number of affiliated clubs, trades and councils. Caroline Benn says, 'the new movement was the product of many minds but it had Hardie's stamp'. The Pankhursts were among the first to join. So developed the hugely significant and important friendship that was to shape not only Sylvia's life, but also the growth of the women's movement and the Labour Party.

In May 1895 the new ILP invited Dr Pankhurst to stand in Gorton as its candidate for the general election, and this time the 13-year-old Sylvia was campaigning by his side, with Emmeline collecting subscriptions in her open umbrella. When her father was defeated – by a slim majority – Sylvia was at the count and wept bitterly, for which she was reprimanded by her mother for 'disgracing the family'.

By 1897 Christabel was taking lessons in French, logic and dressmaking. Sylvia was studying with Elias Bancroft, a well-known Manchester artist, and developing an ever-deepening relationship with her brother. He was eight years old, she was fifteen, and since repeated fainting and headaches had kept her away from school, they had had more time together. Harry was a lonely boy, prone to wandering by himself, to find friendship with local builders or workmen, who often took him, protectively, under their wing.

Adela, at the age of 12, was 'more and more unhappy'. She believed that Sylvia hated her, and when she put on adolescent puppy fat, she suffered cruel taunts from other girls as well as from her sisters. 'She is a lump, a lump, a lump' they would cry and, sadly, her remote and preoccupied parents never thought to reassure her that her siblings' behaviour was all a part of normal growing up.

Both Dr Pankhurst and Emmeline were working at fever pitch on their respective local commitments, and although outsiders were unaware of his health problems, Sylvia realized, instinctively, that something was wrong. She had several times seen her father cry out with pain, which he passed off lightly as 'indigestion'. One evening, seeming sad, he took her on his knee and talked about his work. 'Life is valueless without enthusiasms,' he told her, while Sylvia experienced a sense of terrible uneasiness that she could not understand.

During the summer of 1898 the Pankhursts decided that Christabel should go to Geneva for a year to perfect her French. She would stay with Emmeline's friend of her own youth, Noemie Rochefort, now Mme Dufaux. The dressmaking preparations for Christabel's wardrobe took weeks. Emmeline and Christabel were very conscious of fashion, a pleasure they enjoyed sharing. As for Sylvia, who knows whether her windswept, disorderly, dishevelled attire and apparently total disregard of her appearance was developed as a defence, or defiance, at the prospect of competing with Christabel's pretty red curls, or whether she was simply born untidy. As she grew older, her workload increased with her years and her sartorial concerns diminished; friends have described her wearing a blouse inside out or arriving to speak at a meeting with her fly-away hair piled high and in danger of collapse.

Emmeline and Christabel left for France, putting Sylvia in charge, a duty she undertook with characteristic seriousness. It was the first time in nineteen years of marriage that Richard and Emmeline had been parted; the last letter he wrote to her was tender, as he had always been: 'When you return we will have a new honeymoon and reconsecrate each to the other in unity of heart. Be happy. Love and love, Your husband R.M. Pankhurst.' It was not to be.

At home the darkness was closing in on Sylvia. On Saturday, 2 July 1898 the three children, Adela, Harry and Sylvia, were having lunch with their father when he suddenly stood up and left the table. He was found, huddled in agony in Emmeline's yellow drawing room but refused to let Sylvia send for the doctor. By next morning his condition had worsened and she began to panic; raging fear overwhelmed her and she decided to call the doctor without asking her father's permission. The doctor eventually arrived, but through Sunday and into Monday, Richard Pankhurst was becoming delirious.

There is a long letter written by Christabel to Sylvia,[1] which is touchingly innocent of the turmoil that was overwhelming her younger sister in Manchester. It was from Corsier and dated 1 July, the day before their father collapsed:

> . . . All this morning we have been rowing in the boat. It is lovely and warm at present. Yesterday I went out on the tandem and when we were a long way from home . . . the tyre burst. Armand and I walked home while Henri went on his machine to fetch the motor car. When we were about two miles from the house it arrived much to my pleasure. Tomorrow we are going on a picnic, Mother, M. Dufaux and Mme Dufaux and the daughters of some friends of theirs are going in the motor car and the rest including two friends are to go on bicycles – I hope it will be fine.
>
> . . . Mother says will you make a parcel of 'studios' and put some drawings of your own in – some of your charcoal things etc. Also you must not ride too much on your bicycle . . .
>
> Love to Father and all of you.

1. Pankhurst Papers.

The telegram that his doctors had advised Dr Pankhurst to send his wife on 4 July arrived the same afternoon. Emmeline and Christabel were taking tea in the garden overlooking Lake Geneva. It was a simple but dramatic request for Emmeline to return, saying only that Dr Pankhurst was unwell. She left on her own by the first available train. But she was already too late.

As the train sped across Europe, with Emmeline unaware of what was happening, the bewildered Sylvia struggled to cope as best she could. When she woke on Tuesday, 5 July she went immediately to her father's room, where she was alarmed to find Adela and Harry already standing by his bed. As Sylvia held out the oxygen tube that seemed his lifeline, he turned away his head as though to gaze at something. 'The cook crossed herself, murmuring a prayer. I went to the other side of the bed to see his face . . . The skies were crashing down, the world was reeling. Father was dead.' He had been suffering for several years from an ulcer that had finally perforated.

Sylvia relived that terrible time in *The Suffragette Movement*, the emotion still raw and painful after so many years. 'Sobs and cries were rending me . . . not here, one must make no noise here . . .'. She rushed into the garden and fainted headlong on the grass. Distraught, she battered the doctors with her grief and guilt. Why had they not told her earlier to send for her mother? Why did they not explain what was happening? How could her mother ever forgive her?

Christabel's account is curiously detached, speaking of the effect of her father's death on others but hardly at all on herself and showing little of the isolation of a 17-year-old left alone at such a time in a foreign country. There is no reference in the newspapers to suggest that she came home for her father's funeral.

'It was the collapse of our happy life,' Christabel wrote in her autobiography ghosted some sixty years later. 'Sylvia, poor Sylvia had met the shock alone . . . The responsibility, the shock were terrible for her.' Even then Adela was unsympathetic towards her sister: 'Sylvia was prostrated,' she wrote, 'she would not even try to rally, she considered it treason for the rest of us to do so.'

Emmeline read the news starkly as the train approached Manchester in the small hours of Wednesday morning. The black-bordered evening newspaper headline simply said 'Doctor Pankhurst Dead'. She fainted and was comforted by fellow passengers before travelling on to her darkened home and distraught children. 'Manchester felt the loss of her great citizen, one of the most high-minded and sacrificing public men.'

'Faithful and True, and my loving Comrade' were the words she chose for her husband's tombstone. The secular funeral at Brooklands Cemetery the following Saturday, 9 July has been variously reported as 'gay' and as a 'remarkable and impressive public demonstration'. It was certainly unusual, for the *Manchester Guardian* described how the coffin, borne on an open carriage and covered in red flowers, was accompanied by a large number of representatives of the ILP and a contingent from the Clarion Cycle Club, wearing white rosettes. The Pankhursts were all keen cyclists and belonged to a local Clarion Club. These had been established by journalist Robert Blatchford, to encourage rambling, hiking and cycling. They were an integral part of the growing socialist movement and generally they met above a stable or small room fetid with the smell of tobacco and stale beer.

Several hundred people, from every movement with which the doctor had been associated, were at the graveside to hear the euologies. These included one from John Bruce Glasier and another, most unusually and appropriately, from a woman. Mrs Cliff Scatcherd, who had herself been instrumental in winning the vote for women in the Isle of Man, reminded mourners that the progress women had made towards freedom was largely due to Dr Pankhurst's influence. Time and again he had told her that if women did not protest now, they would regret it thereafter – to those women who mourned him today he would always be an inspiring memory. Keir Hardie was not at the funeral. His wife Lillie was ill in Scotland and he had returned there to nurse her. Years later, he spoke to Sylvia of her father, reminding her that 'the greatest gift a man leaves his race is to have been a hero'.

With true Pankhurst spirit, there was barely time to mourn. In public there was so much to do. Dr Pankhurst left no will and no money. Emmeline knew she had to work, and to her grief for her husband was added anxiety for her children. Sylvia felt she must try now to support her mother and, with Christabel still away, took over the housekeeping. Quite often Sylvia and her mother shared a bed, weeping, talking and planning through the night. It was a rare time of togetherness. 'In those days,' wrote Sylvia later, 'I thought it would be my destiny to be her life companion; that my brother and my sisters might go away into the world, but I should always remain with her . . . How strange is fate!'

After Dr Pankhurst's death, Adela's picture of life was increasingly desolate. 'Mother was now involved in public work. We had no friends, we played no games and went nowhere . . . we children were not companions for her. She took no interest in our affairs. Christabel seemed at a distance, Sylvia hopelessly depressed, hung about her all the time. Public life was a relief to her . . .'.

It was no longer, even outwardly, a happy home. As middle-class Victorian children, they had been used to absentee parents and very close relationships with servants or a governess. This was not at all unusual. Parenting was a remote responsibility and in the Pankhurst case even discipline, though ordered by Emmeline, would often be carried out by the servants. Now they needed the love of their mother even more. Their nurse, Susannah Jones, had been with the family for so long and did her best to ease the pain, but Adela was probably correct that Harry was sadly neglected. Measles had left him short-sighted, and since Emmeline was prejudiced against spectacles, she would not allow her son to wear them; so, unable to read, unhappy at his school, he played truant. When he broke his front tooth, the cook, Ellen, suggested that he should not show his mother until after she had had her tea and even then he asked her forgiveness: 'I couldn't help it,' he pleaded.

Undaunted by the debacle of her previous business ventures Emmeline decided to open yet another Emersons, and helped by her younger sister Mary, who had artistic flare, she put all her energies into making cushions and other items for the new shop.

Meanwhile, all the pictures, books and furniture in the house now had to be sold and a new, much smaller home was found at 62 Nelson Street. Today that house is the home of the Pankhurst Centre in Manchester . . .

'A struggle between two burglars' was how George Bernard Shaw described the Boer War that broke out in 1899. With the memory of their father's earlier support of the Boer Republics, the young Pankhursts were immediately on the campaign path. Emmeline resigned from the Fabian Society because members refused to oppose the war. Even Harry spoke out for peace at his school – and was beaten unconscious by the boys; Adela at the Girls' High School was injured by a book thrown at her face.

To her delight, that year Sylvia won a free place to the Manchester School of Art, where she knew she would find happiness in her painting. But even this was not to be – the neuralgia and chilblains from which she suffered all her life returned and she lost many weeks of work. She was ashamed of holding a free place when she was often absent, and so although Christabel had returned from Geneva at Emmeline's request to help at Emersons, Sylvia offered to take her place as an assistant. Like Christabel, she was soon bored, finding there was nothing to do at Emersons. Consequently, when at the close of the school year 1901 she won the Lady Whitworth scholarship of £30 and fees, she returned, thankfully, to Art School.

On a rainy day in February 1900 the ILP and the Trades' Unions met in Farringdon Hall, London, on the site of the old Fleet Prison. They resolved to establish a 'distinct labour group within Parliament' that was, within six years, to metamorphose into the Labour Party. It was an amalgam of the Unions and various splinter groups, and its secretary was Ramsay MacDonald. Keir Hardie, speaking afterwards, said, 'it has come. Poor little child of danger, nursling of the storm. May it be blessed.'

At the ILP Conference later that year, Hardie resigned as chairman. He hated the formalities and tedium of committee work; he was an ideas man with no wish for personal power – more a philosopher than a politician at heart. Many years later, Frederick Lawrence, then the brilliant young editor of the left-wing newspaper the *Echo*, wrote of Hardie: 'He was the most sensitive person I have ever met in my life, and if he was unconventional it was because he had to be, in order to achieve his purpose ... He dreamed dreams of a more just world ... and if any man is to be accounted the principal architect of the better order, it is he. He founded the ILP and from it built up the Labour Party and inspired both with his spirit.'

The General Election in the autumn of 1900 saw Keir Hardie returned to Parliament as ILP member for Merthyr Tydfil, which was again the cause for great celebration in the Pankhurst household. The news seemed to regenerate Emmeline's political purpose. In November she was elected as Independent Labour Party member to the Manchester School Board, holding the position until the abolition of school boards in 1903.

There had been very little overt agitation for women's suffrage in the 1890s. In 1897 the National Union of Women's Suffrage Societies (NUWSS) had been formed, with Millicent Fawcett (1847–1929) as chairman and the poignant telegraphic address of 'Voiceless London'. She was the wife of the blind Liberal MP Henry Fawcett and the sister of Britain's first woman doctor, Elizabeth Garrett Anderson (1836–1917). The NUWSS was a compilation of the many small societies who had for years been working quietly and efficiently around the country. Like Lydia Becker, Millicent Fawcett believed in gentle persuasion through Parliament and was totally opposed to violence – a view that was soon to bring her into head-on conflict with the Pankhursts.

It would be wrong to assume, however, that because the franchise issue was lying dormant, there were not other, quite dramatic changes and improvements afoot that were to pave the way for the explosion of energetic activity when the Victorian period came to an end. This was the age of the emerging 'New Woman'. In 1895 readers of *Home Chat* magazine were invited to enter a competition to define her; one of the entries ran thus:

Who cuts her back hair off quite short
And puts on clothes she didn't ought
And apes a man in word and thought
New Woman

Who rides a cycle round the town
In costume making all men frown
And otherwise acts like a clown
New Woman

Who's the sweetest of the sweet
Because she throws not sex away
Is always lady-like yet gay
True Woman.

Some of the periodicals available to Sylvia during her adolescence were decidedly avant-garde. For instance, in 1896 the Manchester Labour Press produced a series of pamphlets, 'Love's Coming of Age', by Edward Carpenter, a Cambridge cleric who was one of the first socialists to 'come out'. He and a group of fellow homosexuals had founded a model village community outside Sheffield in co-operation with the Sheffield Socialist Society. His writings invited readers to rethink the conventional wisdom that sex was bad. He maintained that, next to hunger, sex is the most imperative of our needs: 'the state of enforced celibacy in which vast numbers of women live today will be looked on as a national wrong'. He also wrote on homosexuality, the 'Intermediate Sex', at a time when the subject was still taboo and did not shy from declaring his own colours.

The somewhat straight-laced Keir Hardie reviewed the articles ecstatically in the *Labour Leader*, of which he was now editor, and was a regular, uncensored reading in the Pankhurst house. 'It is not often that I feel satisfied with a man's treatment of this subject, which is usually little more than a display of his own ignorance and conceit but in this case I have nothing but commendation.' Homosexuality became an issue of public concern, spotlit by the trial of Oscar Wilde in 1895, but the subject of lesbianism was still taboo.

With the mushrooming of the newspaper and magazine market, advertising also became a growth industry; the first promotions were coy and self-conscious, but they in turn encouraged shopkeepers to promote their merchandise in an entirely new way. Previously, shopping had been conducted in gloomy back rooms, but during the 1890s new chain stores such as Boots and Liptons emerged and thrilling window displays began to entice shoppers. The world was opening out. Attitudes were changing. This was, in turn, to facilitate the way in which the Suffragettes would be able to harness a whole range of exciting new promotional tools and techniques.

Middle-class girls were beginning to rebel against their parents as never before and to demand equal treatment with their brothers. With admission to universities increasing, the Girton Girl[2] became a role model. 'Mrs Grundy' – that symbolic image of pettifogging restriction – was finally on the way out. The emerging word for the middle and upper classes was 'freedom': to dance, to cycle in Bloomers,[3] on bicycles fitted with John Dunlop's revolutionary pneumatic tyres.

Robert Blatchford began writing about the rat-infested slums of Manchester in 1888. His life had been transformed by reading Henry Hyndman's[4] Marxist book *A History of the Principles of Socialism*. Blatchford had founded the *Clarion* newspaper in 1891 to promote socialist ideas, and his articles were then collected in a book, *Merrie England*, which became the decade's best-selling publication. But more than that, Robert Blatchford determined to generate a social spirit: he started Cinderella Clubs to bring street parties to the slums and sent a fleet of mobile information centres around the villages.

Blatchford himself, according to Caroline Benn, was a hedonist, a follower of William Morris's belief that 'fellowship is life'. He invited the puritanical Hardie to speak at a Manchester Club frequented by actors and prostitutes. He was mortified by Hardie's reaction. 'I offered him the warmest welcome that I ever gave another man and he held out a hand that was like a cold toad and ran away.'[5]

Perhaps even more importantly, the new teashops gave women somewhere respectable in which to meet, and easier communication by the expanding telephone network was an additional pleasure. The *Lady's Realm* declared in 1898 that, 'The multiplying of women's clubs and the accompanying facilities for social intercourse, is distinctly a feature of London society.' Only in her club could a woman write or read, 'undisturbed by the importunities of a family circle which can never bring itself to regard feminine leisure and feminine solitude as things to be respected'.

2. Girton College, Cambridge was founded in 1869 as the first all-women university. Men were not admitted until 1977.

3. Amelia Jenks Bloomer promoted the outrageous fashion for women's trousers in her magazine, the *Lily*, in America in 1849.

4. Wealthy old Etonian, Henry Hyndman addressed large audiences wearing a silk top hat. In 1884 he had founded the Socialist Democratic Federation (SDF) to promote Marxist principles.

5. Laurence Thompson, *Robert Blatchford*, Gollancz, 1951.

Now, at the turn of the century, most towns had a girls' high school and technical colleges were being established everywhere. There were 2000 women graduates – eight had even received honorary degrees; there were 400 women doctors and 9000 nurses. Married women retained their earnings and property and there was a network of organizations caring for children's welfare, maternity, emigration, education, employment and politics. But there was still no parliamentary vote for women.

Then, in 1901, the almost unthinkable happened. Queen Victoria died at Osborne House on the Isle of Wight. Her presence on the throne for over sixty years had had a significantly oppressive influence on the nation's family life and morals. However, after Prince Albert's death in 1861 and the Queen's self-imposed retirement from public life, there were signs that the old order was gradually changing. The ideals of the 'domestic woman' had gone virtually unchallenged throughout her reign and had, in fact, formed the basis upon which English social and political life was formed.

The volcanic energy that had been bubbling beneath the surface for half a century was about to erupt. The cause championed by those early, respectable, hard-working campaigners – Mary Wollstonecraft, the Beetons, Helen Taylor, Lydia Becker and, more lately, Mrs Fawcett – was about to be taken over by the controversial and formidable Pankhursts.

Dr Pankhurst would have been proud of his women. Exasperated by the way in which his own sex had obstructed progress towards female emancipation, he often urged them to action with the admonition, 'Why don't you scratch our eyes out?'

4

Deeds Not Words

'Coursing through the Socialist movement to working class circles beyond its confines was the confident, imminent hope of a Labour Party . . . The long, solitary struggle Keir Hardie had waged for it in contests of indescribable bitterness in the Trade Union Congress since he first appeared here in 1887 was about to be crowned with success . . . With the prospect of a Labour Party had arisen the thought – What would the Party do for women?'

Sylvia Pankhurst, *The Suffragette Movement*

In 1902 politics was not yet the driving force of Sylvia's life. She had grown up living and breathing the concept of service for others and especially the belief that in order to be free, women must win the vote. Her adolescence was shaped by the growth of the new young socialist movement and the slow birth of the Labour Party itself. She saw achieving the vote as a single, though vital, step towards achieving a better world

With Keir Hardie's encouragement, Christabel, who was being coached for her final school leaving examinations, was by now speaking at public meetings (she had a particularly beautiful voice). Sylvia was still only dreaming that what she believed was her one talent – as a painter – might beautify life for others and, in particular, the poor and oppressed.

When that year she won a National Silver Medal for mosaic design, a Primrose Medal and the highest prize available to students at the Manchester School of Art, a travelling studentship, she chose to go to Italy. Overjoyed at Sylvia's success, Emmeline decided to travel with her as far as Geneva, to stay again with her childhood friend, Noemie Dufaux, from whom she had parted in some distress four years before, when she was called home to her sick husband. Sylvia and Emmeline stopped off in Bruges, where Sylvia was totally captivated by the old town and almost abandoned Italy in its favour. She and her mother stayed in the ancient attic granary of an old half-timbered building: 'we slept between lavender scented sheets . . . and emerged with a great sense of renewed life . . . We were so happy together . . . My wishes lingered in Bruges, when she tore me away to Brussels, where she revelled in the shops and purchased hats for us all, and where I lost my heart to the ornate architectural riches of the Hotel de Ville.'

The now stout Mme Dufaux met them in Geneva, and Sylvia experienced her first and overwhelming sight of the mountains. The stay was relaxed and agreeable; each morning Monsieur Dufaux, an artist himself, worked on a portrait of Emmeline, which, according to Sylvia, made her look young and beautiful. Sylvia also tried painting her mother, but was ruefully disappointed with the result, in which she appeared, probably more truthfully, older and very sad. 'I was by no means pleased with my drawings.'

Both Mme Dufaux and Emmeline decided to accompany Sylvia to Venice, chattering all the way as if there were thirty years of memories to recover. Eventually they reached 'the promised land of my sad young heart, craving for beauty fleeing from the sorrowful ugliness of factory-ridden Lancashire and the full aching poverty of its slums . . .'. The two older women threw themselves into an orgy of sightseeing and shopping, exhausting Sylvia physically and mentally: 'I toiled after their speeding steps like a tired dog.' Emmeline, with her usual lack of commercial acumen, decided to buy a great deal of Venetian glass for Emersons, with no idea of whether it would be saleable in the industrial north of England. It was not.

Eventually the ladies left Sylvia in the care of a middle-aged spinster from Manchester who was lodging in Venice and who had agreed to act as a chaperone. 'I parted from my mother, my eyes streaming with tears; the anguish of separation seemed greater than I could endure.' The pain was soon dimmed by the sheer joy of painting in Venice, of being followed by crowds of curious people, especially children, eager to watch her work and to be painted too. As the colder weather arrived, Sylvia joined the Academia delle Belle Arti, where as the only woman student in the life class, she was an object of some interest. But, having decided that although, like many educated young ladies, she could speak some Italian, it was best to pretend she could not and so she was mostly left to eavesdrop untroubled on her fellow students' discussions of sex and love.

There was much talk of love and celibacy amongst the young people in romantic Venice. Her closest friend, the beautiful Polish Countess, Sophie Bertelli Algarotti, known as Madame Sophie, widow of an Italian Count, confided to her of her own tragic, great love in middle-age for a man who became insane on the evening of their marriage and who she visited every day until he died. Any idea of moving on to Florence was abandoned in favour of staying in Venice, painting by day and listening in the evenings to Madame Sophie's thrilling stories of her part in the liberation movement in Poland. Sometimes she would play the piano while Sylvia sang some of the arias of *La Traviata*.

Not many of Sylvia's paintings from this period seem to have survived and those that still exist are undated. There are some studies of Italian mosaics, but many reflect her interest in the lives of the ordinary people – streetsellers, children, domestic scenes. One in particular that pleased her (she was a severe critic of her own work) was an untitled view in soft browns, russets and gold of a laden barge drifting through a canal. This hangs today in her son Richard's study in Addis Ababa.

As spring approached, it was time for a return to reality, precipitated by the arrival of a letter from Christabel, telling her sister that since she had decided to study law at Owens University, Manchester, Sylvia must return immediately to help their mother with the shop. Madame Sophie begged her to remain, on the grounds that to do so would be far better for her future. But, as ever, her sense of duty won the day.

Her feelings about this time are recorded in a series of notes tucked away among the Pankhurst Papers and headed 'Decisions that have Mainly Influenced My Life':

> My decision to return to Manchester was made without any hesitation. I was clearly aware that I was leaving a life of security where I was happy and beloved and which attracted me above all because therein I might study and improve the art which was very precious to me. I grieved also at parting from my dear friend but I permitted myself no doubts and no regrets.
>
> Soon after my return to Manchester I realised, that so far as my mother's business was concerned my presence was not required.

In Manchester, Emmeline had hired a studio over the shop, in which she hoped Sylvia could work; however, her days seem to have been spent, as before, on trying to keep abreast of the domestic chores, at which she was not very adept: darning, dusting and housekeeping.

She was intrigued and not a little puzzled by Christabel's developing friendship with Eva Gore Booth, daughter of an Irish baronet. It could be that Christabel, being a little older and increasingly ambitious, was simply engaged in what today would be called 'networking'. Eva and her devoted companion, Esther Roper, had recently arrived in Manchester, and though they are now largely forgotten by history, they quietly managed to fire the imagination of the women trades unionists of their day and at the same time galvanize the respectable middle-class ladies of the city in those pre-'Suffragette' days. They were determined to rid the NUWSS, of which they were Executive Members, of its image as a 'fad of the rich and well-to-do'. They saw the vote not as a 'right', but as a weapon whereby women of all classes could transform their lot.[1]

When Christabel heckled at a meeting at which they were speaking, they astutely recognized her potential and invited her to join them: she was flattered and found herself suddenly and actively on the franchise bandwagon. Christabel had discovered that she had a range of hitherto unsuspected abilities: she was an excellent and intelligent speaker, charmed her audiences with her good looks and charisma, and thrived on leadership. She had the makings of a true, even great, politician, and it was she who began to influence and eventually eclipse her mother.

Esther Roper and Christabel together formed the Manchester and Salford Women's Trade Union Council, one of the affiliates of Millicent Fawcett's NUWSS. Although Sylvia, still only 21, had not yet been drawn into the cut and thrust of local politics, she was fascinated and influenced by her sister's friends. They were resolutely non-militant and had energetically carried their message into the homes of the miners and the factory workers, into the clubs and pubs and football grounds – it was all more entertaining, and 'people entered into a new fellowship in which the common belief in socialism formed the basis for having a high old time'.[2]

At the time it was believed that Eva was dying of tuberculosis and so had left home to care for working women in her 'last few months' (she actually died, unmarried, in 1926). She was extremely beautiful with golden hair tied in a loose bun at the nape of her neck, and Sylvia was astonished to see how her sister, who had never before shown any interest in acting the nurse, would gently massage Eva's head if she had a headache. Even Mrs Pankhurst was uneasy and not a little jealous. Nevertheless, the friendship gave Christabel, in particular, a valuable grounding in politics, a preparation for what was about to happen.

Sylvia was delighted, at this time, to be asked to decorate the lecture hall of the building that the Independent Labour Party had erected in St James Road, High Town, Salford, in memory of her father. The foundation stone had been laid on 26 November 1898,[3] and since it was better than anything the ILP had

1. Barbara Castle, *Sylvia and Christabel Pankhurst*, Penguin, 1987.
2. G.D.H. Cole, *The British Working Class Movement 1789–1927*, Allen and Unwin, 1932.
3. *Salford Reporter*, 3 December 1898.

yet possessed, Sylvia was determined to do it justice. She had just three weeks and no idea at this stage of the dramatic significance that Pankhurst Hall was to have to her family, to the emerging Labour Party and to the Suffrage Movement. Her handwritten notes for décor suggest:

> As this hall bears the name of a pioneer whose life was given for the ideal and for the future, emblems of the future and the ideal have been chosen with which to decorate it.
>
> The Entrance Hall. The symbols are a peacock's feather, lily and rose, emblems of beauty, purity and love; with the motto 'England Arise' and the name of the hall.
>
> The large Hall. Symbols. Roses, love, apple trees, knowledge, doves, peace, corn, plenty, lilies, purity, honesty, bees, industry, sunflower, butterflies and hope.
>
> The panel illustrates Shelley's line: 'Hope will make thee young, for Hope and Youth are children of one mother, even Love.'[4]

The sponsors of Pankhurst Hall had shown some courage in trusting such a major task to a girl of 21 with virtually no experience of painting on so large a scale. It seems they were well satisfied, and Keir Hardie himself complimented her in the *Labour Leader*.

The artist Walter Crane, whose work so influenced Sylvia, was invited to speak at the opening, and reluctantly she agreed to make her first public speech, describing the significance of her decorations. She was so nervous that she forgot to remove her gloves when drawing on the blackboard. It seems somehow appropriate that the girl who never played games herself as a child should have provided such a colourful backdrop to eighty years of community entertainment for the people of Salford. When Pankhurst Hall was finally demolished in 1978, it was a Bingo Hall.

Unfortunately, the Pankhurst family euphoria was short-lived. Sylvia discovered that women were not allowed to join that branch of the Independent Labour Party. To her horror, she also discovered that there were those on the ILP Executive who were actively opposed to votes for women. The groundswell within socialism carried with it the exciting, real hope of the imminent birth of a Labour Party, but it was of great concern to the suffragists that even a Labour Party might drag its heels on the Woman Question. The great majority of people in Britain were indeed still lukewarm about the idea

---

4. *The Revolt of Islam*, canto 8, verse 27.

of parliamentary votes for women, and some politicians were afraid for their respective party followings. Many of the new Labour group believed all men should get the vote first – women later (possibly). Only Keir Hardie seemed passionately committed.

So it was that on 10 October 1903 six women gathered at the Pankhurst house in 62 Nelson Street. Sylvia was not present. After a certain amount of heated discussion, the Women's Social and Political Union – the WSPU – was born, which Emmeline saw, at the time at least, as primarily a women's organization working for social reform and female franchise. It was to be, politically, the women's parallel to the ILP.

The Manifesto drawn up that day said:

Social reform can never be satisfactory as long as one half of the nation is not represented.

Working men have found that political action is needed to supplement trades unionism and so they have formed the Labour Party. Women Trades Unionists and social reformers now realise that the possession of the vote is the most effective way of securing better social and industrial conditions, better wages, shorter hours, healthier homes and an honorable position in the State which will enable women as well as men to render that citizen service which is so necessary to the development of a truly great nation.

From the outset the WSPU accepted the principle of a limited franchise, linked to property qualification, on the same terms as men. Women had taken a step towards this goal when the 1894 Local Government Act gave them the right to vote in local government elections. The cause of universal adult suffrage was considered unattainable. In Parliament itself there had been virtually no change of attitude – the whole idea of women in government was a huge joke. They were too sensitive, frivolous or just ignorant. Besides, it was assumed that most women were not interested anyway.

The WSPU believed that the inequalities women suffered could not be redressed without a vote, which would make individual MPs accountable to their female electorate: 'First of all it is a symbol, secondly a safeguard and thirdly an instrument.' The WSPU motto, which echoed the gung-ho mood of the ladies present, was 'Deeds not Words'.

Frederick Lawrence, the wealthy young barrister who was soon to play a pivotal role in the WSPU, explained later that the main reason for men's opposition to women's suffrage was fear. They were seriously worried that if women got the vote, they would abuse the privilege: women, they claimed, would quickly become the majority voters and use emotional arguments to change policies – especially on sexual and moral issues, imposing impossibly high standards of behaviour. It was also felt women would lose their charm and men their treasured dominance.

It is interesting – and important – to understand the genuine, if sometimes inconsistent, views that well-known women had also expressed on the issue of suffrage. Octavia Hill (1838–1912), the great reformer and philanthropist, probably the first woman housing manager and one who did so much to improve housing for the poor, was hostile to women's suffrage. Her reasoning seems strange to us from one who had herself achieved such professional success. In a letter to the *Evening Standard* in August 1910, towards the end of her life, she explained her unshaken anti-suffrage conviction. Women in Parliament would be lost, she said, to good works. The vote, she felt, was a red herring, drawn across the path of her fellow workers, which hindered them from taking an adequate interest in those subjects with which she considered them best fitted to deal.

The writer and economist Beatrice Potter[5] was another dissenter – but twenty years later she 'recanted'. In 1889 she had joined the notorious Appeal Against Female Suffrage instigated by the Dowager Lady Stanley of Alderney and signed by 'Lady Randolph Churchill and 100 others (mostly titled)'. She wrote: 'Why I was at that time anti-feminist in feeling is easy to explain, though impossible to justify – the root of my anti-feminism lay in the fact that I myself had never suffered the disabilties assumed to arise from my sex. Moreover, in the craft I had chosen a woman was privileged. In those days a competent female writer on economic affairs had, to an enterprising editor, actually a scarcity value.'

Sylvia, a committed socialist, was already uneasy at the growing rift between her mother and the ILP, but she was carried along herself by the drama of unfurling events. She was also taken aback by the 'torrents of WSPU frenzy' poured on Keir Hardie, so admired by her father, when he next came to Manchester. However, Hardie met the anger at the apparent lack of ILP support for the new movement by agreeing to publish a statement, 'The Citizenship of Women. A Plea for Women's Suffrage.' This was mostly written by Christabel but signed by Hardie himself. Furthermore, he organized a questionnaire for the ILP branches to establish what proportion could be regarded as working class among local government voters. Nearly forty

5. Beatrice Potter (1858–1943) married Sidney Webb in 1892 and helped found the London School of Economics. They were active Fabians.

branches of the ILP combined their research and found that of 59,920 women voters, 82.45 per cent could be defined as working class. This was the fuel needed to convince the ILP executive that to press for a women's vote on the same terms as men would hand no advantage to the propertied classes.

At the 1904 Easter Conference of the ILP Mrs Pankhurst was elected to the executive with the express purpose of introducing a Votes for Women Bill to Parliament. For Christabel, suffrage was more of a means to a personal end. The undoubted leadership gifts and revived enthusiasm of her mother complemented her skills rather than competed against them. Votes for Women was the career for which she had been searching. Together she and Emmeline were becoming a team, giving strength to each other. This was quite unlike Sylvia, for whom the WSPU slogan 'Deeds not Words' became not an exhortation to militant action, but to the practical service of others. The cause was never a self-promotional vehicle for her. It became a very personal mission, always driven by the heart and the memory of her father, but at times she admitted that she had actually enjoyed some of the rough and tumble that marked her mother's campaign.

From the outset Sylvia paddled her own canoe, often through dangerous and stormy waters. She never broke ranks and remained, at least publicly, loyal to the family. But as she matured and her under-rated intellectual powers increased, she showed vision and remarkable courage – characteristics that have never been properly recognized. Often she was an intolerable challenge to her increasingly authoritarian mother and sister, and so, eventually, she was cast aside.

Both Adela and Harry suffered, too. Adela, the neglected child who became the free-thinking and outspoken adult, was eventually exiled by Emmeline and Christabel. Since his father's death, Harry had been overshadowed by powerfully independent women. His mother had less and less time to spare for him and, as he tried desperately to hold his own in the family, he became fanatical, as 15-year-old adolescents often do. He chalked WSPU slogans on pavements, heckled at meetings and tried anything that would win him praise. He was, David Mitchell says, 'an honorary suffragette . . . like a sickly knight-errant, weighed down by strange, ill-fitting armour to prove himself worthy of the four ladies of his devotion'. Only Sylvia understood and gave him the love he craved throughout his short life. They comforted each other when he was sent to school in London, and Sylvia, by then a lonely student at the Royal College of Art, took him under her wing.

Mrs Fawcett's NUWSS now had 500 affiliates. Intellectual, professional and respectable, how could they deal with the circus of the WSPU? There was no political party supporting them, and without that, Roger Fulford says, 'It was like backing a race with no runners.' There was no press support either and, on the whole, women's magazines ignored them too.

Although for the next eight years the WSPU was to fill the centre of the stage, attracting all the limelight and diverting all attention from the quieter supporters of their cause, in the background these undemonstrative supporters remained always the heart of the movement, carrying conviction by their very patience and resignation.

Unbeknown to them the WSPU had in Sylvia a quietly potent weapon, for soon she was to win the discreet devotion of the emotionally needy Keir Hardie. Together they were to provide the often unappreciative Union with an additional parliamentary voice. The WSPU became a doubled-headed monster to Parliament, fronted by Christabel and her mother Emmeline, backed by Sylvia and Keir Hardie.

Long before their time, Christabel and Emmeline were mistresses of 'spin' and would have been on every television programme today. Their sense of showmanship was spectacular; their parades and demonstrations were a riot of colourful costumes and banners; their fund-raising merchandizing, long before the day of the T-shirt logo, was worthy of a Hollywood blockbuster. Puzzles, tea caddies, notepaper, all were sold in the WSPU shops that eventually opened around the country.

Nurses, nuns, postboys and policemen – the disguises in which they escaped arrest were also imaginative and successful. Add to this the emotional blackmail caused by respectable women on hunger strike, suffering the torture of forcible feeding, and it is no wonder that public and parliamentary feeling ran high.

But in 1904 the battle lines were only just being drawn up.

5

The Second Pillar

'I have seen him come home on a cold, dark evening after an arduous day, strip off his overcoat, go to the fireplace and light a fire on top of the spent coals left in the grate. In a few moments there would be a cheerful blaze. Then he would bring forth bread, butter, Scotch scones, the main staples of his diet and tea, which he would often cast in a saucepan of cold water taking it off the fire as soon as it came to boil . . .'

Sylvia Pankhurst, *The Suffragette Movement*

Even more challenging for Sylvia than the task of honouring her father's memory at Pankhurst Hall was sitting, in 1904, for the entrance examination to London's Royal College of Art. The questions were difficult and, having failed to complete the geometry at all because her fingers shook and she rubbed her papers into holes, she crept home in despair. The family was at the theatre, and since she had no key, she climbed in through a window and went to bed, her typical lack of confidence having convinced her of failure. When the results arrived, Sylvia's disastrous geometry was forgotten. The examiners had recognized her other talents and she was not only awarded a scholarship, but emerged top in the entire country. 'I was surprised but not elated; the standard is not very high I concluded,' she observed modestly.

The shock of uprooting and finding herself living alone, in a tall house off the Fulham Road, in London, was painful. The rent of her cheerless room was 10/0d[1] a week. Her scholarship provided £5 a month from which all artists' materials had to be bought. In addition to this, Sylvia was worrying about Emmeline's finances in Manchester and that her mother was still paying rent for her studio over Emersons. She wrote to her mother every other day and imposed on herself the task of trying to sell her own designs for cotton prints.

1. Ten shillings – 10/0d – is equivalent to today's 50p. One pound is made up of 20 shillings and each shilling of 12 pence.

Being paid in guineas[2] she kept the shillings to pay her bus fares and sent the rest home to Manchester. Emmeline herself brought this to an end by asking Sylvia to devote her time solely to collecting signatures for a petition in support of the Women's Franchise Bill. This involved travelling around London in the evenings after college and on Sundays attending public meetings at which audiences might be persuaded to sign.

At this time Sylvia also had her first enjoyable experience of public speaking at an open-air meeting in Ravenscourt Park, West London; there she met Dora Montefiore, who had contributed so much towards the enfranchisement of Australian women in 1902, and who was now living in considerable style on Chiswick Mall, overlooking the Thames. Sylvia found RCA life extremely difficult at first and a sharp contrast to the reassuring security of the smaller Manchester School of Art, where she had had such spectacular success. She felt herself surrounded by gloomy and depressed students who were constantly demoralized and criticized by staff. A new College ruling stated that in the first six months, students must spend their days in the architectural school and devote only the evenings to life classes. Non-architectural students felt this was a waste of their precious two-year course. Sylvia, being a Pankhurst, could not let the matter rest and set off to protest to the Principal, Mr Augustus Spencer, only to find herself summarily dismissed from his office: 'thereafter we glared at each other like savage dogs'.

It seems that the Principal was against women students and that very few ever achieved scholarships. This was the first occasion when Sylvia enlisted the help of Keir Hardie, asking him to table a Parliamentary Question on the matter. This he did, but was told that RCA scholarships were awarded in the proportion of one woman to thirteen men, which they all knew was not a reflection of merit. Sylvia's action and her reputation as a 'troublemaker' were noted by the staff.

Even by Art College standards, Sylvia seems to have acquired a certain notoriety among the students, but she found it difficult to mix easily and was 'anxiously miserable' and very lonely. Girls would talk to her, but she didn't realize that if men ignored her, it was not wrong for her to make the first move. They, in turn, labelled her 'snooty'. In fact, she was very shy and very busy.

Her one male student friend was the eccentric and rebellious 18-year-old Austin Osman Spare. She described him as a 'pale flaxen-haired youth in a white shirt and scarlet sash'. The other girls were shocked and a little afraid of

---

2. One guinea is one pound and one shilling.

him, and, since his work was unconventionally bizarre, they felt he could be dangerous. Defiantly, in her second year Sylvia told them that she planned to order a copy of a book of allegorical and satirical drawings that Austin was about to publish, called *Earth, Inferno, Destiny, Humanity and the Chaos of Creation* (published by the Co-operative Printing Society in 1905). Sylvia took orders from those girls too timid to tackle the author themselves. Sylvia and Austin remained friends and for years he supported her many causes, particularly that of Ethiopia.

Another friendship that was to last was with the pretty and unworldly Amy K. Browning[3] (1881–1978), who shared Sylvia's determination to improve the lot of women students. When life was proving difficult, the girls spent many hours in Amy's rooms, talking long into the night. But Amy was no campaigner – she was utterly dedicated to her painting and her exceptional talent was being encouraged by the College. She could never have abandoned her art, whereas Sylvia suffered agonies of indecision: 'Is it just that we should be permitted to devote our entire lives to the creation of beauty while others are meshed in monotonous drudgery?'

When Amy left the Royal College, she went on to exhibit at the Royal Academy every year until 1977. The Paris Salon des Artistes also awarded her a silver medal, and she won international respect but never the fame that her stunningly beautiful paintings deserved. Why? She would have said that it was because she was a woman. She was never at the forefront of the women's movement but she remained Sylvia's friend and went on many Suffragette protests and marches.

Sylvia's time at college confirmed her growing belief in the evils of capitalism. She realized that despite the anxieties felt by students, and the dread that they would not make a living as artists or would not find work even as teachers, they and she were privileged because they enjoyed their painting, whereas the mass of people laboured simply to keep alive. She once asked Keir Hardie, 'are we brothers of the brush entitled to the luxury of release from utilitarian production?'

She was suffering, as she suffered throughout her life, the agonies often occasioned by an overflowing social conscience. She desperately longed to find a purpose for her art but could not make up her mind whether it was 'worthwhile to fight one's individual struggles . . . to bring out of oneself the best possible and to induce the world to accept one's daily bread when all the time the great struggles to better the world for humanity demanded other

3. Joanna Dunham, *Amy K. Browning. An Impressionist in the Women's Movement*, Boudicca Books, 1995.

service.' On balance she felt that 'the idea of giving up the artist's life, surrendering the study of colour and form . . . to wear out one's life on the platform and the chair at the street corner was a prospect too tragically grey and barren to endure'. Neither Amy nor Austin Spare could understand her dilemma – for them there was no choice but the life of the artist.

During Sylvia's first year she joined the Fulham branch of the ILP and occasionally went to the 'At Homes' hosted by Margaret and Ramsay MacDonald[4] at their flat in Lincoln's Inn. Margaret MacDonald was clearly struggling to keep her head above water as a devoted mother, politician's wife and professional lady herself. Sylvia was sympathetically in tune: 'She had little time to attend to her dress and it was no uncommon thing to see her with her blouse put on back to front, several buttons undone and parting company with her skirt at the waist . . .'.

Gradually and almost unnoticed, Keir Hardie began to play a more important role in Sylvia's life and she in his. She often went, alone, to Hardie's lodgings at 14 Nevill's Court, off Fetter Lane. Her brother Harry was at school in London, and every alternate Sunday she took Harry along, too. 'Keir Hardie gathered us both under his benevolent wing.'

There, in his comfortably cluttered room, Sylvia found the happiness and security of mutual affection she had so longed for since her father died. Hardie lived in an Elizabethan, half-timbered building, with a gloomy winding stair that led up to a modest room, painted dark green and divided by curtains into living, sleeping and kitchen areas. There were engravings, busts, socialist memorabilia and curios. Hardie worked by candlelight, cooking his food, blacking his boots, doing his housework. Sylvia was intrigued and enchanted by his domesticity, his firelighting and tea-making skills. He was entertained by her enthusiastic lack of reticence. She 'lightened his soul'. He also had a garden, 'thirty inches wide and fifteen feet long', where he grew primroses, leeks and his favourite ox-eye daisies.

To this simple home came a colourful mix of pilgrims: Russian exiles, Indians, reformers, painters and 'dreamers of dreams', but never the press. Hardie would rarely allow journalistic intrusion into his private world. They were all eager to exchange ideas and ideals with the now legendary founder of the ILP. For Sylvia this was a nostalgic reminder of those days in Russell Square.

With his gentle, rather kindly eyes and beard, there was a messianic quality

---

4. Ramsay MacDonald (1866–1937) was less enchanted by Christabel and her mother and remained aloof and critical. He became the first Labour Prime Minister in 1924.

about Hardie that touched people's hearts and imaginations. Adored by the public too, he loved and cared for people en masse and children in particular, yet had serious difficulties with individual personal relationships. Needy as he was, he found it almost impossible to reach out for close friendship: those who wished it needed to come to him. 'Like Sylvia, he was a visionary, caring deeply for the problems facing the world in general – far ahead of his time he was an environmentalist with real concerns for the rain forests and a true animal lover.'[5]

In Nevill's Court, Maggie Symons, a 30-year-old educated, efficient linguist and utterly loyal woman, served Hardie for years as secretary at a time when it was most unusual for an MP to employ a woman. He paid her a pittance but made some efforts to help her achieve her journalistic ambitions. There was also Frank Smith, a dedicated socialist and teetotal Christian, who identified totally with Hardie's vision of Utopia and had offered his impecunious friend a home in London when he was first elected to Parliament. Frank Smith became, as Caroline Benn describes, Hardie's 'Sancho Panza', devoted to promoting Hardie's ideals but never himself, a quality that appealed to Hardie and to Sylvia. Smith offered to stand and finance his own campaigns at various by-elections, seen as essential ILP propaganda. He spent a great deal of time working among London's homeless, establishing allotments to help the poor feed themselves. He was also a believer in spiritualism and telepathy – concepts Hardie later explored with Sylvia when they were apart. It was Smith who found Nevill's Court for his friend in May 1902 when he was no longer able to offer him a home.

Hardie himself had a very poor self-image. He was a lonely man, haunted by what he saw as failure in his personal and political life. It is true he quarrelled with many leading socialists; he was not even always on good terms with the fledgling Labour party and was eventually blacklisted by King Edward.[6] But he was proud to be an agitator.

Caroline Benn observes: 'The rosy notion of a labour movement built on the foundations of consistent brotherhood is chimeric: likewise the picture of Hardie as a dear old gentleman everybody loved. He had few friends and was reviled by the Liberal press.' On the other hand, she says, 'no other politician drew from such a fund of popular support . . . No other activist of the left stamped humanitarian socialism so firmly into the political fabric; or saw the future so clearly . . .'.

5. Caroline Benn, *Keir Hardie*, Hutchinson, 1992.
6. He was banned from royal garden parties.

Kenneth Morgan describes the impact of this complex, charismatic man –
Labour's only 'acknowledged folk hero' – on his time and on his party:

> Hardie's achievement remains immense. He is amongst the handful of figures
> in British history to have forged a new national party with an abiding mass
> appeal. Further he combined practical achievement with a power of prophetic
> insight and imagination, unique in his own time . . . No historical treatment of
> his career is adequate unless it takes into account the emotional core of
> Hardie's life.

For many years, at a crucial time that emotional core was Sylvia Pankhurst. As
a young woman driven by overwhelming concern for the oppressed, Keir
Hardie possessed understandable magnetism. For Sylvia, at least, their
friendship introduced a heady, intoxicating mix of cerebral and emotional
passion to her life.

Often when Sylvia arrived, he would continue working – nothing could ever
distract him from work – but she was content to sit and read until he relaxed
and read in turn to her: Shelley, Byron, William Morris and Burns. He had an
intense interest in new writers who dealt with social problems, such as Ibsen,
Shaw and Anatole France. They went together to see Shaw's *John Bull's Other
Island*. There were walks in Richmond Park and meetings in one of the new
Lyons Corner Houses.[7] She introduced him to black coffee, which he had
never tasted. He introduced her to childish games, such as 'five-stones', which
she had never played. Later, as the relationship matured and he trusted her, she
helped him with his political work, planning Parliamentary Bills and speeches.
In the winter evenings he reminisced about his childhood and early life,
sentimentalized maybe in the light of the fire, but undeniably tough and
blighted by poverty: 'I never knew what it was to be a child . . . the scars of
those days are with me still.' The soft-hearted Sylvia was saddened and
captivated.

It was a situation that poignantly characterized the contradictions in his life.
In his own way he loved his family and Lochnorris. Whenever he went abroad,
which he increasingly did, his watch, marked by the teeth of Donald, his
favourite pit pony, was set to 'Daddy Time' in Lochnorris, so that he knew
what they were all doing. He loved women too – especially strong women – yet
he relegated Lillie to the status of all those unfranchised, poverty-stricken and

---

7. The first Lyons teashop was opened in Shaftsbury Avenue, London in 1894, and the grander Corner
Houses followed soon after.

neglected wives for whom he had developed a political rescue mission. She had no chance of self-fulfilment and she suffered silently.

Only twice in any of her prolific writings did Sylvia refer, obliquely, to Lillie: in the notes for her first book[8] she mentions Hardie's 'unhappy marriage'. About this time she also began writing short stories under the name of S. Prigionaire, revealing a guilt-ridden young woman. One in particular, unpublished, was called *A Dream from The Devil's Tempting*. The Devil is cast as a woman and is, transparently, Sylvia, tempting the married man to start work he would never finish.

Until Kenneth Morgan's biography, historians did not acknowledge Hardie's love for Sylvia. He had previously embarked on one intense but short-term relationship with a woman, whereas this was Sylvia's first romance. Hardie and she were both emotionally starved but Sylvia generated more than enough passion for them both. They gave each other mutual support and understanding, as well as the excitement of their shared political fervour. There is no doubt that Hardie's almost self-destructive pursuit of the cause of women's political and sexual freedom which dates from this time was deeply motivated by their relationship. The relationship lasted until about 1912 and their love certainly longer. If their friends were aware, they were discreet.

Fenner Brockway, then a rising young socialist journalist and later a Labour MP,[9] was also a friend and regular visitor to Nevill's Court. He was sent there originally to do an interview for a newspaper and was greeted by Hardie, 'his stern features a carving of struggle and strength', with the words, 'young man, if you will put away your pencil and notebook I will talk to you'.

Brockway became a regular visitor and it was here that he met Sylvia. 'It was whispered they were lovers and certainly they loved.' Hardie took her on his knee when Brockway was there. 'I was astonished because I had never seen Keir Hardie so unbent and warm . . . he was stroking Sylvia's hair and laughing with her. I was glad. Hardie had become human. It was the reaction of a father in his late fifties to a daughter in her twenties. And probably it was that. They would hardly have been so open in their affection if they had anything to hide. I do not know. But why worry? They were happy, they harmed no one. Hardie influenced Sylvia, she comforted him when war came. Sylvia was the best of the Pankhursts.'[10]

In Carolyn Stevens' thesis, 'A Suffragette and a Man' (published by the University of Rochester, New York, 1986), which took the Canadian seven

8. E. Sylvia Pankhurst, *The Suffragette*, Sturgis and Walton, 1911.
9. Fenner Brockway (1888–1988) was ennobled as Baron Brockway of Eton and Slough in 1964.
10. Fenner Brockway, *Towards Tomorrow*, Hart Davis MacGibbon, 1977.

years to research, she refers to her belief that for Sylvia this was 'serious, more allied to a sanctified experience, than a romping or frolic. In classic Romeo and Juliet fashion,' she says, 'they breached symbolic walls.' She also claims that 'The love relationship between Keir Hardie and Sylvia demonstrates in miniature the attempts of one socialist man and one feminist woman to deal with the sexual mores they inherited and how they changed the rules to bring culture more in line with what they saw as human personal need.'

Reading the letters and poems that remain in the Pankhurst archives, it seems unlikely that theirs was a platonic affair or that the feelings expressed – particularly by Sylvia – were an expression merely of wishful thinking. Barbara Castle wrote, 'The relationship fused together all the strands of her aching personality.'

Like many men of his age, Hardie enjoyed 'dressing up' for parts, taking on dramatic roles, hiding his real identity, 'knowing more than he would tell'. Kenneth Morgan comments that his frequently changed hats and assumed tweedy image perhaps had nothing to do with his working-class origins but were disguises for a tragically unfulfilled personality. He was, he says, not a typical working man at all: he was at heart a bohemian. His clothes drew almost as much comment as his policies: the deer stalker followed the tweed cap and the trilby came later. A purple muffler, a red cravat or a kimono, he dressed for effect, sometimes padding round the House of Commons in sandals without socks. Small wonder he became known as 'queer Hardie'. Many of his clothes were lovingly made by Lillie, and Sylvia often refers to them affectionately.

Before long, Sylvia moved into two rooms in Park Cottage, in Park Walk, between the King's Road and Fulham Road, Chelsea. It was a cosy, comfortable place, run by a congenial couple, Mr and Mrs Roe, who made riding breeches. Here, for a time, Sylvia's friends from the Art College came to paint with her on Saturday afternoons. The lonely days were over.

6

A Year of Destiny

'Nothing would induce me to vote for giving women the franchise. I am not going to be henpecked into a question of such importance.'

Winston Churchill in response to Sylvia's heckling
at a meeting in Manchester in December 1905

The arrival of Emmeline to stay with Sylvia in February 1905 heralded a change in lifestyle for her and the tolerant Roes. As the new Parliamentary session was about to begin, her mother needed help to lobby Members of Parliament. Increasingly, Sylvia's studies were interrupted by Emmeline's determination to go campaigning. Sylvia had for some time been helping Keir Hardie in his battle to improve the lot of the unemployed and she was delighted that, this time, the King's Speech contained a promise of legislation. Emmeline, on the other hand, was dismissive, claiming that Hardie's priorities were wrong, since such reforms would become a matter of course once women had won the vote.

Each Friday afternoon in the House of Commons was set aside for private members' bills, but their allocation was decided by ballot. Somewhat against her better judgement, for the eight days before the ballot Sylvia sat with her mother in the Lobby, waiting for members to appear and pleading for their support. They met with pitifully little response. Only the loyal Hardie agreed that he would introduce a 'Votes for Women' bill if he were lucky in the ballot, and so every night an anxious Sylvia found herself comforting the distraught Emmeline. Her mother was terrified that 'her life's work, her husband's long struggle, the efforts of all who had striven for this old cause would be thrown away, unless this very year Votes for Women were enacted'. She was justifiably afraid that with the likely arrival at the next General Election of a Liberal government, who supported giving the vote to adult men only, the Woman Question would be lost for years.

Emmeline worked herself into such a frenzy, night after sleepless night, that Sylvia found her college work seriously affected. Rising one morning to be in class by 8.30 a.m., Sylvia heard her mother still declaiming and was concerned for her state of mind. Then, to Sylvia's dismay, Emmeline smiled at her obvious concern: 'don't look at me like that,' she said. 'Bless you, your old mother likes it. This is what I call life.' For Sylvia, to whom the cause of social reform was a serious business and not one to be enjoyed, this was a portent of things to come, and she recalled her reaction in *The Suffragette Movement*: 'It was an awakening to me and caused a revulsion of feeling. To her too, it was perhaps an unusual self-revelation: nor was it entirely true, for she was as many mooded as the sea.'

On 21 February, Sylvia and her mother waited in the House of Commons for Keir Hardie to emerge and break the news of the ballot. He had failed to secure a place and would be unable to present their bill. But that was not the end of the story. Emmeline immediately telephoned Bamford Slack MP, who had been more fortunate and had secured a place in the ballot. Caught between Emmeline and his feminist wife, Bamford Slack agreed to take up their bill. This stated that in all legislation concerning the qualifications for voting, words of the masculine gender should be held to include women. It was set down for the second order of the day on Friday, 12 May. Emmeline had achieved, by arm-twisting determination, what the more circumspect and restrained NUWSS had failed to do in years of quiet campaigning.

Beatrice Potter, now married to Sydney Webb, claimed that feminism – including, but not exclusively, the fight for the vote – was part of a wider spread of ideals and a general move towards the partnership of all human beings. This was exactly Sylvia's philosophy but one which was already causing her internal pain. By now she was well and truly in the thick of things. She found herself forever on the move from meeting to meeting, by bus, to every corner of London, raising support for the bill and gathering signatures on a petition. It was an expensive business for an impoverished student. She went alone to an NUWSS gathering and was amused by its discreet politeness in the genteel hands of Millicent Fawcett; it was different indeed from the rousing socialist meetings to which she was accustomed.

The WSPU, noisy as it was, was regarded by most people as little more than a local Manchester family firm. This was about to change. Emmeline returned to London on 11 May to try, with Hardie, to manoeuvre their bill into first place. This time Emmeline and Sylvia were not alone. The corridors and Lobby of the House of Commons were overflowing with excited, ebullient members of women's organizations from all over the country and abroad, eager for victory. Inside Parliament, MPs were busy wasting time and discussing absurdities in order to leave no time for the franchise bill. It was talked out and the House adjourned.

Despite the disappointment, Sylvia still had much work to do. She had continued to spend long hours helping Hardie and designing posters for his Unemployed Workman's Bill, which occupied the Commons through most of the summer. Hardie wrote to her about this time, clearly concerned for her frenetic workload. His letter, in pencil, is as usual undated:

Dear Sylvia. Under the workmen's compensation act the sum to be paid is not regulated by the number of dependents but by the average wages over three years of the killed or injured worker. Where he had no dependents no compensation is paid. There is some force in what you say about the childless widow but I don't think it is any concern of ours to force women, or men, into an already overcrowded labour market. That is how it appears to me. If a woman with a pension cares to go to work that is entirely her own concern and if she has a pound a week apart from her work she will see to it that she is neither sweated nor overworked. See that you do the same. I am more concerned about that at the moment than anything else. Sincerely as aye . . .

When Prime Minister Arthur Balfour eventually agreed to meet a deputation of 1000 destitute East End women, he was heavily protected by a perfume spray against the stench of poverty. The Bill had a rocky ride, but following major disturbances in Manchester and elsewhere, the Government panicked and within a few weeks it became law. The success of popular violence was not lost on Emmeline.

By the time Sylvia returned to Manchester for the summer holidays, her mother and sisters had recruited some impressive new WSPU members. There were three in particular who, for very different reasons, were to influence the future of the WSPU: the mill girl Annie Kenney, the agnostic socialist and former teacher Teresa Billington and the colourful Flora Drummond, known to the other girls at that time as 'Precocious Piglet'. Eventually, because of her liking for peaked caps, epaulettes and military clothes and her habit of riding at the head of demonstrations flourishing a baton, she became rather more impressively known as 'The General'.

On account of her romantic, mill-girl background, her fanatical hero-worship of Christabel and her devotion to the cause, Annie Kenney was initially adopted as the WSPU 'mascot'. Her ageing thin face and worn hands, from which a finger had been torn by a whirling bobbin in the mill, contrasted with the mop of youthful, child-like blonde hair. As time passed, however, her courage and tireless energy marked her out for an important place in the story.[1] Born 13 September 1879 at Springhead, Lancashire, on the edge of Saddleworth Moor, she was the fifth of eleven children and a happy child who adored her mother. At the age of ten Annie was sent off to work part-time, wearing her shawl and her bright clean clogs, dividing the week between the mill and school. 'I was a little dunce. I could not retain anything.'

When she was thirteen, Annie left school for good: 'My education was finished, my school knowledge was nil. I could not do arithmetic. I was a bad writer, geography was Greek to me; the only thing I liked was poetry. All through my life I have lived in dreams,' she wrote later. By the time she was twenty, Annie had become more politically aware and serious, reading the *Clarion* newspaper and developing an interest in the new Labour movement.

Then in 1905 her mother died. 'I owe all that I have ever been to her . . . the cement of love that kept the home life together disappeared.' To occupy her mind she joined the Oldham Trades Council, who had invited Christabel to address them as part of her already heavy speaking programme. The audience was tiny but Annie was there with her three sisters. They were politically ignorant, knowing nothing of Votes for Women.

Christabel was quick to spot Annie's potential; very soon she was invited to Nelson Street, and by the time Sylvia returned, Annie was already a part of the family. 'One of the wonders to me,' Annie wrote later of Christabel, 'is that she ever roused in me a genuine passion for politics . . . and yet I felt within a few months as though I had been in the heart of politics all my life.' Christabel, she said, had a way of looking vacant as though she were 1000 miles away, 'but she was making indelible mental notes about me'. Sylvia, too, liked Annie – her twinkling blue eyes and her lively sense of fun provided some light relief for the somewhat intense group of women. Like most of the WSPU members, she was unmarried.

Annie was a natural follower, not a leader, not an organizer, but a valuable and apparently indestructible cog in the machinery of the WSPU. As Christabel assumed more and more the mantle of the warrior queen, Annie Kenney did not intend to let her down. She became a lively and courageous speaker, urging her fellow textile workers to rise up and fight. Her political knowledge remained sketchy, and despite plans to improve herself, she was no student. Yet the force of her bright, eager personality held her audiences everywhere. She galvanized the Pankhurst girls to spend their Sundays travelling around the north country fairs and 'wakes'.

1. Annie Kenney, *Memories of a Militant*, Edward Arnold, 1924.

They were all so young and their sincerity so compelling. Men and women at these gatherings were not too bothered about political detail on a sunny Sunday afternoon. They liked and remembered mill-girl Annie Kenney with her simple message of 'Votes for Women', alongside the novelty of listening to Christabel, an elegant, intelligent, middle-class lady, criticizing Members of Parliament.

The arrival of Teresa Billington added a slightly daunting measure of intellectual gravitas to the movement. Here was a contrast, in every way, to the bird-like Annie. Tess, as she liked to be known at this stage, was the child of an unhappy marriage but already had an impressive professional standing. She was a teacher, Hon. Secretary of the Manchester Teachers' Equal Pay League, a worker at the Manchester Ancoats University Settlement and studying for her BSc from London University. A large, rather aggressive woman with strongly-held views, it was her refusal to teach religion in a state school that prompted her to seek the advice of Emmeline Pankhurst, who invited her to join the WSPU.

Tess eventually married Frederick Greig in 1907, joining her name to his as Billington-Greig. Thereafter she preferred to be known as TBG. TBG's memory of Emmeline at that time is useful in that it reveals the atmosphere in which Sylvia and her sister Adela were struggling, while Harry, almost unnoticed, was sinking under the strain:

> To work alongside her was to run the risk of losing yourself. She was ruthless in using the followers she gathered about her as she was ruthless to herself. She took advantage of both their strengths and their weaknesses and laid on them the burden of unprepared action, refused to excuse weakness, boomed and boosted the novice into sham maturity, refused maturity a hearing, suffered with you and for you, while she believed she was shaping you and used every device of suppression when the revolt against the shaping came. She was a most astute statesman, a skilled politician, a self-dedicated re-shaper of the world – and a dictator without mercy.'[2]

Sylvia wrote of TBG in *The Suffragette Movement*, 'She was one of the "new" young women who refused to make any pretence of subordinating themselves to others in thought or deed.'

Flora Drummond was a stout, jolly, working-class Scot. Unusually for a Suffragette, she was married, and, with her husband, had been one of the

---

2. Carol McPhee and Ann Fitzgerald (eds), *The Non Violent Militant*, Routledge and Keegan Paul, 1987.

founder members of the ILP. Her accent and down-at–heel-appearance were initially treated as something of a joke by other members, but Flora Drummond proved her worth, for she was an exceptionally good organizer, a rousing speaker and a stalwart member of the team.

Between these three Titans, the equally determined Sylvia was quietly holding her own: it is particularly noticeable that in many of the books chronicling those heady early days of the WSPU, Sylvia's name features far less than those of Emmeline or Christabel. Adela is almost invisible. Yet Sylvia and Adela were both there – working every hour of the day and soon to be suffering too, but in the early 1900s, when press exposure was as vital as it is today, the younger Pankhursts, perhaps, appeared less photogenic and, certainly at that stage, less newsworthy.

The next WSPU attempt at militancy was tinged with humour, as were many of their later escapades. On 13 October 1905 Sir Edward Grey, a potential Cabinet Minister whose wife was a fervent feminist, was booked to speak at the Manchester Free Trade Hall. The pro-suffragist Winston Churchill, rising young star of the Liberal Party and their prospective candidate for Manchester North West, was also there, surrounded by adoring women to whom he was already 'Winston'.

From now on, WSPU policy was to attack the Liberals at every possible moment – it had been decided that trying to influence individual Members of Parliament was useless. The only way forward was to challenge whichever party was in power, regardless of its colour, and it was assumed that the Liberals would form the next government. Christabel and Annie went to the meeting with the intention of heckling and causing a fuss. For the first time the slogan 'Votes for Women' was heard in public, when Annie stood up and shouted, 'Will a Liberal Government give women the vote?' She was hauled back by a steward and a hat placed over her face. Once again she tried – this time standing on a chair to make her protest. As the girls were dragged by six men to the exit, Christabel threatened assault and unconvincingly attempted to spit at the police. When they attempted to address the crowds leaving the hall, they were arrested, and next day she and Annie were convicted and sentenced respectively to fines of 10 shillings and 5 shillings or imprisonment for seven and three days. They chose prison, but although Mr Churchill apparently went himself to Strangeways, the authorities refused his offer to pay their fines. However, for the moment Christabel, who was by now studying law at Owen's College, Manchester, had to toe the line, for the College authorities threatened to expel her if she behaved badly again. The women's movement was in the headlines for the first time in years, since this was also the first time a woman had been sent to prison for a political cause. Membership grew dramatically.

Back home in Nelson Street, Emmeline announced to Sylvia that Christabel was now to be the leader of the Women's Social and Political Union, explaining that she would never be deflected from her purpose in life by her emotions, as most women are apt to be: 'We are politicians Christabel and I.' In one way Emmeline was right – throughout the Votes for Women campaign Sylvia was the only Pankhurst with the emotional support of a man in her life. Apart from an attempted seduction, when she was in Italy, which upset her, and a brave kiss by a porter on the homeward-bound train, she was inexperienced and naïve and her love of Hardie all the more passionate for that. She seems to have possessed a strangely appealing charisma that was less obvious than Christabel's, but nevertheless she was attractive to men. Reticent Hardie, married to reticent Lillie, was very amused by the un-reticent Sylvia.

This added dimension, of being loved and cared for, especially by Keir Hardie, gave her an inner confidence and maturity. Importantly, it gave her a more rounded view of life and it helped her, finally, to establish her independence beyond the family fold. As the movement became increasingly and stridently anti-men, Sylvia managed to sustain and live by the deep conviction taught by her father and shared by Keir Hardie that men and women should be equal partners.

In Emmeline's autobiography *My Own Story* she outlined very firmly the fundamental and unshakeable policy that she claims made the WSPU so different from all other suffrage organizations at this time and gave them such spectacular appeal:

> No member of the WSPU divides her attention between suffrage and other social reforms. We hold that both reason and justice dictate that women shall have a share in reforming the evils that afflict society . . . Therefore we demand, before any other legislation whatever, the elementary justice of votes for women.

No wonder Emmeline did not approve of Sylvia's hours, locked with Keir Hardie on the unemployed workmen's bill and remedies for other social problems. No wonder Sylvia was so uneasy that her mother was already moving so far from the cherished socialist ideals of her late husband. But Sylvia was loyal and not yet ready for confrontation.

On 4 December 1905 Arthur Balfour's Government resigned and campaigning for the General Election began in earnest. Back in London for the winter, Sylvia's tiny flat was gradually taken over by the arrival of a succession of eager WSPU members. Annie Kenney was the first, and it was she, with TBG, who was given the task of creating the first major London disturbance at a Liberal rally, in the Albert Hall. They let down a 9-foot banner demanding, 'Will the Liberal Government Give Women the Vote', and were promptly thrown out. The celebrated journalist and editor of the *Review of Reviews*, W.T. Stead was there standing on a chair and waving his hat.

Sylvia returned home to Manchester for Christmas to find her artistic talents diverted into banner making. Day after day, night after night, she willingly painted Votes for Women on hundreds of strips of white calico, ready for the election onslaught. It had been decided by Christabel that Churchill was to be their target. This was not a personal vendetta. It was practical. Churchill was selected because he was the only important candidate seeking election within easy reach of headquarters; besides, he was fighting a high profile seat that had been held for twenty years by the Conservatives. She spoke at every election meeting he addressed, heckling and banner waving.

Sylvia, with Harry loyally in tow, was among the gathering to hear Churchill at his first meeting in Cheetham Hill schoolroom. She put her question and was ignored, whereupon Harry set up a chanting demand that Sylvia should be heard. She tried again. Again there was no reply, and the audience erupted in anger. The chairman invited Sylvia onto the platform so she could be heard, and as she was turning to leave, Churchill himself took her arm and said, 'wait until you have heard what I have to say'. He faced the audience and declared that Sylvia was disgracing her family: 'I am not going to be henpecked into a question of such importance.' This was Sylvia's first confrontation with Churchill. It was by no means to be her last.

Then followed the first of the many WSPU antics, most of which would not have been out of place in one of the comic films being produced by the burgeoning cinema industry. Sylvia, having been locked in a side room, managed somehow to squeeze between the window bars and escape to the yard outside where a crowd was cheering and demanding a speech.

Meanwhile, Emmeline Pankhurst was in Merthyr Tydfil campaigning for Keir Hardie – which was just as well because Hardie himself could not be found. In fact, he was racing around the country speaking in support of the fifty Labour Representation Committee candidates. In three days he covered 1120 miles by train, returning just in time for the count – having lost his voice. The election was held between 12 January and 7 February 1906. At that time elections took place over a period of several days. The Liberals won a landslide victory and the press remarked on the extraordinary success of Hardie's group, which trebled its share of the vote to 5.9 per cent. Keir Hardie was returned at Merthyr and elected leader of the Committee, which renamed itself the Labour Party. Sir Henry Campbell Bannerman became Prime Minister, with Asquith, Lloyd George and Churchill as his senior colleagues.

Sylvia was already back at art school in London, and watched the results come in with the crowds outside the *Daily News* offices, and saw the Labour Party – 'our party' – win twenty-nine seats: 'Life was now changed. No more painting parties. The future seemed full of promise.' The Palace of Westminster was agog, a number of new Labour newspapers were launched and Hardie himself was in constant demand by reporters. The first rule he made was that no Labour MP was to be seen drinking in the bars: 'Labour and Liquor don't mix.'

Annie was now dispatched by Emmeline, with a wicker basket and £2 in her purse, to 'rouse London'. Sylvia met her, took her home to Park Street and the following evening the girls went off to Canning Town to begin evangelizing the poverty-racked women of the East End. They described to them the paradise that would be theirs once the vote was won. 'I honestly believed every word I said,' Annie recalled in her autobiography. 'Poor East End women. We gave them something to dream about.'

Sylvia's famous lack of domesticity and doubtful culinary skills meant that an occasional outing to Lockhart's restaurant in the Strand was a welcome escape for Annie. No lentils with egg on top, no tomatoes with egg on top, no egg with tomatoes on top. Reading the menu at Lockhart's was a feast in itself. Annie was bowled over by the romance and the poverty of London; she slept in Salvation Army shelters, took buses to the country and sat, enthralled, at Sylvia's feet to listen to her readings of Shelley and Keats. It was not long before TBG joined them in Chelsea, followed by Mrs Pankhurst to check on how her team was faring, all crowded into Sylvia's tiny flat. For Annie, this was the happiest of times, full of humour, enthusiasm, plots and plans. Here in Park Street gathered the nucleus of the first tiny Committee (Fulham) of the WSPU: Mrs Roe (Sylvia's landlady), Annie Kenney, Sylvia's Aunt Mary Clarke (Emmeline's sister) and Sylvia as the Hon. Secretary.

The first great project Sylvia and Annie undertook together, with Hardie's guidance, was decidedly ambitious. Undaunted by their lack of organizational experience, they decided to stage a major rally in Trafalgar Square on 16 February 1906, the day of the State Opening of Parliament and the King's Speech. But the Square was not free and so Hardie suggested they should book Caxton Hall and sent her off with Annie to rally support from the East End.

This event was to prove a valuable exercise for Sylvia since, as a result of an introduction from Hardie, she met George Lansbury, the man who was known as 'the peaceful warrior' and who would eventually become the Labour leader. She was inspired by his work. George Lansbury was born on 21 February 1859 in Suffolk and in 1880 married Bessie Brine in London's Whitechapel. He was a Christian and a Socialist and had been a friend of Richard Pankhurst.

Annie Kenney described her impressions of the East End years later: 'I have travelled through all the great European cities but I have never seen such drabness, such hopeless despair and such agonising poverty . . . like one big, long funeral.' But there were residents who did have jobs, did pay their rent and did want to improve the area. Lansbury was one of these, and with his encouragement, Sylvia would eventually become another. No politician in this century walked the high wire between utopianism and pragmatism with greater skill or more effectiveness than George Lansbury.[3]

At Hardie's suggestion Sylvia went down to meet Lansbury at his wood yard in St Stephen's Road in Bow and arranged with him for a contingent of some 400 women to travel by train (fares paid) to St James' Park station for the Caxton Hall meeting. Emmeline was furious at Sylvia's temerity in taking so much on herself. She was angry that the girls had booked so large a hall, but it was too late to make changes, as the posters had already been distributed.

By this time Flora Drummond had arrived in Sylvia's lodgings and the press was hovering around the house. How they all fitted in is a mystery. On 16 February 1906, when Lansbury's 'army' arrived carrying their red Labour party flags, they were welcomed, at Annie's suggestion, with a cup of tea and a bun. It was all very jolly. Two curious ladies (one of them Lady Carlisle) turned up from the West End disguised as maids to see what it was all about. The grapevine and publicity was working well, and the Hall was already very full to hear Emmeline's rousing call to battle (she never needed a microphone); Sylvia must have been quietly delighted with the results, especially with the £50 profit that was collected.

When news came that across the road in Parliament the King's speech did indeed contain no mention of the franchise, Emmeline stood and moved that the meeting should resolve itself into a lobbying committee and head immediately for the House of Commons. She marched, 400 women behind her, in the cold and pouring rain to the Strangers' Entrance, where orders had been issued, for the first time in living memory, that no women should be admitted.

3. W. Fishman, *East End 1888*, Duckworth 1988.

Once again, Keir Hardie was to hand. He now persuaded the Speaker to allow some women, including Sylvia, twenty at a time, into the lobby, leaving the rest drenched and shivering outside. Sylvia explains in *The Suffragette Movement* that Hardie was alone in pressing for the enfranchisement of women to be included in the Labour party programme. Her mother decided that she must claim from him Labour's complete devotion to their cause, and so she took Sylvia with her to stiffen his resolve. Emmeline stormed the Commons with Sylvia reluctantly in tow, to berate Hardie, who told them, 'in the muffled voice with which he always cloaked distress', that the party had already made its democratic decision. Emmeline wept and implored and threw a tantrum, while Sylvia sat as a buffer between her and the 'dark-browed, silent' Hardie.

That April, in his first parliamentary speech as leader of the Labour party, he made an attempt to draw suffrage into the arena – something no party leader had attempted before. The political results were negative but the publicity results could hardly have been better. Emmeline and Sylvia were in the public gallery with a number of women who misunderstood the proceedings and leapt to their feet. There was much shouting and disorderly abuse, and Hardie slipped out without speaking to them; he was not amused. Sylvia was mortified: 'I knew that we had angered this generous friend. The knowledge seemed to fall on me like a stone. I felt culpable and that I alone was culpable; for I alone understood the difficulty of his stand for us and that his rivals were taking advantage of it to aid them in decrying his whole policy. At least we should have consulted him, I thought ruefully.' There was general condemnation of the WSPU action, with the exception of W.T. Stead who referred in the *Review of Reviews* to their 'divine impatience'.

Hardie remained silent for a few days. 'They were an age to me,' said the distressed Sylvia, but then, generously, he spoke out, defending the women on the grounds that they did not understand procedure. His support for the women was in defiance of the mood of the party he had founded. It was a magnanimous and politically dangerous gesture that was completely lost on Emmeline but not on Sylvia. She was troubled and embarrassed by the differences and pressures being laid on Keir Hardie.

Meanwhile, on 10 January the *Daily Mail* published an article, appropriately in the circumstances by its war correspondent, Charles Hands. In it he used for the first time the name of 'Suffragette' for the ladies of the WSPU. It was a name that was to launch the campaign internationally as it reverberated around the world.

Said Emmeline: 'there was a spring in it, a spring that we liked'.

7

The Third Pillar

'I have lost one of the pillars of my world, the dearest of long loved friends.'
Sylvia Pankhurst on the death of
Emmeline Pethick-Lawrence, 12 March 1954

In February 1906 the WSPU had no money, no office and no organization. Sylvia, often distraught, overburdened and struggling to cope, was herself in financial trouble. Then, into this shambolic hotbed of revolution and proposed guerrilla tactics was drawn the wisdom and organizational genius of Emmeline and Frederick Pethick-Lawrence.

Emmeline, now aged 38, had all her life believed in the kind of practical socialism which had inspired 24-year-old Sylvia. Born in 1867, the eldest of thirteen children of middle-class, nonconformist parents, her early years were secure but nevertheless 'the only unhappy time of my life'. In her autobiography[1] she describes with sensitive insight the loneliness of the Victorian nursery: 'Outside the walls of the nursery we were surrounded by loving and dear people who cared deeply for us but they lived in another world separated by prison walls . . . Nurseries in those days were prisons, as I realised when I found myself for the first time in Holloway Jail and reverted at once to the old sense of helplessness and misery.' Then came a series of boarding schools, the inevitable 'finishing' establishment and at 16 first a spell in France, where she learned quite a lot about the local boys and not much French, followed by a convent in Germany. At the age of 19 and against the wishes of her parents, she escaped from the conventional fate of unmarried girls waiting to be married off and left home to work at the West London Mission.

Emmeline Pethick, like Sylvia, was influenced by socialism, Edward Carpenter and Keir Hardie. She founded the Esperance Working Girls Club and then opened a dressmaking business that paid employees double the

1. Emmeline Pethick-Lawrence, *My Part in a Changing World*, Victor Gollancz, 1938.

money they were used to receiving; she ran a club for Jewish girls and pioneered the 'Green Lady Hostel' – a holiday home in Littlehampton on the Sussex coast for working girls, at a time when the idea of an annual holiday by the sea was unheard of. She became captivated (as did Sylvia) by the amazing 'vitality and eagerness for life in the half-starved and over-worked young people' of the East End of London.

In 1901 she married 30-year-old Frederick Lawrence, Old Etonian, Cambridge Union President and a former editor of the socialist London evening newspaper the *Echo* and by now a wealthy lawyer. He fell in love with her 'liberal habits of smoking, going out walking without gloves and being able to jump off a moving omnibus'. Like Emmeline, he was a Liberal-turned-Socialist, committed to social reform, and many of the deprived young people with whom the couple had worked were guests at their wedding. Throughout their lives the childless but child-loving Pethick-Lawrences were devoted to giving children and young people the love and affection they had felt deprived of themselves.

Together in 1906, with their names now combined as Pethick-Lawrence, this popular and well-connected couple were to take the embryonic WSPU under their wing and launch the name of Pankhurst on the road to international fame. Frederick Pethick-Lawrence became known as 'Godfather' to the women of the WSPU. After their marriage they rented a large flat in Clements Inn, where Frederick created a sunny garden room to which only his wife had a key. This was to be her own private, flower-filled retreat. They also bought a house, 'The Mascot', near Dorking in Surrey, designed by Edwin Lutyens.

Emmeline Pethick-Lawrence (and through her, Sylvia) was also friendly with the distinguished musician Cecil Sharp and his sister Evelyn, whose love of folk music and dance was encouraging a revival of English country music and folklore – in particular Morris dancing. As an artist, Sylvia was fascinated by the fluid movements of the dancers.

Keir Hardie, a close friend of Frederick's and regular visitor, astutely judged that the Pethick-Lawrences were the couple most likely to shape this excitably disorganized but determined group of women into an effective army ready for battle. He persuaded first Emmeline Pankhurst and then Annie Kenney to plead with Mrs Pethick-Lawrence for help. Mrs Pankhurst appeared immediately to Mrs Pethick-Lawrence as having 'a temperament akin to genius. She could have been a Queen on a stage or in a salon.' She was, as she herself instinctively felt, cast for a great role. However, it was Annie's child-like simplicity that first deeply touched Emmeline Pethick-Lawrence, and so, 'by a very extraordinary sequence of events, I who am not of a revolutionary temperament, was drawn into a revolutionary movement . . .'. Annie Kenney wrote of her: 'Mrs Lawrence is not a woman who will play at work or work without method or from pure inspiration. She must see where she is going, where the road will lead and what obstacles may be to block the path. She was the person we needed. Christabel, Mrs Pankhurst and I were too temperamental and purely intuitive. So Providence sent the right woman at the right time to help in turning the tiny vessel into a great liner.'

Mrs Pethick-Lawrence agreed to attend a meeting at Sylvia's house in Park Street, where she met the six-strong committee, including Sylvia, her aunt Mary Clarke, TBG and Annie Kenney. It was the friendship between Mrs Pethick-Lawrence and Sylvia, not that with Christabel nor with Emmeline Pankhurst, which would endure into old age. Emmeline Pethick-Lawrence came to admire and even love Emmeline Pankhurst and was captivated by Christabel, who became one of the children she never had, but it was the quieter Sylvia, earnest and intense, who was to be most influenced by her and with whom she corresponded and maintained a touching friendship long after the franchise furore was over. Their letters, exchanged over many years, reveal a respect and affection that Sylvia longed for but was never able to find in her mother.

Of that initial meeting with Sylvia in Park Street, Emmeline observed, 'I found her a baffling personality.' She was intrigued by her appearance, reminiscent of the young Russian students who had given up their careers to go amongst the workers and prepare the ground for the revolution. Sylvia's obviously strong will, 'trained to endure', and the apparent hardness did not match her childlike face. Thirty years on, Emmeline had come far closer to understanding Sylvia's complex personality: 'I know now that under that outer coat of mail there hides a sensitive and tender child . . . quiet and shy in those days, she surprised her friends by one brilliant success after another . . . The expression of Sylvia's real self was to be found in her creative art and in the depth of her emotional attachment to very few persons.'

It was several months before Mrs Pethick-Lawrence met Christabel, who was studying in Manchester, and noticed the gulf between the girls. Christabel, she said, embodied 'youth knocking on the door'. Like all the Pankhursts, she had great courage and, in addition, a cool, logical mind and quick wit, but she had none of Sylvia's 'passion of pity': she detested whatever she saw as weakness. In the end, as Sylvia dedicated herself to the fight not only for the vote, but also for over-worked poverty-stricken people, there was no longer room in her life for the art and devotion to beauty that had inspired her youth. 'She has never wavered in her loyalty to the victimised and the oppressed in every part of the world,' wrote Mrs Pethick-Lawrence in 1938, at a time when Sylvia was still fighting, this time to alert the world of the dangers of Fascism.

Initially, Emmeline Pethick-Lawrence was reluctant to become involved because her enthusiasm, like Sylvia's, had been focused on work that would directly improve the lives of the toiling masses. 'The days when women's suffrage was a live issue were over before my time. The story of the betrayal of the suffrage movement by Parliament has been told to weariness. The young do not waste time sitting on graves.' Despite this, and despite her many existing welfare commitments, she admitted, 'It was not without some dismay that it was borne in upon me that somebody had to come to the rescue of this brave little group and that the finger of fate pointed at me.' Indeed, 'It became my business to give their genius a solid foundation.' And so she allowed herself to be 'sucked into that whirlpool of the WSPU'. In 1906 she became the Hon. Treasurer.

The early gatherings in Sylvia's one-time workshop had taken on the noisy ribaldry of Angela Brazil's school stories that first appeared in 1904 and were devoured by girls of all ages in many countries. In *The School by the Sea* she wrote, 'the old order had changed indeed, and yielded place to a rosy, racy, healthy, hearty, well grown set of 20th century schoolgirls, overflowing with vigorous young life and abounding spirits, mentally and physically fit and about as different from their . . . forerunners as a hockey stick is from a spindle'. According to Sheila Rowbotham,[2] this creation of a body of fiction, concentrating on the adolescent middle-class female market, actually aided the expansion of the women's role in society.

Not all the Suffragettes were young, of course. Some, like the now venerable Mrs Wolstenholme-Elmy, with her pink and white complexion and white bobbing ringlets, had been fighting for the cause all their lives, but it was the young who caught the public imagination. There was a high-spirited youthfulness and optimism, regardless of age. In those evenings plotting and planning, Mrs Martell read graphic accounts of the murders of Dr Crippen (out loud); TBG urged the flouting of 'Mrs Grundy' and enlightened the young women with titillating details of her love affair with a Scotsman, who she had refused to marry until women had the vote; Annie Kenney encouraged her with adulation; and Mrs Roe supplied constant cups of tea. The underlying deadly seriousness was leavened by a great deal of merriment and banter. There was plenty of feminine feeling, but their common dedication to the cause did not prevent the formation and fracturing of intense relationships.

2. Sheila Rowbotham, *Hidden from History*, Pluto Press, 1973.

After the death of Queen Victoria, women enjoyed much greater emotional freedom, but even in their twenties and thirties many were still emotionally adolescent. Within the Suffragette movement, passion was intense, even violent – whether for the cause or for the new female friends who shared that cause.

Much has been made in recent years of alleged sexual relationships within the movement – did Emmeline Pankhurst have an affair with self-confessed lesbian Dame Ethel Smyth?[3] Was Annie Kenney in love with Christabel? Is this what held the WSPU together? The emotional (though probably non-physical) chemistry between many of these women certainly cemented the movement and gave it (and them) strength, but there is very little, if any, historical evidence to support recent allegations of sexual activity. The fact that Emmeline Pankhurst and Dame Ethel shared a room on at least one occasion would hardly be proof of an affair in a court of law.

Martin Pugh, in his excellent study of *The Pankhursts*,[4] suspects Mrs Pethick-Lawrence of sexual ambivalence and, on fairly shaky evidence, he says that she 'never concealed the fact that as a girl she had been very troubled by her sexuality and the "tangle of emotions" it caused. As a result she had rejected the whole idea of marriage and suffered from a "vague feeling that I was not the kind of girl to attract a mate".' But this is a very understandable fear. Many women (and men) who are comfortably heterosexual but who have been educated in a single sex school will appreciate only too well Emmeline Pethick-Lawrence's confusion and anxiety approaching puberty. Not so long ago, this painful transition was often marked by having a 'crush' or a 'pash' on a senior girl or gym mistress – it was a phase that usually passed. Barbara Winslow, in her book *Sylvia Pankhurst. Sexual Politics and Radical Feminism*, refers to an essay by Blanch Wiesen Cooke in which she mentions, 'the world of women's friendships and the crucial role played by female networks of love and support, the sources of strength that enabled independent, creative and active women to function'. In the new freedoms of 1906 the valuable and enriching discovery of the power of women's emotional bonding was exciting – but it was not necessarily lesbian.

Sylvia, on the other hand, did not make close personal friends so easily, and seemed to stand back from entanglements with individual WSPU members. She had no need, for her relationship with Keir Hardie was rich on every level and seemed to satisfy her emotionally, physically and idealistically. Ethel Smyth once

3. Dame Ethel Smyth (1858–1944) was the celebrated composer who wrote the music for the WSPU anthem 'The March of the Women'.
4. Martin Pugh, *The Pankhursts*, Allen Lane, Penguin, 2001.

wrote to Emmeline Pankhurst, much later, in 1912: 'I couldn't help reminding [Christabel] that I always said . . . that Sylvia would never fall into line and would always be a difficulty given the fact that since C. is not on the spot Sylvia will never be an Amazon. If it isn't JKH it will be somebody else.'[5] In fact, this encouragement of hero-worship within the WSPU caused it to develop, in time, some of the potentially sinister characteristics of religious cults.

The messianic Christabel herself had many of the reckless and dangerously exciting qualities of a cult leader. She possessed a magnetic charisma that attracted recruits of all ages. Her rule was absolute, and when she eventually took the WSPU along the road to vandalism, they followed willingly. Also typically of cult leaders, she ruled from afar – living for most of the campaign in Paris and going to prison only three times. Not for Christabel the nightmare of force-feeding. She explained, and her explanations were accepted, that a leader cannot lead from prison.

In her autobiography Emmeline Pethick-Lawrence described, perhaps without recognizing the dangers, the relationship between the young Annie Kenney and Christabel:

> Her strength lay in complete surrender of mind, body and soul to a single idea and to the incarnation of that idea in a single person. She was Christabel's devotee in a sense that was mystical: I mean she neither gave nor looked to receive any expression of personal tenderness: her devotion took the form of unquestioning faith and absolute obedience. St Paul says that the truest freedom is to be the slave of Christ. I understand that to mean that in absolute obedience there is no division of will and therefore no sense of external discipline . . . that surrender endowed her with fearlessness and power . . . that was incalculable . . .

It is arguable that in later years the adulation of 'Queen' Christabel had become dangerous and that, far from winning the vote, her fire could well have consumed the movement her mother had founded. George Lansbury even likened Christabel to Christ:

> Let us teach this make-believe Liberal Government that this is a holy war and is a war of mens' and womens' rights the world over, that it is a war that shall not end until our end is accomplished and that it is a war in which we shall endeavour to protect human life but that will have no regard for property of

5. Ethel Smyth, *Female Pipings in Eden*, Peter Davies, 1933.

any kind whatsoever . . . In taking away your leader[6] remember some words uttered two thousand years ago: 'they have taken away our master' . . . sometimes people say there is no religion in the 20th century . . . this movement has made me believe there is. The women are proving there is a bigger thing in life than materialism. They have proved their bodies do not matter but you shall not crush their spirits . . .

Certainly in 1906 Christabel the Suffragette was worshipped both by members and by the public, even by her mother, but not by sister Sylvia: she was already aware of its dangers. As she wrote in *The Suffragette Movement*:

I was wounded by her frequent casting out of trusty friends for a mere hair's breadth difference of view; I often considered her policy mistaken either in conception or in application, but her speaking always delighted me; her gestures, her tones, her crisply-phrased audacity, I admired her, took pleasure in her, as I had done when we were children together in Russell Square. I avoided crossing swords with her; for six years I refrained from dissent from her decisions in words or deed . . . I could not have done this so consistently were it not that I regarded myself as one who had come into active political life only as a sacrifice to the urgency of the need, departing from the path I had marked out for myself and to which it was my intention to return. There came a time when I could efface my desire for the development of another policy no longer; but this was not yet.

On 9 March Sylvia and thirty women went to Downing Street to be greeted – and sent away – by two detectives. They had hoped to obtain an interview with the Prime Minister, Sir Henry Campbell Bannerman. Irene Miller knocked again and rang the bell pull, the door opened and she and Sylvia were both arrested. Annie Kenney then tried jumping onto a motor car to make a speech, with the same result. The three, detained at Cannon Row Police Station, were sent a message from the Prime Minister.

Two hundred Members of Parliament then formed a supportive Women's Suffrage Committee, urging the Prime Minister to receive a deputation from the pro-women's suffrage organizations. This he agreed to do. The date for this confrontation was fixed for 19 May 1906. About 350 suffrage delegates, representing some 260,000 women and including the non-militant suffragists, finally met the Prime Minister on the agreed date. There were not only

6. Christabel was in prison.

Pankhurst followers, but also temperance and co-operative workers, graduates, East Enders, Liberals and Socialists.

Whilst he was sympathetic and promised support, Sir Henry Campbell Bannerman also said that many of his Cabinet were opposed to the idea, and he 'preached the virtue of patience'. Keir Hardie spoke out and little Mrs Wolstenholme-Elmy protested that she had been working for the cause since 1865, but since her voice was too frail to be heard, her speech was read for her. Annie Kenney, in her shawl and clogs, once again jumped on a chair and shouted 'the agitation will go on'. Some 7000 women then reassembled in Trafalgar Square for the first major public open-air meeting for women's suffrage in London.

Following this demonstration, the suffrage movement became even more fragmented. There was a frenzy of superficial excitement and drama as the confrontational tactics occupied more and more space in the press. Underlying the WSPU success, dissent was brewing, not only amongst the Suffragettes themselves, but within the entire suffrage movement. More worrying to Sylvia, within the Labour party there was grave concern at Keir Hardie's determination to support the women's cause, even in the face of opposition from most of his parliamentary colleagues. There were those, like the NUWSS, determined to continue their protest within the rules, but the WSPU was now bent on increasing the disruption of the parliamentary process and distancing itself from all political parties. Christabel explained: 'The only way for either men or women to get what they want is to interfere with the peace of mind of the Government ... nothing is a greater disappointment to them than to find that the attention of their audience is distracted ... and that newspaper reports contain more about the Suffragettes than about themselves.'[7]

WSPU militancy was escalating; more and more women were being imprisoned for short terms, having refused to pay fines, and the press was vitriolic, calling them 'martyrettes' and 'hooligans'. In June, Lloyd George and Churchill appeared together in Manchester to be confronted this time by Adela Pankhurst, then a primary school teacher. She had slipped through the 'no Suffragette' cordon, 'disguised' in a very respectable pretty white muslin dress and a rose be-decked hat. She stood to ask a question, was set upon by a gentleman with an umbrella and promptly arrested.

Sylvia, too, heckled Churchill and was roundly reprimanded. Her thoughts on the incident did not match those of her sister or mother: 'I felt a

7. WSPU, 'Why we Protest at Political meetings', undated.

contemptuous interest in seeing the desperate eagerness of the candidate to win the election, his uncontrolled exasperation at our interruptions and arrogant determination not to deal with us as other questioners . . . Then the whole thing would appear to me as a sordid business and I would wish myself out of it for the rest of my life.'

Emmeline Pethick-Lawrence wrote in the *Labour Record*, 'There can be no going back.' She spoke particularly of Annie Kenney, who, like Christabel, seems to have touched the mother in her: 'That frail woman-child . . . who, if I could have my way should be shielded from every blast of the bitter wind.' Indeed, the Pethick-Lawrences were before long to offer Annie Kenney a home at 'The Mascot', where Christabel also spent much of her time later on.

But first Annie was sent to be an official organizer in the West Country at £2 weekly, and Sylvia, loaded with bundles of Dr Pankhurst's papers, was delegated to write the story of the Suffragette movement. Her time at the Royal College was coming to an end. Her talent had been acknowledged and she was advised to apply for a free, five-year place. Characteristically, Sylvia felt this would be wrong, as there was no way she could support herself for so long and was, she said, 'emphatically determined' to maintain her independence.

Only with Keir Hardie was she able to share her anxieties. She went often to Nevill's Court to pour out her troubles – he was always a good listener. She talked of her fears of giving up the life of an artist, 'laying aside the beloved pigments and brushes'. Ideologically, she longed to use her considerable talent in the cause of reform and, for the time being, spent much time and energy on designing posters and postcards for the WSPU. But she was already finding the Pankhurst name a hindrance rather than a benefit for earning a living, as editors tended to assume she could only write about the franchise. They were unwilling to promote the family name and certainly not to pay for the privilege. Only the *Westminster Review* agreed to accept material of women's interest – and then under the pen name of 'Ignota'.

She was ill with neuralgia, she was worried about her brother and also uneasily aware of an increasing difference with Christabel. The precarious future, which she realized she shared with her fellow students, made her extremely anxious, and she longed for support from her mother. It never came. Sadly, she wrote, 'we were no longer a family, the movement was overshadowing all personal affections. I had written to her regularly every second day, all the years of my absences. Now, my last letter unanswered I ceased to write at all . . .'.

She was exhausted, uncertain that she could even pay the rent. So it was that towards the end of June she wrote out her resignation from the secretaryship of the Fulham WSPU and left it on the table for Mrs Pethick-Lawrence. Emmeline Pethick-Lawrence wrote: 'For her own sake she should have done it long before . . . many months of work had been interrupted and spoilt by the agitation that was so foreign to her true nature.' Her mother, on the other hand, was furious that Sylvia had not waited until Christabel was free to come down from Manchester, and immediately appointed two joint honorary secretaries, Mrs Despard and Mrs How Martin, in her place. Christabel was appointed chief organizer at a wage of £2.10s weekly. Adela, who had been in prison, was also appointed a paid organizer.

Sylvia decided the time had come for a move, and she rented two unfurnished rooms in Cheyne Walk on the Thames Embankment, next to the house once occupied by the artist Turner. So painful was the neuralgia, it took Sylvia a whole week to transfer her meagre belongings from Park Street in a handcart. An easel, camp bed, packing cases of books and paints and one little bag of clothes: 'I sat among my boxes, ill and lonely,' she wrote, 'when unexpectedly Keir Hardie came knocking at my door. With quick discernment and practical kindness he took command of the situation. He lifted the heavy things into position, and when all was, so far as it could be, in order, he took me out for a meal at the little Italian restaurant where Harry and I had lunched on many a happy Sunday. I was immensely cheered.'

8

Prisoner

'Prisoners were scrambling for dresses of dark, chocolate coloured serge in the heaps on the floor. "Make haste! Make haste!" cried the officers. I pulled from the pile a skirt, many feet too wide, of the same pattern as the petticoats and a bodice with several large rents badly cobbled together. The broad arrows daubed with white paint on the dresses were fully four inches long. The bodices were fastened by only one button at the neck and gaped absurdly.'

Sylvia Pankhurst, *The Suffragette Movement*

In 1906 Keir Hardie was 50 years old and went home to celebrate his birthday. He looked 60, his complexion grey and his hair almost white. Yet he wrote from Cumnock, 'I am younger in spirit than I ever remember to have been.' Sylvia – the likely reason for his high spirits – was now 24. She gave him youth. He helped her towards maturity, and while they each endured endless 'unutterable torments of internal conflict' over human suffering and world problems, they were uplifted and united in their mission to convert the vast masses to socialism.

Hardie outlined their shared Utopia in a book, *From Serfdom to Socialism*, published in 1907. Socialism was, he wrote, 'fundamentally ethical, a vision of justice and equality born of a new society'. Both were prophets more than politicians, and the far-seeing Hardie, according to Sylvia, was already warning of the threat of war ahead in Europe. To his adoring public, Hardie was an eccentric, inspiring, endearing leader, cleverly illustrating his speeches with popular, old-fashioned tub-thumping allusions from the Bible, which was still the bedrock of much working-class belief. He touched their hearts just as he touched Sylvia's.

In June, Christabel graduated with honours, but since she was a woman, she was not allowed to practise law professionally. As WSPU chief organizer, she stayed with the Pethick-Lawrences in London. As Emmeline Pethick-Lawrence said, 'it was a visit that was to last five years'. Christabel then launched herself on a punishing programme of lectures, travelling and organizing. The bored girl who had sulked, head in book at Emerson's, was now unrecognizable. She had already decided that too much reliance was being placed on Sylvia's East End women and that their presence at demonstrations could be a deterrent to some badly needed wealthier supporters. Besides, she explained loftily, 'Parliament prefers a feminine bourgeoisie to a feminine proletariat.'

Emmeline Pankhurst understood the need to move their base nearer to Parliament as the focus of their action, but was worried about the finances. She had no need to. The Pethick-Lawrences were now in control of money and the WSPU never looked back on that account.

To Sylvia's obvious concern, Harry remained in Manchester. He had left West Heath School in Hampstead and was, she felt, being inadequately cared for in Nelson Street by his well-meaning Aunt Mary on a too limited budget. There was no prospect of the frail boy qualifying in anything, because his poor eyesight and his mother's inexplicable objection to glasses made studying impossible. With excitement running so high in London, neither the house in Manchester nor its occupants were a priority for Emmeline or Christabel. They seemed unaware of the emotional starvation experienced, in their different ways, by the younger children.

Adela's own memories of her brother at this time conflict utterly with those of Sylvia. Years later, she angrily blamed Sylvia for Harry's gradual decline in his adolescent years, writing, 'Money had been spent on him – what he had wanted was love and care beyond the ordinary. That was impossible to give him, except at the abandonment of Mother's public career, unless Sylvia had made some sacrifice of her Art and stayed at home to keep house and look after her brother . . . none of us did what we could have done for the dear boy . . . but for that our training, outlook and particularly father's influence were to blame . . .'.[1] Sylvia, on the other hand, tended to blame her mother's dedication to the cause for her blindness towards Harry's needs. But despite Adela's view of the way things were, whenever Harry was in distress, it was, in fact, to Sylvia, not to Emmeline or even to Adela, that he turned.

Meanwhile, life was frenetic in London. An initial £100 raised by Keir Hardie, a second donation from Mr Pethick-Lawrence himself, a secretary and the use of a room in his Clements Inn home all gave the movement a more solid foundation for the future. Within a few years that single room had mushroomed to become, with twenty-one rooms, the largest headquarters of

1. *My Mother: a Vindication and an Explanation*, Pankhurst/Walsh Papers, Australian National Library, Canberra.

any political party in London. The movement had been miraculously transformed by the Pethick-Lawrences into a powerful organization, with a national string of offices, shops and libraries. There was a huge army of increasingly middle-class volunteers across the country, who were able to write articulate letters to the press and encourage more and more donations. The value of literature sales alone rose from £60 in 1906 to £9,000 by 1909.

The day-to-day running of the WSPU was informal – too informal for some members. No minutes survive from this time, but TBG commented later, 'A certain routine/semblance [sic] was observed but it had no *guts*, "it was decided" in the minutes might mean Mrs P announced it as decided, – or no one objected – or there was a vote in favour.'

At the same time, poisonous anonymous letters poured in. Travelling to over 5000 meetings that year, the women were often unwelcome in hotels and guesthouses, and were daily treated to insults and indignities. TBG's record of her own experiences sheds some light on Sylvia's troubled conscience too, and helps us to understand how the Suffragettes were able to persevere in the face of such hostility:

> More than compensation was given us by the adhesion of numbers of women of character and principle who recognised the spirit of emancipation, the great hunger for human progress and liberty which was seeking utterance through the channel of militancy. We knew that the channel was narrow and ill-chosen, though as yet we had scarcely dared to admit this even to ourselves, for it seemed to us that so long as it served to give outlet to the great forces of feminine revolt against injustice it was uplifted and vindicated by its purpose. This was the doctrine we preached and believed.

And Sylvia? Well, Sylvia continued on her now increasingly lone championship of the working women who had no voice, while Hardie was equally absorbed, still collaborating with her, exchanging ideas by letter and whenever they met.

In August 1906 Sylvia appeared openly with Keir Hardie on the House of Commons terrace. There they heard of Christabel's apparent disloyalty at the recent Cockermouth by-election, where she had astounded electors by declaring that she 'cared not a jot' if they voted Tory or Labour, provided they ousted the Liberals. Her object was to oust any government – even a Labour government – that would not give women the vote. In this case, the Liberal candidate was in her firing line because the Liberal government was not yet playing the franchise game. The speech was treachery to the faithful Hardie, and Sylvia recognized, in Christabel's brilliant oratory and shrewd parliamentary analysis, a devastating destructiveness that was taking her far from their father's principles and could split the WSPU. 'How much easier to win applause . . . than for any constructive scheme . . . I detested her incipient Toryism,' she wrote in *The Suffragette Movement*.

Parliament reassembled on 23 October 1906, and immediately a number of WSPU members tried to hold a meeting in the lobby of the House. The fracas resulted in mass arrest and appearances at Cannon Row police station next day. Sylvia, intent on seeing fair play, went along to the hearing, only to find her friends, including Emmeline Pethick-Lawrence, had already been sent to the cells. She protested, was manhandled, arrested for abusive language and sentenced to fourteen days in the third division.[2]

That first night in her cell in Holloway, Sylvia was chastized for not having made her bed. 'May I have a nightdress?' she asked. 'No,' said the wardress. 'Sleep? Certainly not. The mattress and pillow, round like a bolster filled with a kind of shrub seemed as hard and comfortless as stone. The blankets and sheets were too narrow to cover one, the cell airless and cold . . . all night I was cold . . .'. In the morning the door opened: 'Where's your pint?' asked the wardress. Sylvia held out the measure and a thin gruel of oatmeal and water was poured into it and 6oz of brown bread thrown on the tin plate. At 8.30 all prisoners were marched to compulsory chapel. 'The majority seemed quite old,' Sylvia wrote:

The chaplain spoke with harsh severity and many a hard word for the sinner. Old women bowed their heads and wept. At his mention of children the mothers sobbed. Tears flowed at the playing of the organ and voices broke with weeping in the hymns. To me all this was misery. I wept with those poor souls; and when the cell door closed on me again, the shrunken forms of frail old grannies, with their scant white hair, their shaking hands and piteous, withered faces and the tense white looks and burning eyes of younger women, haunted me . . .

At twelve o'clock came the clatter of tins: dinner, a pint of oatmeal porridge unseasoned, like the breakfast gruel but cold and stiff instead of thin and hot. Two days a week 8oz of small sodden potatoes of poor quality, and on the remaining days, 6oz of what was called suet pudding, a small stiff waxy slice,

2. The Prison Act of 1898 decreed that prisoners were to be detained in one of three divisions according to the nature of their crime. Those in Category 1 were allowed their own food, some alcohol and clothes, were not forced to work and could receive some visitors. Categories 2 and 3 were much tougher, ordering prison dress and food, compulsory stitching of mailbags or hard labour and often solitary confinement.

heavy and unsweetened. 6oz of bread were added to each meal. The diet contained no sugar at all, no fat, save in the pudding.

Even Sylvia, uninterested in food as she had always been since those lumpy nursery porridge breakfasts as a child, was distraught by the effect of this cruel diet on her fellow prisoners.

Although over the years Sylvia endured appalling treatment, her many imprisonments engendered an outpouring of prose, painting and poetry, some of which she eventually put together in a book, *Writ on a Cold Slate*, a reminder that prisoners in the third division used ingenuity to keep their minds busy:

> Oh, weary sisters, you who cannot fight
> The cold world's battle but have missed the way
> And are cast out from peace, who tread the lowest path
> Or sit, chafing behind the prison bars.

The earliest known of Sylvia's poems to Hardie was written during this first experience of Holloway prison, of which there are several drafts. Sylvia's poetry is often embarrassingly immature and amateur, with none of the technical expertise she brought to her paintings. But it is, like everything she did, without artifice, straight from the heart. It is not great literature: it is sentimental, romantic and very personal. But it is the touching, often hidden human face of history. Usually undated, smudged, scratched out and often written in fading pencil on scrappy lined notebook paper, it is part of Sylvia's life.

The correspondence and poetry between Sylvia and Hardie has been largely ignored by biographers and historians as too maudlin or too personal. But it is significant that, before he died, Hardie returned Sylvia's letters, suggesting that she should decide what to keep for posterity and what to destroy. Those remaining – hers to him and his to her – were found among her papers after her death and are too long to reproduce in full:

> Dear face, so fond to me,
> Rugged with thought, with many lines of pain
> And with the milk of human kindness filled.
> Dear sturdy neck that my arms love to twine
> My fingers placing in the little curls
> Curls that are white before their time perhaps,
> But bonnier as they are than any else

Dear arms that hold me close, dear
Dear breast on which my head lies when I am tired
To which I cling and sob my sorrows out
Dear heart profound
Not to the cities art thou kin
Although in city thou art come to dwell,
But to the open country and the sea
Like to a mountain is thy character
Steadfast and strong . . .

Dear heart profound.
To peace thyself last, first the commonweal
Sunshine is distilled in your eyes and your dear length
Pressing upon me till my breath comes short . . .
Forward I tried to look to my release
I saw myself at home, upon my couch
And you bending to take me in your arms
But a doubt asked me 'will it ever be?'

The poetry touched Hardie deeply. So deeply that some Labour party members were now afraid his friendship with the Pankhursts and his determined support of the WSPU were affecting his judgement.

Keir Hardie replied to Sylvia with several rather formal letters, written obviously for the eyes of the censor:

Dear Sylvia, When your mother told me about the drawings I mentioned the article, and thought they might be meant for that as you had given her no instructions. I think therefore I had better stick to my idea for the present. They will add greatly to the value of the article. The books I send herewith are varied and I hope you may find them interesting. Noctes Ambrosianae had a great vogue in Scotland fifty years ago, now one scarcely ever hears it mentioned.

I have agreed to be at the breakfast[3] next week. This week I am giving an hour each morning to an artist who begged hard to be allowed to paint my portrait for this year's Academy. He comes here from ten to eleven each morning. He is a big, decent sort of chap and looks more like a farmer than an artist. I hope, for his sake that he may be successful.

---

3. Celebration breakfasts on prisoners' release provided a convenient vehicle for obtaining press coverage.

I hear that McKenna is putting a new clause in the bill making it clear that married women with the necessary qualifications are to be included in the franchise, and already the false friends of the measure are making that an excuse for saying they cannot support it. When the time comes they will change their mind.

Try and do as much work as you can both in sketching and writing. It is the one way of making the time pass. I have you often in my thoughts and shall be happier when you are again free. I don't think you should again take risks. But the cause, I know, has first claim. With every good wish. Yours, as ever J. Keir Hardie.

One of those most badly affected by her first experience of prison was Emmeline Pethick-Lawrence, for whom claustraphobic childhood terrors were reawakened as she bounced along in the darkness of the prison van. Her reaction was so bad that the prison governor showed surprising sensitivity and realized she was seriously unwell. 'It seemed to me that I was in my grave, forgotten by the world,' she recalled later. Her father and husband were sent for and allowed to take her home, before accompanying her to Italy for recuperation from what, in reality, had been a nervous breakdown. Fortunately, she was able to record in her autobiography, 'I was to have several later experiences of the inside of prison and was never again to be seriously disturbed by the routine of the system.' Emmeline's response to her first gaol sentence was what prompted her husband to totally harness his considerable legal brain to the cause of women's suffrage and emancipation.

Meanwhile, in the world outside, Hardie and others were demanding political status for the women, and on 29 October 1906 all Suffrage prisoners were removed, on the order of the Home Secretary, into the first division. This meant that the WSPU women would be allowed books, paper, sketching and writing materials, and that Sylvia could at last begin recording some of the miseries to which she was witness. After the initial shock, Sylvia's time in prison was turned, as everything she experienced, into a crusade on behalf of the poor and oppressed.

When in prison, TBG also made good use of the new permission to have access to writing materials, by prolific and often illuminating essays, some of which were later collated:

Woman is denied the rights of citizenship. She is an outlaw . . . Woman has tried, while submitting to the law to achieve her freedom. She has tried to act as though she were a citizen . . . She has pulled all the strings of what is called legitimate agitation – but the machine has not worked . . . She must employ some new force . . . all history is full of examples that liberty is only won by revolt . . .

Sylvia was released on 6 November and a party in her honour was thrown at WSPU headquarters. The campaigning maverick journalist W.T. Stead was there, wearing prison garments, as he traditionally did, on the anniversary of his own spell inside.[4]

To Christabel's annoyance, Hardie had arranged for Sylvia's article on her harrowing experiences to appear in Stead's *Saturday Review*. When it was eventually printed as a series between January and June 1907, Sylvia was paid a badly needed £10. Her mother, on the other hand, who was imprisoned nearly as often during the campaign, barely mentioned conditions inside. For her, the suffering of prisoners was an unwelcome distraction that would be put right when women had the vote, and she disliked Sylvia's constant protests in the press.

Surprisingly, Millicent Fawcett, President of the non-militant NUWSS, wrote a warm letter to the press in which she expressed some solidarity with the women: 'I, in common with the great majority of Suffrage workers, wish to continue the agitation on constitutional lines: but I feel that the action of the prisoners has touched the imagination of the country in a manner which quieter methods did not succeed in doing.' On the release of the last prisoners from Holloway, the NUWSS gave a banquet at the Savoy Hotel. Sylvia noted in *The Suffragette Movement* that she was not invited because, she assumed, 'the name Pankhurst savoured a shade too strongly of militancy for the non-militants, even in that expansive moment, to extend any special courtesy to one who bore it'. She may well have been right.

A year later, as their tactics became increasingly violent, Mrs Fawcett changed her mind. That autumn, after her release in November, Sylvia was invited to join Emmeline Pethick-Lawrence in Italy for a fortnight's recuperation. There she re-lived the freedom of her student days, painting and sketching. But there was a major difference now: prison had fired her with an even greater sense of commitment to social reform. She went with Emmeline to visit the women's prison in Milan, which, to her surprise, seemed bright and homely after the overpowering grimness of Holloway.

4. W.T. Stead was imprisoned in 1885 on a charge of unlawfully kidnapping a young girl for prostitution. This was, in fact, merely a part of his campaign to arouse public indignation towards the suffering of children in the East End, and he had no intention of employing the girl in this way.

At the Labour party conference in Belfast, in January 1907, the cauldron of dissent came to the boil. Earlier, it had been agreed that women's enfranchisement was to be among the possible measures to be supported in the coming session. However, at the conference an amendment was proposed: 'to extend the franchise on a property qualification to a section only is a retrograde step and should be opposed'. This amendment was carried, to Hardie's distress, by 605,000 to 268,000. In other words, the party had now decided to reject the Pankhurst Votes for Women campaign and to support the broader but more elusive goal of universal franchise.

Hardie's position, according to Caroline Benn, was not easily understood, but his justification for support of the limited bill was this: 'If the women have a bill of their own, short, simple and easily understood and they concentrate on that, even though it should never be discussed in Parliament until the general Adult Suffrage Bill is reached, they would by their agitation, have created the necessary volume of public opinion to make it impossible for politicians to overlook their claims.' Shortly after, he made an announcement that shocked the movement and horrified Sylvia. He threatened to leave the party. Everyone, it seems, was 'left sprawling'. He explained:

> Twenty-five years ago I cut myself adrift from every relationship, political and other, in order to assist building up a worker's party. I thought the days of my pioneering were over; but of late I have felt, with increasing intensity, the injustice inflicted upon women by our present laws. The intimation I wish to make to the Conference is this: if the resolution which has been carried today is intended to limit the action of the party in the House of Commons then I shall have seriously to consider whether I can remain a member further . . . The Party is largely my own child, and I cannot part from it lightly, or without pain; but at the same time I cannot sever myself from the principles I hold. If it is necessary for me to separate myself from what has been my life's work, I do so in order to remove the stigma resting upon our wives, mothers, and sisters of being accounted unfit for citizenship.

It is hard to imagine what such a statement must have meant to a man of Hardie's extreme sensitivity. Frank Smith and Sylvia were probably the only ones who appreciated the toll being taken on his health and 'the deep currents of emotion surging beneath his outer calm'. She wrote, begging him to reconsider such a sacrifice, knowing that despite her youth, she had considerable influence over him. Fortunately that influence was not needed, for the Parliamentary Labour Party agreed to introduce a 'conscience clause', enabling members to vote according to their beliefs and Hardie, therefore, to remain chairman.

Sylvia was surprisingly depressed. She realized that the compromise would leave the Labour party in a hopelessly weak position in a fight for electoral reform. Christabel's disdain for Hardie's role was more and more apparent and his closeness to Sylvia seen as an unwelcome distraction. But the old family ties were still too strong for Sylvia to break, however much she felt the need to urge the Labour party to flout the WSPU and fight for whatever they felt was right. Frederick Pethick-Lawrence announced in the *Labour Record* that if Hardie left the party it would mean, 'the final severance of the Women's Movement from the Labour Movement'. Sylvia reluctantly agreed with much of what was said in that article.

Early in February the NUWSS, inspired by the publicity hungry WSPU, held its own march, from Hyde Park Corner to Exeter Hall. Because the weather was appalling and the half-mile long procession of women, mostly dressed in black, were drenched by the sluicing rain, the event became known as 'The Mud March'. Keir Hardie was there, assuring them that he still supported their fight.

Parliament reassembled on 12 February and Votes for Women was omitted, yet again, from the King's Speech. The following day hundreds of Suffragettes assembled at Caxton Hall for a meeting of the 'Women's Parliament', followed by a mass protest march. Sylvia was among those, including Christabel, who were rushed by mounted police, thumped, bumped, generally manhandled and finally arrested.

That night, she walked over to Nevill's Court only to be bitterly disappointed that although she could see the faint light of Hardie's familiar candle, she could not make him hear. The following day, 14 February, she was once more in prison (number 1635), serving a three-week sentence. Hardie wrote to her on 21 February 1907:

Dear Sylvia, I duly received the m.s.s. you sent and also the drawings and am having a clean copy typed of the former. I shall try what can be done with it next week. Your mother sent up two of the drawings this forenoon just as I was starting out and these I have not yet seen, but if they refer to the same subject as the others I shall send them with the article unless I hear from you to the contrary.

I cannot understand how I missed you when you called the evening before your imprisonment, as I must have been in at the time. Perhaps you did not try the door and the candle light shows but dimly through the blind. My book is not yet out but may be any day now. I shall, if the regulations permit, send you a copy as soon as it reaches me. If you are allowed to receive books and can let me know, I shall send you one or two. With kindest regards and all good wishes, yours aye, J. Keir Hardie.

The book to which he was referring was *Serfdom to Socialism*. In it he speaks with sentimental reverence of the old-fashioned wife who 'ruled her little kingdom in love and gentle firmness . . . never idle . . . never fussed, patching, darning, knitting or sewing, keeping the cradle gently rocking with the light touch of her feet . . . She was a National Asset of priceless worth.' This was Lillie. It could never have been Sylvia.

So flustered had Sylvia been the night before her gaol sentence, she had even left the window of her flat open near a large cartoon of Boadicea on a Chariot which she was drawing for W.T. Stead. She was lucky that the picture was not spoilt and was able to deliver it to him on her release, but was utterly taken aback and 'enraged' to find herself in one of his famous bear hugs. Annie Kenney, too, had had to learn how to deal with Stead's exuberant advances, although in her case she was flattered by his declaration of 'grandfatherly' affection! 'He was a highly emotional and impulsive individual.'

The spring of 1907 brought the pain of Sylvia's only recorded disagreement with Hardie. On 8 March he had been guest speaker at a WSPU meeting in Exeter Hall, where he made the speech that was to increase the agonizing rift between Sylvia, the WSPU and the Labour party. He admitted that he was changing his mind and that if a women's suffrage bill was not granted within two years, he would organize a movement himself, which would stop at nothing short of full adult suffrage.

For the Pankhursts and the WSPU membership in general, the suggestion that they should wait even for two years was treason. Christabel was adamant in her belief that all politicians were humbugs unless they put Votes for Women at the top of their agenda. She believed that all reforms should be stopped until women could participate in their implementation. 'She could not brook a divided allegiance: she wanted to build up a body of women caring for no public question save the vote, interested in no party or organization save the WSPU.'

Sylvia and Hardie went for a walk that evening, wandering along the Thames Embankment. It was a deeply distressing walk for them, as she tried to explain her fears that he had abandoned the cause they had championed together for so long. She knew him so well by now and was afraid that these changing views were about to part her from the man she loved. She told him that given a choice between their love and her loyalty to the WSPU, she would remain faithful to the Union. Hardie said nothing until, as they passed a queue of homeless men waiting for night shelter, he turned to her and asked, 'Do you ask me to desert these?'

Oliver Goldsmith's grave in The Temple is in a quiet corner, distant from the roar of traffic, and for Sylvia was a place of reflection and retreat. It was here that she went one Saturday in April. Having called in at Nevill's Court, she had found Hardie ill, awaiting the doctor. She wandered into The Temple, her mind turning over the 'strange tangle into which our lives had been wrought'. She returned to Nevill's Court to find him worse, with a flustered Frank Smith acting as nurse and secretary and spilling medicine all over the floor. Every day, for an hour or two, Sylvia was there by his side. The following Thursday he heard that his beloved old age pensions had been again omitted from the Budget. He was bitterly disappointed. Sylvia watched him, distressed by his unhappiness and insistent that despite his weakness, he must dictate a reply to the 'brutal budget'. It was an effort that exhausted him, and next day he was sent by his doctor to St Thomas's Hospital. Again she sat with him, this time in the hospital garden by the River Thames, only to hear that he had decided, as he always did when he was ill, to return to Cumnock. He did not wish to risk an operation (for what is not clear), and asked his doctors to allow him to try alternative therapies first. A sense of panic runs through Sylvia's description of Hardie's troubles. Although she is never critical of his treatment of her, it must have been hard to see him fly to the care of someone else, wife or not.

She wrote to her mother to alert her that she was afraid their friend was dying, and Emmeline arrived just in time to see his frail, pale figure on the station platform. Too painful were the memories of his 'beautiful rugged presence . . . his gallantry and kindness'. The two women clung to each other and wept, Sylvia reliving the death of her father and 'the misery of our great loss nine years before'.

But Keir Hardie did not die. He went first to a hydro at Wemyss Bay, where Lillie and his daughter Nan took turns to accompany him, and then it was decided that a world cruise might help. He sailed in July for a fact-finding tour of Canada, Japan, Malaysia and India, where he urged independence, causing mayhem at home and attracting hundreds of thousands of devoted followers in the subcontinent. 'I honestly believe . . . I am being worshipped,' he wrote.[5]

5. Letter to Bruce Glasier, 8 October 1907, Glasier Papers.

He left all his work in England to Frank Smith, and Lillie, alone again, in Cumnock.

At the same time Sylvia, lonelier than ever, packed her own bags and headed north to drown her sorrows in a revival of her earlier determination to use her painting talents for social reform.

9

The Mirror Cracks

'There had been a clashing of temperaments and personalities: the split had ended it . . . The spirit of the WSPU now became more and more that of a volunteer army at war.'

Sylvia Pankhurst, *The Suffragette Movement*

'Never have I seen so hideous a disregard of elementary decencies in housing and sanitation . . . Roads were too often but beaten tracks of litter-fouled earth; rubbish heaps abounded; jerry-built hovels crumbled in decay. The country was utterly blighted . . .'

This was Sylvia Pankhurst's picture of Cradley Heath, Staffordshire, in the heart of the Black Country in 1907.

When Sylvia arrived, unannounced, with her customary small bag of clothes, her easel and her painting materials, this was the centre of the chain and nail making industry and a vital part of the industrial process. At the suggestion of the Pethick-Lawrences and at their expense, she had embarked on an artistic pilgrimage such as she had dreamed of while at college. Her brief was to paint the working women of Britain. She lodged in the local sweet shop and went out daily to paint pictures of the women working in the forges and tumbledown workshops. Regardless of her concern for poverty and her awareness of urban slums, she was quite unprepared for what she saw. Writing on her return, she described how, 'The air smells and tastes of soot and from the low hills on every side rises the smoke of mill chimneys.'

Sylvia was a good listener and the women crowded around her, eager to talk. Despite the fact that they laboured a ten-hour day, they earned at most 25p a week and appeared to accept their lot. Chain making was the local tradition and there was little alternative employment, but even so, they were only permitted to work at the most menial level on the 'slap chain', which required speed rather than skill. The Trade Union saw no purpose in looking after women and so did nothing to ease their lot. With their babies and toddlers beside them, their aprons were often singed by dangerous flying sparks, which occasionally burned the little faces, too.

Needless to say, Sylvia was not allowed to indulge her artistic travels for long. As she was preparing to leave Cradley for Leicester, a telegram arrived from her mother, telling her to join the Suffragettes at the Rutland by-election.

There were already signs that Christabel was assuming an ever more dominant lead in the Suffragette show and causing concern to some members, in particular TBG, who had been posted to Scotland. After all, Christabel was only 26. Emmeline, so experienced, so popular for her grace and eloquence, was 49, and yet she appeared to be totally dominated by her daughter. 'If I can obey so can you,' she told members, and undertook a punishing, almost non-stop round of missionary journeys all over the country to wave the flag and carry Christabel's message. When Sylvia reached Rutland, Emmeline had already moved north to Jarrow.

By this time the Suffragettes had become celebrities, or notorieties, so that wherever they went on their hired wagons, they were greeted not only by curious villagers, but also by gangs of sky-larking youths rattling handbells and cans of dried peas. Sometimes the lads released mice in the hope of scaring the women, and carts were even tipped, with their occupants, into village ponds. Sylvia did her best to support her friends, but she escaped from these meetings as soon as possible and made her way to Leicester to continue her odyssey. There she met Mrs Hawkins, the local WSPU secretary and active Bootmakers' Trade Unionist. Mrs Hawkins introduced her to the owners of a small shoemakers' co-operative factory, where she was permitted to set up her easel in the workshops. She painted the women wearing pale blue smocks, hunched over benches, machining toe-caps, stitching and cutting, 'skiving' or 'thinning off the edges'.

Next stop was Wigan, in Lancashire, where the 'pit brow' girls laboured in the coal industry. Despite her previous experiences at Cradley Heath and Leicester, the life of the women in Wigan distressed her even more. She wrote about her time spent among the coal workers both in Keir Hardie's newspaper, the *Labour Leader*, and later in the Suffragette magazine *Votes for Women*. The term 'pit brow lassies' applied to all kinds of work on the mine surface. There were bankswomen working in pairs and heaving coal tubs from the mine shaft onto railway lines; there were pit brow lassies themselves guiding the trucks to the sorting sheds, where the screenwomen picked out stone and debris as the coal moved past on a conveyor belt. These women wore picturesque corduroy knickerbockers, over which was a blue print apron known as a 'coat'; this was a safety measure, since the skirt could be easily removed and so would prevent its wearer from being trapped and dragged into the machinery. The air was full of coal dust and Sylvia's face became blackened like theirs as she sat painting. Even so, she admired their jollity and generally uncomplaining good spirits.

From Wigan she was summoned again, this time down to Bury St Edmunds in Suffolk. She was upset to find there was no Labour candidate and blotted her copy book by declaring that she was a socialist and looking thoroughly miserable at the Tory victory. She returned to her painting as soon as she was able.

In Staffordshire she visited the potteries where working conditions were, if anything, worse than those in Wigan or Cradley. Women were, once again, not allowed to undertake such skilled work as throwing pots, although Sylvia, it seems, was allowed to try her hand. She was appalled by the haggard pallor of the workers suffering from the effects of over-exposure to lead, and was so overcome herself by the choking, deadly dust that she fainted twice. The china produced was contrastingly beautiful, destined as it was largely for the tables of the rich. Sylvia also visited the factory of Josiah Wedgwood. There had been a long family association between the Pankhursts and the Wedgwoods, and she must have been relieved that conditions there were far better than in the other factories she has seen. The Wedgwoods had originally taken over her great uncle's pottery in Stoke-on-Trent, and Josiah remained a great help to Sylvia, especially during her later anti-Fascist years.

Meanwhile, trouble was brewing in London. TBG had been uneasy for some time, partly with the Pankhurst–Pethick-Lawrence clique, but even more with the insidious shift of policy towards increasing militancy about which members were not being consulted. Neither she nor the other malcontents approved the decision that the WSPU had to become a women-only group, owing no allegiance to any male-dominated organization. 'I did not approve of the line of protest determined upon . . . It was reckless, small and unfair.' She had refused to take part in the protest meeting in Manchester in October the previous year, at which Adela was arrested, but did not then express her anxieties.

In June, Emmeline had written to Sylvia in Wigan, hinting at revolution within the ranks. She told her that the democratic constitution was to be abolished and that she had agreed to become 'the autocrat' of the Union: 'I have just written to KH about Teresa BG. He promised me he would help with Mrs CS[1] if it became necessary and judging from what I hear the time has come to act . . . As for the TBG affair, we have to face her and put her in her place. She has gone too far this time.' Sylvia was in an increasingly difficult position and alarmed by her mother's decision. However, she wrote immediately, urging Emmeline not to fear a democratic constitution – a plea about which she commented later, 'I might as well have urged the wind to cease blowing.'

All through the summer there were continued rumblings of discontent from those who disliked the increasing power of Emmeline and Christabel and were defying the new anti-Labour stance. Unbeknown to most provincial members (and to Sylvia), Emmeline, Christabel and the Pethick-Lawrences had decided to cancel the annual conference scheduled for October.

In September, Sylvia was not best pleased to receive yet another summons, this time from Christabel, asking her to report on a WSPU Members' meeting in London. She explained that she was off to stay with the Pethick-Lawrences in Surrey and wanted Sylvia to send the result to her there. It was a friendly letter:

> I am sorry to trouble you with my affairs, you, poor child have not much family assistance in your worries. This is more than my affair tho', it concerns the Union as a whole.
>
> T.B is a wrecker.
>
> Mrs Lawrence will I think be at the 'At Home' on Friday. I have told Mrs L that I think she ought to speak out [to Mrs Despard] and she agrees.

There were two meetings on 10 September, the first a committee meeting, in the afternoon, at which Mrs Pankhurst announced the cancellation of the Annual Conference and the annulment of the constitution. In future, said Mrs Pankhurst, she would have no one on the committee who did not agree with her. In fact, the new committee never met. Their names were on the Union's headed paper but policy and finance were controlled and acted on by the Pethick-Lawrences, Christabel and Emmeline (who continued her evangelizing around the country and abroad). In future, all members would be required to sign a pledge: 'I endorse the objects and methods of the Women's Social and Political Union and hereby undertake not to support the candidate of any political party at Parliamentary elections until women have the vote.'

---

1. Mrs Annie Cobden Sanderson had issued a joint statement with Mrs Charlotte Despard at the ILP Conference in April, rejecting the policy of the Women's Social and Political Union.

At the second meeting, in the evening, the London members rallied in Essex Hall to be presented with a *fait accompli*. The dissenters – TBG, Mrs Despard, Mrs How Martyn and Caroline Hodgson – refused to accept the authority of the afternoon meeting and announced that they would hold an Annual Conference as planned, claiming that they were the real WSPU. But Emmeline moved fast and by 17 September had sent all members in the country pledge cards along with membership of the WSPU. The breakaway group then called themselves the Women's Freedom League. TBG wrote in her memoirs, 'The "coup d'etat" was a stupid, unnecessary mistake . . . By denying votes to her followers Mrs Pankhurst has belittled the very function which it was her desire and intention to magnify above all other rights.'

It is not clear from Sylvia's own description of what had happened if she was at these meetings herself, although the assumption must be that she was. She shared many of TBG's ideas but remained a loyal Pankhurst, although a Pankhurst without power. Her talents were welcome, her indefatigable energy and her eventual 'martyrdom' on hunger strike applauded, but it is clear that there was no place for Sylvia alongside her mother and sister. It was their names, not hers, on the letter paper, the newspaper and the handbills. She was certainly not mentioned or consulted in decisions and cleverly avoided the issue of commitment. She did not sign the pledge (though neither did she contravene it).

In October 1907 the Pethick-Lawrences launched a three-penny monthly journal titled *Votes for Women*. The leader in the first issue, probably written by Christabel, declared: 'If you have any pettiness or personal ambition you must leave that behind you before you come into this movement . . . There must be no double-dealing in our ranks. Everyone must fill her part . . . those who come must come as soldiers ready to march onwards in battle array . . .'. Sylvia was now invited to contribute a serialized history of the movement and act as a freelance reporter for the WSPU. She accepted the first commission but not the second, which she judged 'monotonous bondage, of no great service to anyone'.

With the split, the majority of mature, experienced campaigners had gone. More and more, the movement assumed a worryingly religious fervour, attracting younger and younger girls ready to worship at Christabel's feet. A spin-off group of women under 30 was formed, who named themselves the YHB (Young Hot Bloods). They were dedicated admirers of Christabel and some of the other youthful single girls, and, from the security of a teashop in the Strand, declared that they were ready to undertake particularly dangerous tasks.

Sylvia, being only too glad to escape, went on her travels again, with several bags of family papers in order to write her history of the movement and to paint. This time she wanted to study women farm workers in the village of Chirnside near Berwick-on-Tweed, 'a crowd of tattered womanhood, lost to all reticence and respect. Their eyes inflamed as though painted with blood, their faces ingrained with dirt, their garments a collection of rags.' When the cold weather set in, she moved on to Glasgow, staying in a two-room flat with a middle-aged couple, their daughter and a family of Yorkshire terriers. She slept in a typical cupboard in the wall. Her subject in Glasgow was the cotton mills, where the heat and bad air made her so sick and faint that she was unable to work. She wrote in the evenings or lectured for the WSPU, but the highlight of this particular journey was her Saturday and Sunday weekend meetings with her brother Harry.

Poor, docile Harry, misunderstood and misjudged, had been sent by Emmeline to work as a builder on Clydeside in March. At 18 he was 6ft tall, frail and more cerebral than practical. He was curiously, as Martin Pugh observes, now much more like his father than his mother was aware. Sylvia was fascinated by his growing interest in Eastern philosophies and Buddhism and horrified at the thought of such a gentle boy, alone in Glasgow, climbing scaffolding on dark, cold winter mornings. At last, with Christmas coming, Sylvia decided to return to London, where she was to meet her mother and sister. She invited them to a restaurant, which had been a favourite of hers and Harry's when he was at school in Hampstead.

On the way out from her flat, she picked up a letter from the hall table but did not open it until they were seated. What she read, laid out secretly on her knee under the tablecloth, was cataclysmic. Who was it from? There is an undated, unusually agonizing letter from Hardie among the Pankhurst papers in Amsterdam. It has no salutation and is also unsigned, but expresses Hardie's lifelong dilemma of how to pursue his personal goal of moral puritanism whilst indulging his naturally passionate instincts:

I feel as though I had passed through fire and water and a long valley of bitterness and had come out duller and wiser as though I should never feel so acutely any more but that may or not be – probably not. At the same time I feel as though I should never feel keenly, fervently, other things that I would wish to feel but only calmly and with reserve and with a double sensation of looking all round them into the past the present and the future. I prayed. I longed. I cried in my agony to be more stollid and self contained – I feel I <u>am</u> now, so I would be in one way, but I would not lose the power to pour myself out for others to forget myself in enthusiasm for persons and things almost I feel that if I lose this liability to be cast down to be all but consumed with grief even for slight things in any direction, so too I shall lose the power to be without reserve in that same direction too. I suppose like nature [illegible] nature has its changing seasons too and maybe I have stepped into a new phase of life and maybe only into another transient mood who [illegible] and the only answer to that is work while you may – so that I will do now.

I wonder when will you write to me again.

Is this the mystery letter that caused Sylvia such pain and about which she wrote in *The Suffragette Movement?*

It roused in me a storm of misery which seemed to be killing my inner life.

Transforming an inner shrine which had been as pleasant a garden of singing birds, to a waste and barren place. Snakes and writhing creatures, fire and destruction passed before my eyes: yet neither of the two sitting before me perceived my anguish . . . They asked me to go with them to Teignmouth in mid-Devon, where an election was pending. I refused, feeling that I must be alone with my grief. But after three days, with a desperate longing to flee from it, I followed them to Teignmouth on Christmas Eve . . . I could not escape from my misery and regretted that I had come . . . on Bank Holiday, to my mother's disgust I insisted on returning to London, unable to control my restless misery in the face of their cheerful chatter. I could not forsee that my sorrow would presently be dispelled as suddenly as it had come.

10

Nauseating Brutality

'If you had power to send us to prison, not for six months, but for six years, or for our lives, the Government must not think they could stop this agitation.'

Emmeline Pankhurst

By 1908 the Suffragette show was well and truly on the road. Sylvia, despite her differences, was drawn heart, soul and paintbrush into the parades, exhibitions and the razzmatazz. In February the 'Trojan Horse', a furniture van, drove into Parliament Square, packed with twenty-one women who attempted to rush the Palace of Westminster. It was then that women adopted their most celebrated tactic of chaining themselves to the railings of Downing Street, Buckingham Palace and even the gallery in the House itself. The annual total of Suffragette prison sentences rose sharply from 191 weeks in 1906–7, to 350 weeks in 1907–8 and over 960 weeks in 1908–9. Mrs Pankhurst was among the prisoners sent to gaol for six weeks. Respectable middle-class women found themselves standing in gutters (to remain on the pavement was counted as obstruction and meant possible arrest), selling *Votes for Women*, chalking on walls and parading with sandwich boards. For them, 'bliss was it in that dawn to be alive'.[1]

There were two more Women's Parliaments and a massive meeting in the Albert Hall in March, at which a symbolic empty chair was placed on the platform for Mrs Pankhurst. For unaccountable reasons she was released from prison a day short of completing her sentence, and so, with the usually brilliant WSPU stage-management, walked unexpectedly into the Hall amid uproar, to take her place.

Due to the excellence of the Pethick-Lawrence's fund-raising and a week of self-denial, donations were now pouring in, and many famous names, such as John Galsworthy, Mrs Bernard Shaw and Dr Elizabeth Garrett Anderson, were

1. Wordsworth, *The French Revolution*.

listed as supporters. Funds became available for ever more massive demonstrations.

Much as Sylvia had disliked what had happened during the split in September 1907, she was totally committed to her own ideological dreams, which she privately hoped could be achieved alongside what she judged to be the narrower goal of her mother. For the time being she helped as much as she was able.

Behind the scenes, young Harry was still causing her great concern. He had turned up on her doorstep in January, having lost his job in Scotland when his employer went bankrupt. He had no money and nowhere to go; Sylvia, with some reservations, took him under her wing. Her own finances were precarious. 'I counted my cash, dividing it to make it last for us both on short commons for nine days, hoping that before that time had expired a cheque would arrive.' Harry was, as ever, affectionate and eager to please, but Sylvia was rightly worried about his future prospects: 'I saw him as a skater on thin ice, who at any moment may descend into an anxious sea of discouragement.'

When Mrs Pankhurst arrived, Harry was clearly an unwanted problem. Christabel suggested, somewhat impractically, that he should qualify as a secretary, but since he had never been allowed glasses to correct his poor eyesight, or proper schooling, he was not equipped for such work. His mother, equally unrealistically, told Sylvia that if he got a reader's ticket to the British Museum, she would pay for some shorthand and typing classes. The minute she returned to the provinces, Sylvia and Christabel arranged for his much-needed spectacles, so that for the first time in his life he could read without distress. But any plans for his education were thwarted by Harry's own determination to play a part in the family crusade.

At Easter, when Campbell Bannerman resigned, Asquith became Prime Minister, and after a Cabinet re-shuffle, a series of by-elections followed. Christabel led the sucessful move to oust Winston Churchill from Manchester North West. There in 1908 on campaign, Harry met and fell in love with a 20-year-old Suffragette, Helen, daughter of Sir John Craggs. Many years later, Helen was to become the second Mrs Pethick-Lawrence. Harry drove the WSPU four in hand, with Helen by his side. When the election was over, he wrote to her, and to his delight received a reply. He then followed her to Brighton and spent the night on the cliffs outside her school, hoping for a sight of her passing by. First love was a painful process for Harry, who, like his sister Sylvia, found a release for his emotions in poetry:

> I saw thee, beloved,
> And having seen, shall ever see,
> I as a Greek and thou,
> O, Helen within the walls of Troy.
> Tell me, is there no weak spot
> In this great wall by which
> I should come to thee beloved.

Once back in London, Harry joined the women at whatever activity was the order of the day. Sylvia became more and more anxious about his lack of serious application and his long-term job prospects. It was unfortunate that his mother, having heard that Harry had been speaking at an ILP meeting on the virtues of a return to the land, decided he should gain agricultural experience, for which he was again totally unsuited.

Mrs Pankhurst had heard through Hardie of his friend, Joseph Fels. In 1900 this small, wiry, Jewish American had arrived in Britain and bought a mansion, where he proposed to pioneer a scheme of farm colonies to ease East End unemployment. When he and his wife lost their only child, Joseph Fels had turned to philanthropic work. He was introduced to George Lansbury, who had attempted a similar allotment scheme in the 1890s. He was to prove a generously unstinting, idealistic and practical source of support for many of their social and political projects. Fels financed many of Hardie's foreign travels and supported his election campaigns. Emmeline saw the farming enterprise as a healthy prospect for the sickly Harry, and so the hapless boy was despatched to rural Essex. This was a disaster, for Harry endured, uncomplaining as ever, the harsh conditions in which he was expected to work and live. The family did not discover his suffering until it was too late.

On 5 April 1908 Keir Hardie returned triumphant from his world tour (largely financed by the ever-generous Fels, who had accompanied him, Lillie and daughter Nan on the first stage), and Bruce Glasier announced, 'we are in for a big Hardie boom'. There is no record of Sylvia's response to his return: she does not mention it in her book, yet significantly she had cut out and treasured all her press cuttings covering his long journey. Nor is there any evidence that she went to the massive 'welcome home' celebration organized by Frank Smith in the Albert Hall. Although Hardie had resigned the Labour party leadership while he was away, in order to 'be free to speak out', every seat was taken. When he rose to speak, he was unable to utter a word for fully ten minutes while the audience cheered, waved handkerchiefs and sang 'The Red Flag' and 'For He's a Jolly Good Fellow'.

He told his euphoric friends that he did not believe he had been a success as a political leader: he had indeed neglected his parliamentary duties and had found himself at odds with his Labour party colleagues, but, he explained, 'I am an agitator. My work has consisted of stirring up divine discontent with wrong. With what remains of my life I intend to follow the same course.' These were words with which, had Sylvia been present, she would have identified, and despite the fact that Hardie then returned to Lillie in Scotland, it was not long before Sylvia and he were meeting and working together again.

Hardie, who had been distressed by Mrs Pankhurst's behaviour in 1907, wrote to Glasier that her actions had been 'folly . . . and will in time drive all the better spirits out of the WSPU'.[2] Nevertheless, like Sylvia, he decided to sit it out and to continue his fight for the women's cause overall, which they both judged more important than the unbalanced behaviour of one particular group. Their friendship renewed and revived, they were seen more and more together, although the Suffragette banner provided a convenient cloak for their intensifying intimacy.

In June there was a heatwave, and as temperatures soared, so did the women's spirits as they planned the largest-ever meeting to be held in Hyde Park for Midsummer Day. The constitutional suffragists, not to be outshone, slipped in first, with a far smaller 13,000-strong rally on 13 June.

Perhaps for the first time, Sylvia came fully into her own. She had her official role to play as voluntary organizer of the Chelsea, Wandsworth and Fulham districts, where she had already been breaking new ground with open-air meetings. Now she was excited to be a part of the most ambitious demonstration so far and glad to be able, like the other volunteers, to pay her own expenses.

In May, Mrs Pethick-Lawrence had suggested the Union should adopt its own colours – purple for dignity, white for purity and green for hope – and on 21 June those colours were emblazoned for the first time on the nation's consciousness. For once the entire Pankhurst family was working in unity. There were to be thirty special trains bringing demonstrators from seventy towns. For Sylvia the memory remained forever fresh:

There were 40 platforms and 140 speakers, nine chief marshals, seven group marshals, 30 group captains, 40 banner marshals as well as over three thousand standard bearers, all wearing badges and regalia in the colours. There were ten huge silk banners and five hundred smaller ones, thousands of flags and a large

2. Glasier Papers.

number of brass bands, each item paid for by some ardent donor, its price
announced and appealed for in Votes for Women.

Sylvia was asked to produce designs and heraldic devices for the factory
making banners, bunting and regalia: 'There was no great artistry . . . it was
mass-production at breakneck speed.' Impact rather than perfection of detail
was the order of the day. Decorated buses drove through the streets, and a
launch, laden with banner-waving women, anchored off the House of
Commons terrace where MPs were taking tea in the sunshine. The ladies
shouted invitations to join the rally; 'with police protection – there will be no
arrests,' they assured.

The pace was exhilarating and Sylvia was clearly enjoying the excitement, as
crowds of young people, including Harry, went off at her direction, chalking
and fly-posting. They worked continuously for four days and three nights as
21 June approached. Each of the main processions in the Park was headed by
a four-in-hand, in which rode the rich and famous, such as Mr and Mrs H.G.
Wells and Mrs Thomas Hardy. Keir Hardie marched, in procession, carrying
a banner proclaiming 'The World for the Worker', and George Bernard Shaw
was present in flamboyant mood.

All the women had been asked to wear white decorated with the Union's
new colours. Sylvia's own procession from Chelsea numbered 7000, and by the
time they reached the Park itself, she said, 'the ground was already thronged
with an unprecedented mass . . . as far as the eye could see was a sea of human
beings . . . the predominating gay hues of the women's clothes and the white
straw hats of the men suggested a giant bed of flowers.' *The Times* reported: 'Its
organisers had counted on an audience of 250,000. That expectation was
certainly fulfilled; probably it was doubled; it would be difficult to contradict
anyone who asserted it was trebled. Like the distance and numbers of the stars,
the facts were beyond the threshold of perception.' The *Daily Chronicle*,
patronizing but courageously supportive, noted, 'the beauty of the needlework
should convince the most sceptical that it is possible for a woman to use a
needle even when she is wanting the vote.' According to Sylvia, the whole affair
had cost £4,813, not including expenses, salaries or local costs. It is probably
true that many of those who had attended were there in the spirit of spectators
at a gladiatorial fight and eager for police action, but there was none.

Immediately afterwards, Sylvia and Christabel rushed back to Clements Inn
and sent a messenger to the Prime Minister, asking what he would do in
response to such a powerful demonstration. The answer was 'nothing'.
Exhausted but undaunted, they immediately announced a public meeting to be

held in Parliament Square on 30 June. Some 5000 policemen were detailed to control the crowd and, in the furore that followed, Sylvia lost her keys and her purse as gangs of hooligans tried to whip up a frenzy. Women were abused, manhandled and thrown to the ground, and in fury two protesters ran to Downing Street, where they threw the first-ever Suffragette stones – at the windows of the Prime Minister's house. Twenty-seven women were charged that day and sent to Holloway. They were incarcerated in the sweltering heat of the unventilated, unsanitary prison cells, where conditions had become so unbearable that inmates were fainting even in the exercise yard.

From 1908 released prisoners who needed medical care were sent to a nursing establishment in Pembridge Gardens run by the redoubtable Nurse Catherine Pine, who was to become for so long a rock for the organization. Nurse Pine (1864–1941) had trained in St Bartholomew's Hospital, London. She remained there as a sister until 1907, when she opened her own nursing home.

Quietly, in the background, Sylvia's meetings with Hardie were becoming more frequent, though still discreet. He wrote to her:

Little Sweetheart.

I find there is to be a Shop Assistants' meeting in Hyde Park tomorrow, which I declined going to on the plea of another engagement. That closes the Park against me for lunch.

For other reasons, which I can explain when we meet, I want you to come here. The menu will be a light one but we can go out in the cool of the evening and have a decent meal somewhere. Come along Holborn and down Chancery lane. That is the best way for you.

I shall wire you re this evening, probably about 6.50.

Affectionately K.

These intimate tea and toast evenings, focused as they certainly were on serious issues, provided for the couple a degree of much needed closeness and calm. To her great pleasure, Sylvia was encouraged to begin work on an unfinished chalk sketch and then a sensitive final watercolour of Hardie; the only known portrait of the founder of the ILP, it hung for years in her study. Sometimes there were walks, sometimes a theatre, always there was politics.

In October that year Emmeline Pankhurst and 'General' Drummond were arrested for inciting the public to rush the House of Commons. Sylvia and a large contingent of women, some on horseback, distributed thousands of leaflets inviting people to join them, which drew a crowd of some 60,000 and 5000 police to Parliament Square. The situation became potentially ugly and

Sylvia was hysterical, while Chancellor Lloyd George and Home Secretary Herbert Gladstone, son of William Ewart Gladstone, 'the Grand Old Man', watched from safety.

Mrs Pankhurst, Christabel and Mrs Drummond were summoned to appear at Bow Street on 21 October, and Sylvia, with her old art school friend Amy Browning, went along to give support. Sylvia's romantic reporting of events in the *Suffragette* was in tune with other journalistic hyperbole of the day: Christabel, she said,

> . . . was dressed in a fresh white muslin dress, whose one note of colour was the broad band of purple, white and green stripes around her waist. Her soft brown hair was uncovered, the little silky curls with just a hint of gold in them clustering around her neck . . . her skin looked even more brilliantly white and those rose petal cheeks of hers even more exquisitely and vividly flushed with the purest pink than usual She triumphed not by her grace and freshness but by the force and depth of her arguments.

In a brilliant publicity coup, Christabel conducted her own defence and subpoenaed a very reluctant Lloyd George and Herbert Gladstone to appear. Her sense of theatre and cross-examination were unassailable and both ministers were tied in knots, but the following day it was very different and she was a shadow of her earlier self. Amy confided many years later to her family that she and Sylvia knew that for Christabel this was the wrong time of the month and they had been rushing backwards and forwards to the chemist for pills to help relieve her agonizing stomach pains. According to the *Evening News*, sobs and tears interrupted her defence and 'Portia [their name for Christabel] Breaks Down and was quite unable to continue.' Emmeline Pankhurst and Mrs Drummond were sent to prison for three months and Christabel for ten weeks. For her, the time in prison proved altogether too great; she was frustrated at being removed from power and none too pleased that Sylvia was, for once, asked by Emmeline Pethick-Lawrence to deputize for her.

Sylvia's first major challenge arrived in the shape of Lloyd George, who decided to make a friendly gesture to the women's movement and wrote to the Women's Liberal Federation, suggesting that he should address their Albert Hall meeting in December. The WSPU was implored not to rock the political vote by heckling: they refused unless Lloyd George was prepared to support government action on Votes for Women in the next parliamentary session.

Sylvia threw herself wholeheartedly into the public relations opportunities on offer and secured all the seats in the front of the arena. It was planned that the women, dressed in prison clothes under their coats, were to sit there. She knew that hecklers would be man-handled and told the women that after they had removed their coats, made their protests and were thrown out, they should return immediately to Clements Inn. There she arranged for journalists to wait wanting to see the results of this treatment.

While the rowdy meeting was taking place, Sylvia waited at Clements Inn for the return of the hecklers, bruised and bloody, their dresses ripped and even corsets torn. For once the press appeared sympathetic and reported 'unnecessary violence' and 'nauseating brutality'.

Not so the King. The Archives stored at Windsor Castle include a vivid record of Royal responses to all manner of day-to-day events. On 3 December 1908 the King's Private Secretary wrote to Mr Asquith:

My dear Asquith,

The King desires me to say that he is rather disgusted at seeing in today's Times that Mr Lloyd George intends to preside at a meeting at the Albert Hall in favour of Women's Franchise.

He considers it a most improper thing for him, holding the high and important office which he holds as Chancellor of the Exchequer to do and if he continues to show in the future as he has done in the past such an entire absence of good judgement and propriety he shall have no more to do with him than what is absolutely needed.

The reply was prompt and dismissive:[3]

10 Downing St, 7 Dec 1908

I think your letter about Lloyd George's meeting was written under some misconception of the facts.

He was invited months ago – not to preside – but to speak at a meeting of the respectable and constitutional section of the supporters of womens suffrage and agreed to do so.

When he found that the Suffragettes were threatening to intervene and create disturbances he was anxious to get rid of the engagement and tried to do so but it was not found possible.

On the general question, I must point out that in this Cabinet (as would also be the case if the Unionists came to power) female suffrage is an open question. I myself am opposed to it but the great majority of my colleagues

3. The Royal Archives, Windsor, R29.

including some, such as E. Grey and Haldane whose opinion I greatly value are
in its favour.

The Albert Hall meeting had, undeniably, stimulated public interest, and
everyone was now drawn into the argument. Sylvia was to remain at the heart
of affairs for some time while her mother and Christabel were in Holloway.
The next major Suffragette project was a Women's Exhibition to be held 13–26
May 1909 in the Prince's Skating Rink in Knightsbridge.

In the meantime, as the unofficial 'official' artist for the WSPU, Sylvia's
skills were greatly in demand. The hugely increased output of speciality items
for sale in the Union's shops meant that she was working flat-out on designs
to be used on tea services, banners, badges and greetings cards. Probably best
known were her Angel of Freedom and the portcullis badge that she designed
as an award for members leaving prison. Much of her work still shows the
influence of her early years in Manchester and of the art of William Morris
and Walter Crane. She was distressed that, because of the pressure, she had
not achieved her best and was dissatisfied with results.

Many of the London departmental stores were now taking half-page
advertisments in *Votes for Women*, a sure sign of their recognition that many
of the readers had spending power. Indeed they had. One Suffragette, returning
from prison to Clement's Inn, noticed the silks and furs worn by those now
established there. Since the split with the Women's Freedom League,
Emmeline Pankhurst had campaigned for a less working-class membership.
Parisian chic was becoming increasingly popular and affluent Suffragettes were
now as likely to be found in the new Trocadero or Café Royal as in the
Coventry Street Corner House.

Sylvia, now deep into planning the exhibition, had scarcely time to eat or
sleep. The Prince's Rink measured a vast 250ft by 150ft and she had problems
finding a suitable workshop in which to prepare the massive 20ft high canvases
to decorate the walls.

Once again, Amy Browning, 'my right hand', came to her rescue, and they
co-opted two other girls and four male friends from their student days. The
girls allowed themselves 30 shillings a week in order not to rock the WSPU
financial boat. The men were paid decorating rates of 10 pence an hour. It was
a thrilling, Michelangelo-sized challenge for them all, for none of them had had
to work on such a large scale, at such heights and at such speed before. They
had three months to complete the task.

Sylvia was the mastermind behind the designs, which were then to be
enlarged and painted, sometimes using ladders, sometimes kneeling on mats,

and not always to her satisfaction. At the end she was exhausted, having worked relentlessly, often through the night. The finished work was breathtaking and she was thrilled with what they had achieved. Over one door was a 13ft high figure of a woman sowing grain and at the far end another bearing the harvested corn. The whole effect was a riot of symbolism and hope: angels, flowers, trees, doves and wildlife amongst the delicate tracery of the arches. Years later, when she was living in Ethiopia, she spoke of her enormous pleasure and pride in this project, even though her work was only on view to the public for two weeks. The original paintings were destroyed during a clear out at her studio while she was in prison.

Despite Suffragette pressures, family affairs were still very much on Sylvia's mind. Harry was ill again. He had been sent from the Fels farm to Sister Pine's nursing home suffering from an acute bladder infection. Mrs Pankhurst was summoned and distressed to be advised that Harry should be examined under anaesthetic. But when the results were reasonable and his symptoms abated, she took a tougher line and, overruling the doctor, decided to send him back to Essex. After all, he was tall and well proportioned and the outdoor life, she judged, must be good for him. He had to learn to cope – just as Keir Hardie had done as a boy, and look what he had achieved! Then off she went again on the campaign trail.

Sylvia, worn out and longing for country air, took a short holiday. She went first to Ightham in Kent and then to Penshurst, where she spent her days painting and writing in a rented cottage on Cinder Hill.

In July the first Suffragette went on hunger strike.

11

The March of the Women

Life, strife – these two are one,
Naught can you win but by faith and daring.
On, on – that ye have done
But for the work of today preparing
Firm in reliance, laugh a defiance
March, march – many as one
Shoulder to shoulder and friend to friend

'The March of the Women',
music by Ethel Smyth, composed 1910

In the summer of 1909 the popular, fun-seeking, womanizing monarch King Edward VII was many miles away from Holloway Prison. On holiday in the fashionable watering place of Marienbad on the borders of Bohemia, he asked his private secretary to write to Herbert Gladstone: 'His Majesty would be glad to know why the existing methods (i.e. forcible feeding) which must obviously exist for prisoners who refuse nourishment, should not be adopted.'[1]

Marion Wallace Dunlop, a sculptor and writer,[2] had lit a touch paper when she went on hunger strike on 5 July. The hunger strike had been used by political prisoners in Tsarist Russia but was a new weapon in Britain. Marion Wallace Dunlop had been sent to prison for stencilling a sentence from the Bill of Rights on the wall of St Stephen's Hall in Westminster. 'It is the right of the subject to petition the King, and all commitments and prosecutions for such petitioning are illegal,' she wrote. The words took two hours to remove. Despite being offered plates of luxury food, she refused to eat for ninety-one hours and was released on 14 July 1909. At that time she was not fed forcibly, but from then on until the outbreak of World War I in August 1914, the

1. Royal Archives, Windsor.
2. Daughter of Robert Wallace-Dunlop, author of *The Magic Fruit Garden, Fairies and Elves and Fairies*.

images that the Suffragettes projected onto the public consciousness were violent and shocking. Everything changed.

Sylvia was not force-fed until much later, but her vivid description of her own experiences mirrored those of all those women who were tortured between 1909 and 1913:

> Presently I heard footsteps approaching, collecting outside my cell . . . I was strangled with fear . . . There were six of them all much bigger and stronger than I. They flung me on my back on the bed and held me down by shoulders and knees, hips, wrists and ankles . . . Then the doctors came stealing in . . .
>
> My eyes were shut . . . I set my teeth and tightened my lips over them with all my strength . . . A man's hands were trying to force my mouth open; my breath was coming so fast I felt as though I should suffocate . . . His fingers were trying to pull my lips apart . . . getting inside. I felt them and a steel instrument pressing round my gums, feeling for the gaps in my teeth . . . a steel instrument pressed my gums cutting into the flesh . . . 'No that won't do! give me the pointed one . . .' then something gradually forced my jaws apart as a screw was turned . . . they were trying to get the tube down my throat . . . they got it down I suppose though I was unconscious then of anything then . . . for they said at last 'that's all' and I vomited as the tube came up . . . Day after day, morning and evening the same struggle. Sometimes they used one steel gag on my jaw, sometimes two . . . sometimes but not often I felt the tube go right down into the stomach, a sickening terrifying sensation . . . now as soon as I could pull myself together after each feeding I struggled till I brought up what had been forced into me, choking and straining, the cords of my streaming eyes feeling as though they would snap. The flesh round the eyes and the eyeballs themselves grew daily more painful: the eyes shrank from the light . . .

On 21 July 1909 Mr Gladstone wrote, 'with his humble duty', to the King:[3]

> Your Majesty may like to know the full reason for the discharge of Suffragette prisoners from Holloway this week. The Women's Freedom League, of which Mrs Despard is president, is, on the whole, acting quietly. The League prisoners in Holloway are well-behaved and give no trouble.
>
> Fourteen members of the Women's Social and Political Union (Mrs Pankhurst President) were committed last week to Holloway for breaking windows in Government offices. They declined to be searched, to change their

3. Royal Archives, Windsor, VIC/R 39/58.

clothes, and to obey orders. And they broke their cell windows . . . The prisoners refused to leave their cells and force was used. Most of them resisted with violence. The wardresses were scratched and bruised, their uniforms were damaged and two were bitten. Varying punishments were awarded. Two prisoners refused food and subsequently at intervals others followed their example . . . The reports of the Medical officers were of a grave character . . . In these circumstances there were four alternatives.

1 To let the prisoners starve in the hope that ultimately they would give in. This risk, obviously could not be taken.

2 To feed the prisoners forcibly. This is a very unpleasant operation though frequently resorted to in lunatic asylums and occasionally in prisons. On grounds of policy Mr Gladstone decided against this course.

3 To concede the demand of the prisoners to be placed in the first division. Such a concession is, in Mr Gladstone's opinion, impossible.

4 To discharge the prisoners when, in the opinion of the medical officers, it would be dangerous to detain them.

After full consideration Mr Gladstone has adopted the latter course. It has the great advantage that it is precisely what the prisoners don't want. They impose on themselves more discomfort than would be caused by a month's imprisonment. They are foiled in their demand to be treated in the first division. The whole affair becomes rather grotesque.

Mr Gladstone humbly submits this for Your Majesty's information.

Perhaps the King did not fully appreciate just how cruel these suggestions were.

The Suffragettes' suffering may have been self-inflicted, their martyrdom a controversial matter of choice, but their convictions and courage were undeniable. None more so than Sylvia's, who between 1913 and 1921 was arrested fifteen times and endured more hunger, sleep and thirst strikes than anyone else.

Sylvia was never involved in the reckless phase of vandalism and arson that would soon sweep the country. At first stone-throwing had been a tentative affair. Windows were carefully broken, then pebbles wrapped in cloth were dropped through the holes in order to protect any people inside from harm. Later, first Emmeline and then Sylvia, being poor shots, had to be taught how to aim, but Sylvia was never very happy with this degree of violence and not very good at it either.

The response of officials and the public to the new tactics was also violent. Fractured collarbones, broken ankles, pond-ducking and clothes-ripping were becoming commonplace, and several women suffered injuries that were to affect them for life. Lady Constance Lytton[4] was sent to prison. Lady Constance was the daughter of the Viceroy of India, granddaughter of the novelist Bulwer Lytton (who wrote 'the pen is mightier than the sword') and great grand-daughter of Mrs Wheeler, who had so influenced William Thompson during the franchise campaigns of the early nineteenth century. She had been a supporter of the WSPU since she was left some money for which she had no need and decided to do something useful with it. In 1906 she had become involved with the revival of folk dancing, and at the Esperance Club in Worthing she had met Emmeline Pethick-Lawrence and Annie Kenney. She was gradually converted to the women's cause and by 1909 had her first experience of prison. She was so disgusted to discover that her social status brought her privilege that she soon adopted the disguise of 'Jane Warton', seamstress, to hide her true identity. Her courage had tragic consequences, for she became paralyzed as a result of force-feeding and was to remain an invalid for the rest of her life.

In the midst of the drama there was humour and Suffragette laughter. Many of the women kept journals that recapture these memories: the policeman chasing a Suffragette backwards when he charged onto the wrong moving catwalk and found she had passed him in the opposite direction; Suffragettes in white, replacing 'horses', to draw a demonstration carriage; Suffragettes dressed as orange sellers; a girl swinging from a chandelier; another hidden in an organ.

Clementine Churchill,[5] signing herself 'The Clem-Pussy Bird', wrote to Winston: 'My Darling, A letter came . . . yesterday describing how both the PM and Herbert Gladstone are black and blue from the repeated pummellings of the three Suffragettes. Uncle Lyulph Stanley (the Alderney Bull) says he would have no mercy on them, he would feed them with a stomach pump, put them in punishment cells and give them penal servitude, hard labour etc . . .'. Churchill wrote to her later in the year: 'My darling, I hope you will not be angry with me for having answered the Suffragettes sternly. I shall never try to crush your convictions. I must claim equal liberty for myself. I have told them I cannot help them while the present tactics are continued. I am sorry for them . . . ever my darling, your loving husband W.'

On 24 September 1909 the Home Secretary ordered the medical officer of Winson Green Prison, in Birmingham, to force-feed the women who were on hunger strike. Keir Hardie, increasingly made physically ill by anxiety,

---

4. Royal Archives, R39.
    5. Winston Churchill married Clementine Hozier in 1906. Quoted from Mary Soames' *Speaking for Themselves*, Doubleday, 1998.

immediately tabled a Parliamentary Question, to which the Home Secretary's office responded that force-feeding was merely 'hospital treatment'. In a frenzy of rage, Hardie wrote to the press: 'I was horrified at the levity displayed by a large section of Members of the House . . . I could not believe that a body of gentlemen could have found reason for mirth and applause in a scene which, I venture to say, has no parallel in the recent history of our country.' Various respected medical men joined in the uproar, asserting that there was a serious risk of permanent damage or death from force-feeding.[6]

Sylvia, meanwhile, was back again in the beautiful wooded, hillside country of the Weald of Kent. Keir Hardie went down to visit her there regularly, although it is questionable whether he assisted her recuperation greatly, since he was overwrought on so many issues. Much of the legislation that had been so dear to them both – the right to work, child nutrition, pensions – was being introduced by a so-called reforming Liberal government but in a half-hearted and watered-down form. Hardie had also been agitating about reforestation, the state of the roads, coastal erosion and hospital building – in fact, problems that chillingly continue to face governments of the twenty-first century.

One of the current topics that occupied their walks in the Weald was that of the developing nightmare in the prisons. Sylvia felt that her duty was to join the women in Holloway, although Hardie urged her not to do so, not to become a martyr and to finish her paintings in Cinder Hill. 'What is the use of making one more?' he asked. Sadly, her dilemma was soon resolved by another tragedy within the family.

A telegram, waiting for her when she came in from the woods one day, said that Harry had been brought from Joseph Fels' farm to Nurse Pine's nursing home in Pembridge Gardens, where he was seriously ill. Harry had poliomyelitis, about which so little was known in those days. Sylvia was by his side immediately and found her brother paralyzed and in terrible pain.

Their mother was due to sail for a tour of America. She was faced with an unenviable decision. Not a natural carer and uneasy with the sick, she managed to salve her conscience by persuading herself that the trip would raise funds for Harry's health care. She was, in fact, right about this, but her decision left Sylvia, once again, in charge. In Adela's judgement Sylvia was hard and self-serving. Yet in those long hours at his bedside it was Sylvia who was able to give her brother hope that he would walk again. She reassured him that they would go together to Venice for his convalescence, although she knew in her heart that he would never regain the use of his legs. Harry had confided in

6. In 1910 two criminals were force-fed – the man died immediately, the woman committed suicide.

Sylvia about his love for Helen Craggs and so one day, in a stroke of imaginative compassion, she decided to find the girl. Helen arrived within an hour of receiving a message from Sylvia, who begged her to lie if necessary, but to give Harry that last happiness of knowing that his love was returned. Was Helen, too, in love? Sylvia never knew, but she saw how tender and apparently happy the young couple were: 'he had reached the highest pinnacle of joy,' she wrote. 'He dreamed of her, had nightmares that she had been taken away so that we could not believe this radiant boy was dying.'

Harry died on 5 January 1910 and was buried at Highgate Cemetery. Emmeline was, according to Sylvia, 'broken as I have never seen her . . . an old, plain, cheerless woman'. But Emmeline and Christabel dealt with their very real pain by leaving immediately on yet more campaigning journeys. Sylvia remained in London to deal with the practicalities but moved from Chelsea to 42 Linden Gardens, Notting Hill, near Catherine Pine's nursing home. She wrote Harry's obituary in *Votes for Women*: 'There never lived a human spirit on earth who attained earlier to beauty than the human spirit all members of the Union mourned last week. Harry Pankhurst was courageous in action, unselfishly devoted to the public good, a fighter in the cause of justice for women. Happy, even in her grief, must be the mother who has borne such a son.'

In the General Election held between 14 January and 9 February, neither of the main parties gained an absolute majority, a situation for which the WSPU claimed credit. The balance of power was now held by forty Labour MPs and eighty-two Irish Nationalists. Keir Hardie, who had campaigned vigorously with his wife Lillie and daughter Nan by his side, enjoyed his best-ever result, and Arthur Balfour commented despairingly, 'I do not believe there has ever been a parliamentary situation at all parallel with the present one.' Hardie and Sylvia were delighted, too, that their friend George Lansbury was among the new Members of Parliament. Cheerful, bewhiskered Cockney Lansbury, says Caroline Benn, was 'flamboyant in manner and ardent in intent. Hardie declared that he brought quite a new spirit to the party.'[7]

Life was not all politics, however, although this was the subject discussed on Sylvia and Hardie's many walks in Richmond Park. According to Bruce Glasier, Hardie was intrigued by the letters of George Sand and her excessive sensuality . . . could he have been hoping to understand Sylvia better? Certainly Caroline Benn is interesting on the issue of their relationship. She says: 'Reverence for Hardie as Labour father figure seems to prevent our seeing him

7. Keir Hardie to Glasier, 13 February 1911.

as a man like any other; attracted to sex with the innocent. The "child" in all but years.'

Despite their shared anxieties, this was also a time of developing closeness. There is no clue in any of Sylvia's writing as to what her long-term hopes were at this time and certainly none from Hardie. It is hard to imagine that with all her honesty, freely expressed love and sensuality, Sylvia would not have wished to take their friendship to its limits. Certainly her poetry suggests that she did, but she would have feared the results, for Hardie's sake if not her own. Throughout his life Keir Hardie remained a puritan. However deeply he was flattered and no doubt benefited from Sylvia's attentions, his character was that of an emotional but not a physical philanderer, revelling in what he knew he could not have and, at least bodily, faithful to his wife.

One upshot of the General Election was the formation of a cross-party parliamentary committee, the Conciliation Committee, to further women's suffrage. Lord Lytton was the chairman.

Violence was suspended, and in the somewhat uneasy peace of early spring and summer, many of the Suffragettes took advantage of hospitality offered by wealthy supporters in the country, such as philanthropist barrister Henry Harben, a Fabian. They enjoyed a brief rest and gracious living in various stately homes. During this period before the storm, political pressures were eased, but intense personal relationships and high-spirited frolics not surprisingly took their place. The 'lesbian' state was still not openly acknowledged, or even understood, in society, and although it was quite usual for girls and young women to kiss, touch and even share a bed without comment, such behaviour was judged endearing, romantic and not particularly shocking. But in the rather hothouse, enclosed community of the WSPU, such friendships developed with ever-increasing strength – strength that seems to have been directed back into the movement when hostilities were resumed.

Emmeline herself became the focus of the attentions of tweed-wearing, pork-pie hat-sporting composer Ethel Smyth, a self-confessed lesbian who had been introduced to the WSPU when Lady Constance Lytton wrote asking her opinion of the women's cause. She decided to give the movement two years of her time and then to return to her music. Her immediate impression of Emmeline was her authority. She admitted that when she met Emmeline, she had been 'swept off my feet at once'. The letters she showered on Emmeline are lurid, but one letter says, 'I think it is the crowning achievement of my life to have made you love me.' Sylvia was very uneasy about her mother's friendship with Ethel Smyth but, once again and unlike Christabel, tolerated the position in preference to confrontation. Her description of Ethel, 'the tremendous genius', is amusing and benign:

> Ethel Smyth was a being only these islands could have produced. Individualised to the last point she had in middle age little about her which was feminine. Her features were clean cut and well marked, neither manly nor womanly, her thin hair drawn plainly aside, her speech clear in articulation, and incisive rather than melodious, with a racy wit. Wearing a small, mannish hat, battered and old, plain-cut country clothes hard worn by weather and usage she would don a tie of the brightest purple, white and green, or some hideous purple cotton jacket, or other oddity in the WSPU colours she was so proud of, which shone out from her so incongruously, like a new gate to old palings.

Sylvia was clearly present at some of the gatherings in Ethel Smyth's modern cottage near Woking, when she would entertain the Suffragettes to a solo performance of one of her own compositions, intended for full choir and orchestra. 'Voices of sailors drinking in a tavern, rude rough fellows, wild adventurous spirits, voices of merriment, coarse large laughter, hideous laughter, mad, wild laughter, the voices of women, foolish, fierce, merry, sad and grieving: voices of horror, voices of Death – all these enwrapt in the rude, wild blast of the storm one heard in that chorus, given by that one magic being.'

Christabel appears to have remained aloof from all this and kept a distance between herself and her many fanatical young devotees, which is possibly what made her increasingly dangerous as time went on. Sylvia, with her heterosexual love for Hardie, was an outsider.

At Easter the Pethick-Lawrences went to Europe to see the Passion Play at Oberammergau, inviting Sylvia and Annie Kenney to join them. The performance thrilled her, but she was even more excited by the skills of the villagers – carving, potting, toymaking. In the glorious beauty of the mountains Sylvia's thoughts were constantly beset by darker anxieties. The white upright stones lining the hairpin mountain roads reminded her of the tombstones of the workers who had constructed them: the craftworkers in the village of Partenkirchen reminded her of the waste of talent in English prisons and made her impatient to end the suffrage campaign in order to focus her mind on more constructive work. At the age of 27 she was moving ever closer to a declaration of independence.

At 3.00 a.m. on 7 May 1910 Prime Minister Henry Asquith, on holiday aboard the Admiralty yacht and heading for the Mediterranean, received a telegram: 'I am deeply grieved to inform you that my beloved father, the King, passed away peacefully at a quarter to twelve tonight (the 6th). George.' King Edward VII, known for his international bridge-building as 'The Peacemaker' and himself increasingly worried about the way that things were going at home and abroad, had taken a short break in Biarritz. There he had caught a cold, which got worse and ultimately proved fatal.

Sylvia heard the news with apprehension. She could see uproar and disaster ahead and of course she was right. She wrote in *The Suffragette Movement*: 'Two ideals strove for mastery: imperialism and aggressive armaments versus arbitration and conciliation with the ultimate goal of international citizenship in the United States of the World.' A section of the Liberals strove to turn the Government towards internationalism, or neutrality at least, and thereby found themselves, willy-nilly, in frequent alliance with Keir Hardie and the pacifist section of the Labour party, which most of them were eventually to join. The death of Edward left the way open for the disaster ahead.

Christabel, daughter of republican socialist Richard Pankhurst, suspended all WSPU activities until after the Royal funeral, and *Votes for Women* appeared, black-bordered, lamenting the death of a great monarch. Sylvia painfully wrote:

> . . . it was as though she knew nothing of the struggle convulsing the groups of political thinkers through which she had passed; heard no protest against the race of naval armaments; no cries of alarm at the division of Europe into two armed camps. She had been untouched by Keir Hardie's impassioned protests against British aid in stabilising the Tsarist Government which had exterminated the popular uprising of 1905–6 with torture and massacre and executed upwards of 3,000 political prisoners and butchered 19,000 people . . .

The new King George V, inexperienced, respectable and with a reputation for having a bad temper, was crowned on 22 June.

Hardie was away in September as the ILP delegate to the International Socialist Congress in Copenhagen. He wrote to Sylvia from the Hotel Kongen af Danmark:

> Sweet, nay but did you not promise to have no more imaginings. There was nothing, darling, only on the typewriter it seems to come easier.
>
> From 9 a.m. to 9 p.m. I have been at it every day. Today there is a pleasure sail to which I go not and so I write you instead. Voila!

We have been having the usual trouble with the SDF [Social Democratic Federation] but have now got them finally in hand ... I have accepted invitations to speak at two meetings in Sweden next week and from there I go on to Frankfurt on Main for a demonstration on Sunday 11th. After that is uncertain. I shall post card you from place to place but dearie, do not expect letters. If there is anything very special I could get it Poste Restante, Stockholm on Wednesday or Frankfurt Sunday next. I am in splendid condition and thoroughly enjoying the work. With affection and bundles of kisses. Yours K.

In the false dawn of the summer of 1910 the Suffragettes remained, largely, quietly optimistic. Sylvia, however, was less sanguine and privately warned Emmeline that she did not agree with the terms of a bill that had been proposed by the Conciliation Committee in June.

The bill was far too narrow, Sylvia felt, allowing only for votes to all women householders and occupiers of business premises with a rateable value of not less than £10. 'The Bill,' she warned, 'invited many lines of attack and it would franchise only one woman in thirteen and these mainly elderly widows and spinsters.' She need not have worried. To the fury of the WSPU in November, the Conciliation Bill was finally abandoned. A ninth Women's Parliament was hastily organised for 18 November and the truce was called off. Three hundred women marched to the House of Commons, where they were subjected to an unprecedented onslaught by the police. Kicked and punched, grabbed by the hair and breasts, battered and bloody they returned to headquarters determined to fight. On that one night, which became known as Black Friday, 115 women were arrested.

Christmas was overshadowed. Sylvia, now busy with her writing and determined to forge a career in journalism, had decided to remain alone in her new rooms in Linden Gardens. Emmeline had spent the holiday with her sister Mary Clarke and their brother Herbert in Winchmore Hill, where Mary was recovering from recent imprisonment. After they had enjoyed their Christmas dinner, Mary retired suddenly, and when Emmeline went to see if she was unwell, she found her sister already dead from a brain haemorrhage.

At a time of such distress it was once again on Sylvia's shoulder, not Christabel's, that the tears were shed. Emmeline arrived at Linden Gardens on Boxing Day and stayed with her daughter for several days; Sylvia's easy compassion, her warmth and her willingness to listen and to share the tears, an embarrassment to her sisters, was a comfort to many others throughout her life.

Despite the fact that her mother had only recently returned from America, Sylvia was persuaded by her agent, Feakins, that she should undertake a promotional tour for her first book, *The Suffragette*, due to be published in the United States and England. Shortly after Christmas 1910, Emmeline went with her daughter to Southampton, where she watched her embark on the liner *St Paul* for New York.

– 12 –

America

'March 11 1911.

In one letter you say you hope to be back in New York first week in March and that seems clearly impossible. I am not grumbling, sweet, but only telling you of the difficulties in keeping up with your movements . . .'

Keir Hardie to Sylvia

Hardie was not alone in his confusion!

Sylvia undertook two exhausting tours of the United States, one in January 1911 and another in January 1912. She was away on each occasion for three months, a long, lonely time during which she wrote copiously to Hardie at home and he, less often, to her. It is perhaps best to look at these undated letters as Sylvia's paintings in words, as reflections of emotion and experiences, with the occasional encouragement from Hardie, and not to treat them as a diary.

The timing of the first trip, in particular, was excellent for her, as the American suffrage movement was also 'on the boil' and suffrage bills were before the legislatures of many States. Sylvia was met in New York by Harriot Stanton Blatch of the Women's Political Union and from then on travelled throughout the country, speaking at two or more meetings a day. The second journey was less successful. Emmeline Pankhurst had returned to England in January 1912 just as Sylvia crossed the Atlantic to New York, and so Sylvia's tour, hard on the heels of her mother, turned out to be a disappointment. Meetings were sporadic, and after the intense activity in London, she was homesick.

Sylvia absorbed and learned from everything she saw but was no diplomat. She was equally eager to offer ideas for change and reform in return, which were not always greatly welcomed. She did her best to fulfil her mission and speak on suffrage only, but her interest in the welfare of others was far ahead of her time and she was critical of much that she saw.

Moreover, these journeys do not appear to have been particularly well organized by her literary agent, Feakins, in New York. Even so, on the first trip at least, Sylvia was very well received and the press was kind. They reported that Miss Pankhurst was confidently charming, flirtatious and engaging, but this was seen as attractive and not as indecorous. According to the newspapers, she was also a master at gauging public responses accurately. The *Boston Globe* on 10 January commented: 'He would have been a marble hearted man who could not have become a woman's suffragist at least temporarily while listening to the pathetic voice and story of the pretty girlish English Suffragette.'

Her breathless letters (one runs to ninety pages) in pencil and on lined and scrappy paper, are so vivid, reflecting the artist's eye for detail. They also show a deeper understanding and curiosity about America than Emmeline seems to have achieved on her own long journeys. Wherever she went, all her life Sylvia was an insatiable sponge, eagerly engaging totally with and responding forthrightly to the people and places she encountered. This probably accounts for the confusing chronology in her letters and books. Time was not an issue for her. Sylvia wrote to Hardie:

My dearest Love,

You mustn't dream those dreams about me. My darling, when I read about it I felt ashamed that I so often worry you by telling you of things that worry me and of things that I think may go wrong and of the periods of depression that come to me, and I half felt as though you were my own dear baby, as though I could take you up in my arms and send you to sleep, a real peaceful, dreamless sleep. I longed so much to have my arms around you. I wanted to wake you with kisses and tell you I was there.

Love I hadn't any more adventures on board ship. I never shall have, I shall take more care. It was silly of me that time to let him [the ship's doctor] take me to see his cabin, even if it was the place where his patients went to be doctored and I was quite lucky that the incident wasn't more unpleasant than it was. Now I know more about ships and how they are planned and how very much of a sleeping place a doctor's cabin is and how even a silly old buffer of a doctor may be quite a dangerous person, I'll never be silly again and altogether am getting older and wiser so don't you ever worry again.

Well, Dearie, as I told you, we had a very stormy crossing but Friday and Saturday, not Sunday was the day I minded most. That day I stayed in bed all day and felt ill and got the blues very badly and wasn't good but cried for you many times in the day and night too. There was one night though that I burnt my arm. I burnt the left arm between the wrist and elbow . . . on the hot water bottle in the bed. I had forgotten my indiarubber one and they put a nasty tin one in the bed, which seemed nearly red hot. It was a bad enough burn for the scar to be still plainly showing . . .

During the night I dreamt vividly that I was climbing in the dark up a stone dilapidated staircase without a handrail. It was in a narrow well and went up to a great height. As I was nearing the top, a man in dirty white overalls and a red and white striped knitted cap caught my ankle from behind with a wire which seemed to sting . . . I was a man too I think, but I am not sure. I got to the top, a sort of stone ledge, he was below me coming up the steps. He got me by the wrists. He had to lean across like this [drawing] . . . Oh I haven't the patience to draw it properly but it was a struggle . . .

Extremely controversially and against advice, she visited a Negro University, insisted on seeing prisons and was particularly appalled by the total darkness of cells in Chicago's Harrison Street Jail and the Tank in Tennessee. There a huge cage enclosed smaller cages in which prisoners had wooden benches to sit and sleep on, and were only let out into the larger cage to 'prowl to and fro like animals at the zoo'.

She was horrified by the nightmare industrialization of Pittsburgh, where the workers were in 'horrible conditions', and was disgusted by the many American women on a fevered quest to 'get culture', who assured her there was no need for American women to take an interest in politics because conditions were so good. In St Louis she missed her train connection and courageously wandered through the streets around the station, experiencing her first pornographic 'Dime Museum' and saloons where free meals were offered to customers who would buy drink:

My Darling, I am longing to be in your arms away from it all . . . Oh these long long journeys for a single meeting! How desolate the country is that we are passing through . . . great open wasts [sic] where the snow has fallen . . . there are none of those dainty silver birches that abound in Massachusettes [sic] . . . The trees here have stems and boughs all blackened and seem mostly to have writhing and distorted shapes. We pass by frozen swamps and rivers, the very shrubs that stick up from them are black . . . Sometimes there is an isolated factory with great chimeys pouring forth black smoke, as we go further west, the ice is often melted and there are great pools in the badly paved streets . . . Even in the towns one rarely sees a human creature for hours . . . only a negro standing by the line, a man waiting with his lean horse and ricketty old carriage till we pass by, a woman and child in grey faded garments dejectedly crossing a muddy road.

Well might one think that this country, instead of being one where huge fortunes are being made, were a land of bankruptcy and decay. But the men who grow rich here are for the most part too much in a hurry about it either to live decently or to let others do it. New machinery is put in, the old is thrown out and left to rot by the roadside . . . The very houses built of wood are run up anyhow, there is no time even to level the ground on which to build them . . . And now we are stopping at Indianapolis . . . Oh what a tragedy mankind has made of this poor land . . . I wish I'd never seen the ugly place . . .

She arrived in Boston in a snowstorm and was taken on an exciting ride by sledge to stay with a local family in St John.

Grandparents, parents, children were living together under the same roof in a patriarchal family. Sylvia was not at all impressed with the interior décor and furnishings, which, she judged, were old-fashioned with no artistic merit. 'The house was heated from a central furnace and there was also a big open fireplace in every room where English coal and local logs burned . . . Grandmother presided over the tea cups and formidable looking silver teapot on the long table while at the opposite end sat the mother with a gigantic turkey before her. The daughters . . . served huge portions of vegetables – potatoes, jelly, "squash" – a mashed compound of carrots and turnips – enormous slices of beetroot four times as large as those generally seen and enormous of carrot.' The helpings were so large that even Sylvia was spurred on to eat twice as much as usual.

Back in Boston she wrote again to Hardie:

Oh Dearie, I do wish I were with you. How is my Darling? . . . Are you well? . . . Oh Dear, I don't want anyone but you but I want you so . . . I am afraid I shan't get a letter from you before I go West but what is the use of a letter anyway . . . if I can't have my Darling always he is dearer and better than anyone in the world . . . only I want you now and I can't bridge over the distance. Why can't we Dear? . . . Just think if we could only have half an hour, even ten minutes to talk to each other every day . . . Don't you sometimes feel as though a door was going to open in your mind and teach you something quite outside your knowledge and imagination? Oh I am so sure just outside the circle of the things we know, there it is waiting for us to find.

If such a clumsy thing as wireless telegraphy can exist, surely there isn't anything unreasonable in being able to communicate our human thoughts . . .

Something has come into my head now. It is that when people have discovered the full power of thought transference, the joy and satisfaction and profit of being able to intermingle our ideas with all their finest shades instead of having to rely on clumsy words which were invented for buying and selling and superficial intercourse will be greater than anything we can understand . . . we shall be able to play with our minds producing sparkling shafts of new thought . . . of course there will no longer be misunderstandings and mistakes. They spring from poor, foolish, inadequate words . . .

I'm not sure when one looks into it that all this isn't going to work a more tremendous social change than at first one supposes . . . and much as I love my Darling's arms about me, sweet as kisses are, I rather think it will tend to make us less dependent on those things. If you carry that idea through it leads you a long way . . .

Now you will say perhaps this is all nonsense. Socialism is the cure for all ills. Ah well may be but Socialism couldn't bridge over for me that ocean wide. Moreover, I don't think I go the right way to work. When we are parted I pine and long and eat my heart out . . . but when I am with you I chatter away and use silly words feebly to express my mind and thoughts and I prattle about nothing whatsoever . . .

When I come home I shall sit and look deep down into your eyes and try to know what you are thinking and to make you know what I would say . . . then we must have just one time each day to send a message you see one begins like that . . . and the power gradually grows and some day the door suddenly opens and it is clearer than day. Well, writing has made me feel better. Love and kisses. Goodnight my love. S.

Hardie to Sylvia:

Don't you think the satisfaction which comes from the pressure of my arms around you must be the transference of something from one to the other? And so too with kissing, And if this be so surely the transference of something from the one to the other could be effected without actual physical contact. To that extent I agree with you but without the touch of the actual pressure there could not be the same satisfaction and the wordless talk wd only make distance more terrible. That at least is how I feel about it. But tonight I am sleepy. We sat from three yesterday afternoon till ten this morning and had to be back at the House by noon. Beyond feeling sleepy I am no whit the worse. I am in good fettle . . .

I understand just how you feel dearie and the time will come I like to think, of you going over the same ground, speaking in the same halls and meeting the

same people as I have. I can think of myself as a pioneer smoothing the pathway
for the coming of my little sweetheart . . . May it be ever so . . . K'

Sylvia to Hardie:

Dearest. Unless a change takes place I shall not do very much more than pay
expenses out of this trip. So far, I have two meetings and five more bookings
have been made. These are all spotted about far away from each other . . .
Darling I haven't had a letter from you yet. Dear . . . I think perhaps you
haven't got Feakins address . . . or I think old Feakins may have sent a letter or
letters from you astray . . . I fear he is a fool . . .

And later:

Darling,
Things are going to look up now I hope. I have been stirring up Feakins and
trying to manage things a bit myself. I have determined to go South where no
one ever goes much, where mother did not go and where, above all things,
there is much much to do. Awful conditions of labour for women and children
especially children and everything generally backward. Moreover it is warm
there and the country beautiful I am told. Oh Dearie, I can't write of my
present place of abode with my cousins. Feakins manoeuvred my staying here
against my inclination because he thinks it the proper thing . . . Dear oh Dear
how awful is the home of a wife who is absolutely empty headed poor thing,
I probe incessantly to find some interest in anything but food and clothes . . .
but find it not . . . love and kisses my sweetheart. Don't notice my grumbles.
It will all come right . . . I haven't had a letter yet, Dearie but perhaps
tomorrow. Love I'm longing for a sight of you but it wont be so very long will
it? . . . I must stop. This place makes thinking too hard to bear and I'm longing
to be sitting with you in the firelight . . . my Angel Dear. If only wishing could
bring me to you. Heaven bless you my angel. S.'

Sylvia undertook a gruelling journey south by train. 'The strangest and most
desolate country. What indeed possessed any body of people to settle here?'
The red soil, the faded browning shrubs and grey sage bushes depressed her.
In the distance purple mountains were sprinkled with snow and appeared to
be made of heaps of sand. Gradually the wide tracks of dried river beds
intersected the soil. 'It is all sad and lonely . . . The sky is grey and lowering for
miles one never sees a living thing.' The occasional lean horse grazed near a tiny

Above left: The first pillar.
Barrister Dr Richard Pankhurst
before he abandoned his legal
career for radical politics and the
women's cause.

Above right: Happy days in
Russell Square.
The three sisters – Christabel,
Sylvia and Adela in 1890.

Right: Sylvia in 1896.

Above left: Student days. Sylvia in 1904.

Above right: Sylvia in 1910, the year of the truce.

Right: The dove of peace brooch designed by Sylvia for the Suffragette movement and given by her to Maria-Floria Petrescu, mother of Arcadiu Petrescu, during her visit to Romania.

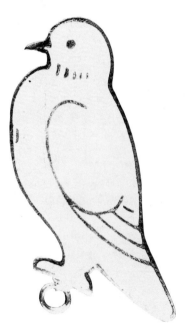

Above: The second pillar. Keir Hardie *(left)* at Nevill's Court with George Bernard Shaw.

Left: Nevill's Court, Hardie's hideaway. Demolished by bombs during World War II.

VOTES FOR WOMEN.

Mrs. WOLSTENHOLME ELMY,

Nat. Committee, Women's Social and Political Union.

Above left: The feisty and dedicated Annie Kenney, 1879–1953.

Above right: Charlotte Despard, 1844–1939. 'The lady in the black mantilla'.

Left: Elizabeth Wolstenholme, 1833–1918, whose bobbing ringlets became, in old age, a symbol of Suffragette endurance.

Above left: 'General' Flora Drummond, 1879–1953. Ready for battle.

Above right: The forceful, argumentative Teresa Billington-Greig (TBG), 1877–1964, who broke away from the WSPU in 1907 in protest at their undemocratic methods, and accused them of megalomania.

Right: The third pillar. Emmeline Pethick-Lawrence, 1867–1954, with her generous and devoted husband, Frederick.

Left: Sylvia's brother, Harry Pankhurst, an 'honorary Suffragette', 1889–1910.

Below: Busy making banners for the Women's Exhibition, Princes Skating Rink, 1909.

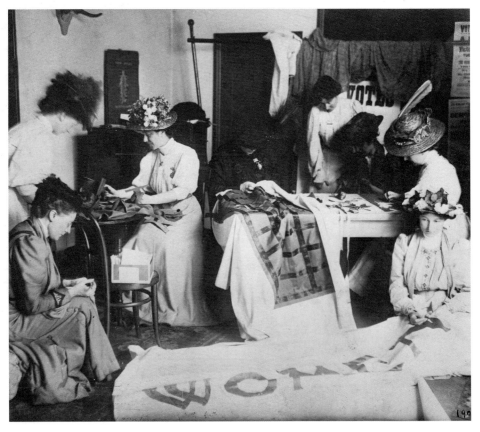

'Sewing Seeds' and 'Angels'. Two of Sylvia's designs for the Skating Rink Exhibition, 1909.

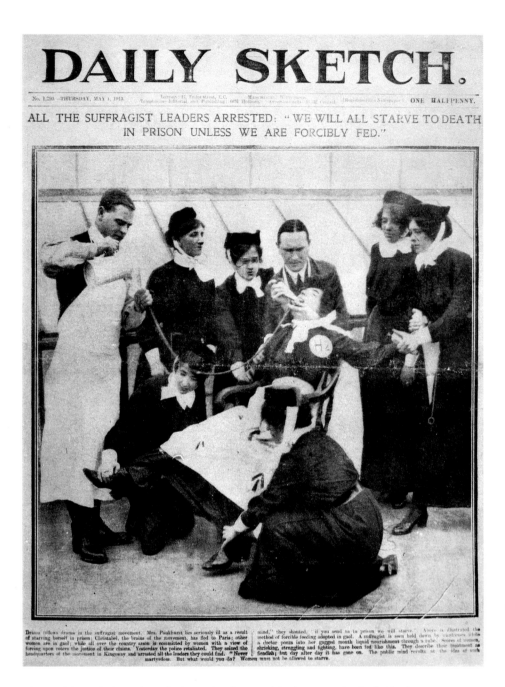

The terrible truth about force-feeding. The illustrated lead story in the *Daily Sketch*, May 1913.

Indian hut built of square earthen blocks often without windows. Standing beside these huts were men, women and children in nondescript looking rags with black hair and copper coloured skin.

Little by little, as there was more water, the country began to change and there was some attempt at cultivation. There were little pieces of ground tilled and pegged out with Indians in loose red and blue clothing running across the ground. It was a barren and forlorn land. 'It is here,' wrote Sylvia, 'that they have driven the poor Indians and now they say they are lazy and will not work! Small wonder indeed that they are fast dying off . . . and that with the buffalo that once roamed round here they will soon be gone.'

During a short stop in Albuquerque, Indians in colourful blankets crowded round her, selling jewellery, pottery and baskets. Inside the depot were more elaborate things. Women were spinning and little chubby faced girls weaving bright coloured rugs, some with a papoose strapped to their back. Later they stopped again by the wayside and a crowd of little Mexican urchins with long grey pants and bright coloured shirts came rushing up crying 'please give us five cents'.

At last Sylvia's mood began to lighten. The sun came out and the mountains in the distance were topped with soft white clouds nestling among their peaks: 'How wonderful it is! . . . It is beautiful, glorious in its immensity and yet awful in its lonely space.' The beauty made her long even more for Hardie: 'if you were there . . . I should hear the buzz of the myriad insect life that no doubt is there, a bird would start up at our feet – we should find lizards and strange cactus plants. But now I can see bones whitening on the sand. We pass the dead body of a horse lying beside a dried up stream. NO dear it is too sad Heaven take care of my dearest 'till I come home.'

In the deep south the grass became green, there were palm trees and oranges and cactus, tall eucalyptus – and sunshine. The *Nashville Banner* ran a heartwarming headline, revealing that for all her celebrity, Sylvia was still very much herself!

Noted Suffragette displays distinctly feminine proclivities . . .

Miss Pankhurst stood in the center of a very interested group of local suffragists shortly after the train pulled in and searched in vain for her trunk check.

First she dived into a huge grey velvet bag and although the check was not forthcoming she did dig up various handkerchiefs, stray gloves, and other articles that one might expect to find in the reticule of an ordinary human being but never in that of a militant suffragette. Then Miss Pankhurst invaded the various pockets and sub pockets of a sort of wallet and one of the station officials politely picked up some of the articles she dropped from this in a vain attempt to locate the missing check. The pockets of her grey fur coat were searched . . . in her confusion Miss Pankhurst dropped several bills of various denominations and several pieces of silver coin which were duly returned to her by the porters . . .

Finally she was allowed to go into the baggage room . . . after which she signed a release, the trunk was sent out and things were smooth again.

At the end of her first journey Sylvia had felt elated enough to write: 'Life in The States seemed a whirl, with harsh rude extremes, rough and unfinished yet with scope and opportunity for young people and with more receptivity to new ideas than is found in the old countries. I thought that some day I might become an American Citizen'

But by the end of the second trip it was a very different story. The American dream had turned into a nightmare. Then she wrote, 'I neither could, nor would, now withdraw to another country.'

13

Norah

'We are worried about Christabel.'

New York Times, 6 April 1912

In May 1911, just after Sylvia had returned from her first trip to America, the death of a man she didn't know, in his stately home in a faraway village she had never visited, was to open the way to a remarkable friendship and so to the next stage of her life.

Hugh Lyle Smyth – very distantly related to composer Ethel Smyth – was chairman of the Liverpool-based family firm of Ross T. Smyth, the world's third largest grain merchants. He died, leaving his fortune to be shared between eleven children. Seventh in line was his daughter Norah, who received about £20,000. It was Norah's generosity with this legacy that was eventually to give Sylvia the opportunity to form her own breakaway movement.

Born in 1874, Norah had grown up in the family home, Barrowmore Hall, in the Cheshire village of Great Barrow. Specially commissioned by her father, the turreted mansion was embellished by terracotta heads of the entire Lyle Smyth family. The 220-acre gardens were among the finest in Cheshire and included a large mill pond with gates that could be opened to flood the meadows for skating in winter. A dutiful army of servants cared for the household and collection of antiques and Constable paintings. It was all a long, long way from Sylvia's chosen world of the deprived and underprivileged.

Norah Smyth, like Sylvia, was a woman whose heart was with the downtrodden poor. She was 38 years old when her father died; he had prevented her from marrying a cousin and had not allowed any of his daughters a university education. Norah grew up a rather studious and artistic woman, finding an outlet for her considerable intelligence in village activities. She was deeply involved with the local church (she played the organ) and was regarded as rather eccentric, largely due to a taste for ties and her fondness for a pet monkey called Gnome.

Norah and her sister Georgina developed an interest in the Suffragette movement and became active locally. In 1906 they went together to the Trafalgar Square Rally, where for the first time they saw the Pankhursts. But it was probably not until her father's death that Norah finally left home and travelled to London to live, where, dressed 'as much like a man as possible', she became a chauffeur to Emmeline.

In May 1911 the Conciliation 'carrot' was once again debated in the House and deferred on the promise to devote a week to a Bill to be debated later in the life of that parliament. Christabel and Emmeline accepted this assurance with optimism and set about organizing a massive 7-mile parade to take place on the Saturday before the coronation of King George V and Queen Mary.

On 17 June 1911 militants and non-militants joined together for the first time to celebrate. Sylvia describes it as 'a triumph of organisation, a pageant of science, art, nursing, education, poverty, factory-dom, slumdom, youth, age, labour, motherhood, a beautiful and imposing spectacle'. Mrs Wolstenholme-Elmy, at the age of 78 now 'the oldest Suffragette', stood watching from a balcony in St James's Street, where she took the salute as almost 1000 former prisoners, including Sylvia, passed by.

The summer and autumn of 1911 were a creative and, on the whole, happy times for Sylvia. She was comparatively unaffected by the trouble fermenting beneath the surface at the Clements Inn headquarters, although she was continually concerned about unrest in Britain and Europe. Hardie had been busy distributing a book by Norman Angell of the *Daily Mail* entitled *The Great Illusion*. It had been published originally in 1908 but echoed the views that Hardie himself had been propagating for years: 'You might sink the German fleets, you might even by a miracle destroy the German army but the invasion of the German trader will continue.' At home strikes spread and Hardie declared sadly, 'the machinery of national life is slowly stopping'.

On the lighter side, Sylvia had developed an unexpected interest in country dancing, to which she had been introduced by Emmeline Pethick-Lawrence's friend, Cecil Sharp. She started work on some studies of girl Morris Dancers in preparation for a large picture but never finished it. One of Sylvia's East End helpers was Ada Walshe, who recalled one of the displays with affection: 'Some of the dances were religious in style, some pagan, prayers to the sun etc . . . the floor of the platform had not been washed and the dancers feet became black. The audience roared with laughter and behaved very badly and for once I saw Sylvia almost crying with laughter and trying to hide it.' Irrepressible mirth did not come easily to Sylvia.

She was also working closely with Hardie on amendments to the National Insurance Bill, which would increase the proposed benefits. The WSPU had been opposed to the Bill, just as they were opposed to all government measures in which women had not been involved, but Sylvia judged that this was unnecessarily destructive to an important, far-reaching piece of legislation. On one occasion she tackled the elderly anti-suffragist Lord Balfour, appealing to him to take up her amendments in the interest of lowest paid workers, who were mainly women. He agreed and she admitted modestly later, 'I felt like a pigmy walking beside this huge figure.'

As the year drew to a close, Sylvia was asked by Emmeline Pethick-Lawrence to organize a week-long fund-raising exhibition and Christmas Fair in the Portman Rooms. She was thrilled and gratified to discover that most of her plastercasts, drawings and models made for the skating rink event were re-useable, and together with some new arches, they looked 'as solid and permanent as stone'.

Some time before, Keir Hardie had given Sylvia a beautiful eighteenth-century book of costumes illustrated by the renowned artist Pine. 'I hope indeed he picked it up at less than its value,' she comments in *The Suffragette Movement*. 'It was stolen from me some years later.' Sylvia used an illustration of a village fair in the book as inspiration for the stall holders' late eighteenth-century costumes: gentlewomen, fisherwomen, market women, weavers, workers of all sorts, a gipsy fortune-teller with her two green birds, a roast chestnut seller, a town crier, a 'zanny' with his odd fool's cap. There were coconut shies, old London cries and much music arranged by Ethel Smyth. Sylvia, however, was so exhausted by her efforts that she went home, fell asleep on the floor and missed the fun of witnessing Keir Hardie riding on the hand-propelled roundabout made specially for her by local carpenters; 7000 people visited the fair.

But behind the jollity, WSPU members were also now in training for their proposed stone-throwing onslaught. They would drive out at dusk down country lanes looking for flints, which were later put into black bags ready for the attacks. Sylvia found an excuse not to go with the women, explaining that she was so committed to the Fair she did not want to risk arrest, but her conscience was clearly troubling her. A few days after the Fair, Emily Wilding Davison, first class graduate, governess and teacher, who was too much of a rebel even to be employed by the WSPU, carried out the first arson attack. On her own initiative, not Christabel's, she set fire to a letter box.

By the time Sylvia returned from America after her second tour early in 1912, she had become even more alarmed by the mood of the movement being directed by her mother and sister. On Friday, 1 March 1912, while Sylvia was still on her second trip to America, well-dressed women suddenly produced hammers from their handbags throughout central London. They smashed the windows of Marshall and Snelgrove, Fullers teashops, Lyons Corner Houses and moments later attacked Swan and Edgar, Liberty and many government offices. The *Daily Telegraph* reported that many of the finest shop fronts in the world had been destroyed. The following day 200 women, including Mrs Pankhurst, were arrested in Downing Street. They all refused bail and were remanded in custody.

On Tuesday, 5 March there was a police raid on the WSPU Headquarters. Documents and papers were seized and the Pethick-Lawrences were arrested and charged with 'conspiracy to incite certain persons to commit malicious damage to property'. A huge haul of papers was removed for investigation. Mrs Pankhurst was included in the charge, although she was already in prison; Christabel was nowhere to be seen. In fact, she was in her new flat in another part of London, but on being warned of the drama in Clements Inn, she decided, 'in a flash of light', that her own imprisonment would leave the movement temporarily leaderless and that she should avoid arrest at all costs. She escaped to Nurse Pine's refuge, disguised as a nurse. She then took a taxi, unobserved, and stayed overnight with a friend. Then, disguised yet again, this time in a black cloche hat and a long black coat, she was driven to Victoria Station. There she caught the train to France, where she became 'Amy Richards'. The Drama Queen had given her most theatrical performance. She would continue playing the lead from the revolutionary stage of Paris. As a public relations operation, it was brilliant. The newspapers loved it.

Even in America the press was on her trail. The *New York Times* on 5 April 1912 alleged, 'Miss Pankhurst is in hiding here. She arrived on the Cunard liner, Mauretania, 30 March.' They claimed Christabel was under an assumed name and had met Sylvia, who gave her some money from the proceeds of her tour before sailing for England. Nowhere has this story been supported and certainly neither Sylvia nor Christabel mentions such a transatlantic tryst with each other. However, in 1972 Nellie Rathbone, Sylvia's secretary from 1913 to 1920, told author Brian Harrison that the story was true.

On 6 April the *New York Times* editorial said: 'The transformation of Miss Christabel Pankhurst, one of the most ubiquitous, aggressive, demonstrative personages of her time, always in sight and hearing, into an elusive, silent invisible state has become an international mystery. We are worried about Christabel.' Even the devoted Annie Kenney did not know where Christabel was until she received a mysterious summons to Paris, putting her in 'supreme charge' of the movement – hurtfully over Sylvia's head, while Emmeline and the Pethick-Lawrences were in prison.

For the next few months Annie Kenney made those weekend trips to Paris to receive her orders. 'The very thought of the journeys to Christabel made me feel seasick,' she wrote in her autobiography. 'Before I left my head would be so full that I had to beg Christabel to give me no more instructions for another week.' But by the time she returned to London there would be a long letter waiting for her, full of the things they had forgotten to discuss. 'Christabel's vitality was good for me . . . she revitalised all she came into touch with. The Saturdays in Paris were a joy. We would walk along the river or go into the Bois or visit the gardens. Whoever saw us would also see stacks of newspapers, pockets stuffed with pencils and always a knife to sharpen them.'

At home, industry was in uproar and strikes were threatened. King George V had written in his diary on 2 March, 'I talked to him [the Postmaster-General] about the coal strike and suffragettes who smashed a lot of windows again in the West End last night.' On 4 March he added, 'It has been an awful day with a lot of rain. The Suffragettes broke a lot more windows today of the ministers and shopkeepers in Kensington and about 100 more arrested outside Westminster tonight. Bed at 11.30.'[1]

On 18 March one million miners came out on strike, affecting all industry and bringing misery to families throughout the country, a situation that was barely recognized by the WSPU leadership, who were too occupied with their own affairs. Civil war seemed imminent in Ireland and Keir Hardie and others were continually warning about the future.

Christabel was becoming restless. The Suffragette struggle was being eclipsed and new policies were needed to keep the movement in the headlines. On the whole the mood in the provinces was strongly against militancy and certainly against vandalism, a view shared increasingly by Adela working in the north of England.

On her return from America, resolute with good intent and disguised by Nurse Pine, Sylvia crossed the Channel to see her sister, anxiously peering in all directions to be sure she was not followed. She changed her clothes in railway stations to avoid recognition and arrived, unexpectedly, at Christabel's Paris apartment. Christabel was eager to rush the reluctant Sylvia around the city sightseeing, shopping for clothes she did not want, indeed, anything to avoid the subject she had come to discuss. It was a devastating experience:

---

1. Royal Archives, Windsor, Diary of King George V.

I asked her what I might do to help. 'Behave as though you were not in the country,' she answered cheerfully. 'When those who are doing the work are arrested you may be needed and can be called on.'

To me the answer was ludicrous; with our mother facing a conspiracy charge and the movement limitless in its need. 'You don't expect me to behave as though I were afraid?' I asked her. She conceded amiably. 'Well, just speak at a few meetings.' Instinctively, she thrust aside anyone who might differ from her tactics by a hair's breadth. 'I would not care if you were multiplied by a hundred, but one of Adela is too many' she had said to me.

Now it was clearly evident to me that I might become superfluous in her eyes. I made no comment . . . I had always been scrupulous neither to criticise or oppose her . . . I was still prepared for the sake of unity to subordinate my views in many matters to hers, but her refusal to ask any service of me would leave me the more free to do what I thought necessary in my own way . . . I could not express my views on policy to her, she desired only to impose her own. That, too, I accepted as one accepts the rose bears the thorns . . . I left by the night boat unable to endure another day.

In her autobiography Christabel does not even mention her sister's visit.

Sylvia returned from Paris to find Keir Hardie in high spirits. The mood was short-lived, for they were both aware of an ominous switch in attitude towards the WSPU. Unlike Christabel, Sylvia foresaw the campaign in the wider international context of events in Europe and social and political unrest at home. She could also see that the new policy could rebound and result in draconian, retaliatory measures by parliament.

On 15 April 1912 the first edition of the *Daily Herald* was launched by George Lansbury, with Annie Kenney's brother Rowland as editor. The *Herald* put a page at the disposal of the Suffragettes and Lady de la Warr gave a generous donation. The very first edition carried the terrible story of the sinking of the *Titanic*. The news personally shocked Sylvia Pankhurst, Keir Hardie and George Lansbury, for their champion, W.T. Stead, was amongst those who had drowned. He had apparently, and heroically, held back to let others into the lifeboats before him and was last seen standing at prayer on the deck. For many years Stead had been a constant campaigner for improved welfare in the East End.

Public hostility towards the Suffragettes was becoming more aggressive and women were frequently physically attacked. Sylvia was not alone in her anxieties: the Pethick-Lawrences, naturally peaceful people, were uneasy about vandalism too. However, Sylvia was still determined to keep the movement alive for her mother and especially, at that moment, to secure better conditions for all her friends and colleagues in prison.

The six-day conspiracy trial began at the Old Bailey on 15 May. Serious as it certainly was, Sylvia's description of the scene has a tragi-comic flavour which belies the familiar idea that she was without humour:

> That court of mockery and doom . . . a grim burlesque . . . a caricature of the Middle Ages . . . among the wigged functionaries of the legal sphere, wherein no woman might yet intrude, sat Sir Rufus Isaacs, the Attorney General, with his handsome Jewish face and dark hawk's eye. Beside him 'Bodkin', 'Sir Archibald' as he presently became . . . ruddy and bald with an egg-shaped head, he was the very image of Alley-Sloper, depicted in the comic papers the servants were reading in the kitchen when I was a little girl in Russell Square . . . In the dock two women, each with her special charm, serenely determined to make a platform of it: the one impervious to small points, searching to fathom the inner mysticism and eternal verities of the situation in which they found themselves; the other swifter and more impassioned than a tigress . . . She was now in the flood tide of the last great energies of her personality before the disintegrating ravages of old age should begin to steal upon her.

The three defendants were found guilty and sentenced to nine months in prison but not in the first division category. Frederick Pethick-Lawrence was forced into bankruptcy and expelled from the Reform Club. A major hunger strike was immediately threatened unless the prisoners' status was upgraded. The request was refused. There was uproar, and Prime Minister Asquith was not only overwhelmed with protests from 100 MPs, but in addition representatives from the church, universities and suffrage organizations from all over the world bombarded him. Among those working with Sylvia to help the prisoners was an old family friend, the genial Liberal Josiah Wedgwood, who appreciated her genuine concern for her mother's health and provided her with a shoulder to cry on.

Even then there were light moments in a dark story. On one occasion the conductor Thomas Beecham[2] recalled a visit to Holloway, where he saw 'the noble company of martyrs marching round and singing lustily their war-chant while the composer, beaming . . . from an over-looking upper window, beat

2. Thomas Beecham (1879–1961) was the Artistic Director of the Royal Opera House and founder of the Royal Philharmonic Orchestra.

time in almost Bacchic frenzy with a toothbrush'. On another occasion the prison commissioners reported that Dame Ethel Smyth had visited Holloway with some wine which, she claimed, Emmeline needed for her health. The Home Office wrote solemnly: 'Is Mrs Pankhurst being given wine and, if so, is any particular brand necessary?' To which the Governor replied '14 bottles of Chateau Lafitte have been delivered and locked up in the chief warder's room.'

That same day, 25 May, Sylvia was in Merthyr where she spoke with new poise and power at an ILP Conference and where Hardie referred, to her acute embarrassment, to the status of 'the lover'. In the future, he said, not only would the bonds of poverty be broken, but also the shackles of convention. This could not be achieved until women stood free and equal side by side, 'with their husbands, brothers, lovers, friends'.

The hunger strikes and the force-feeding continued, although Emmeline Pankhurst, perhaps because of her age (she was now 54) was not subjected to this torture. Emily Wilding Davison made three unsuccessful attempts to throw herself from the prison stairway onto some wire netting, 30ft below. On the third occasion she was knocked unconscious as she tried to hurl herself back from the net onto the stairway. She was returned to her cell and left alone. Despite her injuries, she was force-fed again next day. That event brought uproar to Parliament on 23 June in the person of the ever-emotional member for Bromley and Bow, George Lansbury. The *Daily Telegraph* described the scene where he accused the Prime Minister of torturing women and was ordered from the House amid chaotic scenes:

> To the amazement of the whole House – an amazement so profound that the tumult immediately quietened down . . . Mr Lansbury began to stride down the floor in order to get nearer the Prime Minister . . . the member for Bow and Bromley shook his fist at him, pouring out half the time a torrent of incoherent abuse . . . he shouted that he ought to be hurled out of public life . . .
>
> Mr Lansbury's language was quite the least of his offences . . . it was his conduct and bearing that was the blind outrage. For there he stood, or rather crouched, shaking with passion . . . wholly carried away by blind rage . . . as though he were drunk with fury . . .

The *Telegraph* concluded tartly, 'there are limits to the excesses of an overflowing heart'.

The public did not agree. Lansbury became a hero overnight – the congratulatory telegrams and letters which poured in occupy 427 pages of the

Lansbury Collection. Later in the year, in November, Lansbury resigned and stood for re-election on the single issue of the women's vote – a step Sylvia regarded as precipitate. She strongly disagreed with his decision that the Labour party should vote against the government on all issues, including Home Rule, until there was universal franchise. She felt that this policy would involve losing many reforms that would be of benefit to the working classes.

One of the most persistent speakers against the WSPU in Parliament was cabinet minister Lewis Harcourt MP. His beautiful eighteenth-century mansion stood in gardens, designed by 'Capability' Brown, which ran down to the Thames at Nuneham Courtney near Oxford. There, in the early hours of 13 July 1912 two women were involved in another WSPU escapade. They had travelled in a hired canoe and PC Godden found them standing near a wall of the mansion with hammers, inflammable material and matches. Helen Craggs, Harry Pankhurst's would-be sweetheart, was arrested, but the other woman, chased by police dogs, escaped and vanished into the night. Who was the mysterious 'other woman'? Sylvia knew her name, yet she has rarely been fully identified in any of the Suffragette histories. The police thought she was Ethel Smyth because the canoe was hired in the name of 'Smith' and Ethel was now a known Suffragette. But no. Ethel published her own characteristically forceful rebuttal of any such idea.

In fact the would-be arsonist was Norah Smyth, who in the early 1960s, not long before she died, told the true story for the first time to her nephew, former diplomat Kenneth Isolani, when he went to visit her in Ireland. Knowing of his aunt's love of paintings and antiques, he was puzzled that she could have been persuaded, even by Christabel, to destroy the Nuneham Courtney collection. 'The East wing of the house was empty and uninhabited,' she explained. 'I escaped over the fields and took the boat back to Abingdon from where I travelled to Reading. In Reading I changed my clothes in a public toilet before crossing the Channel to Europe where I hid 'til the dust settled.'

It was when she returned to London that Sylvia and Norah joined forces in Linden Gardens. Their friendship grew, based on shared socialist principles, fired by Sylvia's reforming energy, guided by Norah's practical common sense and nourished by her generosity. It was at about this time, too, that Zelie Emerson appears in the story. The dark-eyed daughter of an American industrialist from Michigan, she had developed an intense affection for Sylvia and was eager to play her part in whatever her heroine was doing.

Despite Christabel's request that she should lie low, Sylvia was busier than ever that summer. Her American trip had given her enormous strength, and, well aware of her new if self-imposed responsibilities, she undertook a gruelling round of massive meetings in every principal open space and park around London. Diplomatically, she made sure that Mrs Drummond was in charge and credited for what was arranged, but it was actually Sylvia, with the lively, mercurial mother of seven, Lady Sybil Smith, who provided the ideas and the impetus.

It all came to a glorious conclusion with a WSPU Hyde Park spectacular on Bastille Day, 14 July, the day Emmeline Pankhurst celebrated her birthday. The women were joined by many of the suffragists, the Fabians and the ILP but not Millicent Fawcett's NUWSS. They thronged the Park in their thousands in a glorious display of banners, bonnets and bands. Keir Hardie spoke from a cart, wearing a white suit and a red plaid tie.

However controversial their actions, there is no doubt that the WSPU talent for theatrical splendour has never been surpassed, and much of this was due to the artistic drive of Sylvia herself. She supervised the making of 252 scarlet caps and banners and hundreds of smaller flags, in a little garden studio in Kensington. She calmed her volunteers when the fabrics ran out, scoured London for white fringe and found it in John Barker's hire department, left over from Queen Victoria's funeral. By the light of candles in bottles, the girls worked on through the summer nights, feeding Sylvia cups of tea while she drew dozens of scarlet dragons on banners.

In the morning her legs were swollen to enormous size but she was determined to speak as planned. And then, in the middle of it all, Sylvia received a telegram from Christabel in Paris. It asked her to burn down Nottingham Castle. 'The request came as a shock to me,' she wrote, 'The idea of doing a stealthy deed of destruction was repugnant to me.'

14

The Smile on the Face of the Tiger

'To be asked to leave the WSPU to which we had contributed our lifeblood was like asking a mother to be parted from her little child.'

Frederick Pethick-Lawrence

The hunger strikers had all been released by 6 July. The Pethick-Lawrences planned a restorative holiday in Switzerland but were asked by Mrs Pankhurst to break the journey and join her and Christabel in Boulogne for a discussion about the future. Mother and daughter were staying in Paris and it was while they were together there that the seeds of revolution, planted in 1907, were given their final watering. The four walked on the cliffs at Wimereux and talked about the future.

The glorification of Christabel had not been too well accepted by Emmeline and Frederick Pethick-Lawrence, since they did not approve of the direction she was taking any more than Sylvia did. In turn, Christabel privately saw their softer approach as subversive and a challenge to the leadership, which had become by this time *her* leadership. Sylvia had heard her mother threaten them in a fit of anger before their departure, 'if you do not accept Christabel's policy we shall smash you'. In his biography, *Fate has been Kind*, Frederick Pethick-Lawrence wrote: 'I took the view that the window smashing raid had aroused a new popular opposition, because it was, for the first time, an attack on private property . . . there was a need for a sustained educational campaign to make the public understand the reasons for such extreme courses. I took it for granted that she [Christabel] herself would return to London.' She did not.

Towards the end of July, Annie Kenney and Emmeline met Christabel at Boulogne again for a summit. The Pethick-Lawrences were by this time in Canada. They had suffered a great deal of physical and mental pain, having supported and sustained the movement with calm common sense and a great deal of money. As a result, they were now threatened with financial ruin. On

their way home they arrived at the Waldorf Astoria in New York to find a
letter from Emmeline Pankhurst in Boulogne, dated 8 September 1912. It is a
calm, sweetly reasonable and business-like letter – the smile on the face of the
tiger. It explained that the WSPU was moving from the Pethick-Lawrence's
premises in Clements Inn to palatial new five-storey headquarters in Lincoln's
Inn House, Kingsway. Emmeline wrote:

> It is quite evident that the authorities and also the insurance companies and
> property owners mean to take full advantage of the fact that they can attack Mr
> Lawrence with profit and through Mr Lawrence weaken the Movement . . .
> They see Mr Lawrence as a potent weapon against the Militant Movement and
> they mean to use it. This weapon is a powerful one. By its use they can not only
> ruin Mr Lawrence but they also intend, if they can, to divert our funds . . . So
> long as you are an official of the Union this will be so.

Her answer to the dilemma, 'after long and anxious thought', was to invite the
Pethick-Lawrences to stay where they were and set up the first 'Imperial
Suffrage Movement' in Canada.

Mrs Pethick-Lawrence's reply on 22 September 1912 was predictably
civilized. She said 'no thank you'. She wrote:

> Our answer today is the same as it has been since we entered the struggle. You
> will realise that directly we state it, there is only one answer possible. It is the
> answer which you, yourself would give if asked to choose between the
> Movement (which you and we have so large a measure jointly built up) and any
> other possession in life, however dear and precious. You would not hesitate for
> a moment. Neither do we. Our answer is that we shall continue to be jointly
> responsible with you in the future as we have been in the past and that the more
> we are menaced the harder we will fight until victory is won . . . the harder the
> battle, the more need for every one of the generals and soldiers.

Emmeline Pankhurst decided to take dramatic action: she secretly recalled
Christabel from Paris, again in disguise and under cover, and arranged to meet
the Pethick-Lawrences in London. Sylvia was not invited.

Emmeline and Frederick went immediately to Lincolns Inn House on their
return. They found that they had been allocated no office space and were met
with embarrassed silence in the corridors. It was clear that this plan had been
a long time in the making and everyone but them knew about it. Frederick
Pethick-Lawrence wrote to their friend George Lansbury on 26 October:

The whole situation has come upon us with startling suddenness and at the time nearly stunned us. To be asked to leave the WSPU to which we had contributed our life blood was like asking a mother to be parted from her little child. And yet as we faced the situation in all its aspects we saw that the only alternative was to carry into the public arena our difference with the inevitable result that the Union would be smashed to bits. It was better we felt to leave it intact in the hands of those from whom we differ.

Fate had been far from kind.

Such dignity! Sylvia was appalled by the way in which an announcement about the departure of Emmeline and Frederick was issued without any consultation with the members. It had been agreed that *Votes for Women* would remain in their care and almost immediately the WSPU launched its own journal, the *Suffragette*. The newspapers revelled in the break and *Punch* asked its readers 'Are you a Peth or a Pank?!'

Despite what had happened, Frederick Pethick-Lawrence said that Mrs Pankhurst and Christabel were 'two of the most remarkable people I have ever known. They cannot be judged by ordinary standards . . . and those who run up against them must not complain of the treatment they receive.' Perhaps this was a lesson Sylvia had already learned, and rather than follow the course of confrontation, she had instinctively chosen the passive path to independence. In her autobiography *My Part in a Changing World*, Emmeline Pethick-Lawrence looked back on that time: 'There was something quite ruthless about Mrs Pankhurst and Christabel where human relationships were concerned . . . Men and women of destiny are like that. From that time forward I never saw or heard from Mrs Pankhurst again and Christabel, who had shared our family life, became a complete stranger. The Pankhursts did nothing by halves!'

Sylvia reflected, afterwards, with great admiration, on the Pethick-Lawrences' generosity of spirit when they continued to befriend even those who had turned against them. Certainly when Mrs Pankhurst's book *My Own Story*[1] was published in 1914, Emmeline Pethick-Lawrence wrote to her with extraordinary and inexplicable warmth and effusiveness. She said that 1000 copies had been sold in Suffragette shops. 'It is Spiritual magic . . . my dearest you must know how truly I am yours – the fact has gone beyond words . . .'.

The contents of the Pethick-Lawrence's beloved home was put in the hands of the bailiffs but the auction fetched only £300. Ninety-three firms and various

1. Emmeline Pankhurst, *My Own Story*, Eveleigh Nash, 1914.

London stores put in claims for damage, which had to be settled by them because neither Christabel nor Mrs Pankhurst had any capital.

'The breach was deplorable,' Sylvia wrote. In hindsight the events that developed over the next eighteen months were probably inevitable. Sylvia had already established her own informal and democratic three-way partnership with Norah Smyth and American heiress Zelie Emerson, who, it was claimed, was very happy to leave her affluent life and be a 'scrub lady'. They had become a team and were feeling their way into George Lansbury's East End. They were welcomed there enthusiastically by George – less so by Bessie his wife, who was worried about their middle-class backgrounds. Bessie cherished her own working-class roots: for instance, despite many offers of free holidays from wealthy suffrage supporters, she maintained her independence and integrity. Eventually, once Sylvia had proved that she was prepared to work and suffer with her 'mates', as she called them, the two women became good friends

The despairing picture of the forgotten East End that Annie Kenney had described so graphically when she first came to London in 1906 was only one half of the story. For although living and working conditions were still deplorable and women in particular suffered so much hardship, the East Enders' spirit was alive and flourishing. There was a warmth and resilience amongst its people that had always appealed to Sylvia's own fighting spirit. Families looked after each other.

By 1912 cinemas had begun to compete with music halls, pubs with bright bars were mushrooming everywhere and the arrival of the tram meant that families could sometimes escape to football or cricket in the parks on a Saturday afternoon. Boxing was popular and bathing lakes drew thousands of people in the summer. There were paddle steamers on the river and working holidays in the hop fields of Kent.

The area depended largely for a meagre livelihood on the trade passing through the London docks. They saw children with bare feet and rickets, and met some of the thousands of men and women employed for a pittance in intolerable conditions in the sweated industries: making artificial flowers, sacks, clothing or even wooden pips for raspberry jam. Wages were low and unequal and those out of work or on poor law relief were disenfranchised. Many of these people had loyally supported Sylvia when, against her mother's wishes and with George Lansbury's help, she had called them to demonstrate over the years at rallies in central London. There had been a long tradition of political activism in the East End: women there formed trades unions and religious, social and political groups. In 1906 the Canning Town branch of the WSPU was established by a group of unemployed women, although from the beginning they were ignored by Emmeline and Christabel. The Actresses' Franchise League, formed in 1910 by Ellen Terry and Evelyn Sharp, staged plays and meetings in East London. Women such as Charlotte Despard were regularly invited to speak on the vote and working women.

But there was no real base from which to orchestrate affairs. Now, because the WSPU leadership was becoming remote and even more middle-class, Sylvia was determined to redress the balance. She wanted a women's socialist movement and her personality and generosity of heart made her a focus for them all and gave them hope

When she arrived in the East End she found a galaxy of women whose names were already revered in local politics, but because there was no franchise, they had no national platform. Writing to a friend in 1914 she said: 'I am a socialist and want to see the conditions under which our people live entirely revolutionised, but because I believe nothing will be achieved without the help of women I feel my first work must be to do what I can to secure for women the entrance into the political scheme, without which they can never play anything but a subordinate part in social reconstruction.' In *The Suffragette Movement* she expanded the theme:

> I regarded the rousing of the East End as of utmost importance. My aim was not merely to make some members and establish some branches, but the larger task of bringing the district as a whole into a mass movement from which only a tiny minority would stand aside ... the East End was the greatest homogeneous working-class area accessible to the House of Commons by popular demonstrations. The creation of a woman's movement in that great abyss of poverty would be a call and a rallying cry to the rise of similar movements in all parts of the country.

There was perhaps a degree of romanticism in Sylvia's identification with the East End, but it arose also from her inherent ability to see problems, not only in the context of their own environment and culture, but as a visionary, looking outwards. She knew that one day all women would be given the vote – she wanted them to be strong and self-sufficient and able to cope with the responsibility when that day came and to safeguard their rights.

Sylvia, Norah and Zelie trudged the dingy streets looking for premises and found an old baker's shop at 198 Bow Road (now converted into flats), not far from George Lansbury's home. There they established the East London branch of the WSPU. George's daughter Daisy and his eldest son Willie were enthusiastic supporters, and Willie's wife Jessie became the first secretary. The Lansburys brought materials from the family wood factory and built a scaffolding platform from which Sylvia could paint the words 'Votes for Women' in pure gold leaf on the fascia board, watched by a curious crowd and photographed by Norah.

Norah Smyth came to the East End armed with a camera. She was a gifted photographer and wanted to use her talent, as Sylvia had once dreamed of using her art, for the benefit of others. Her pictures are a very personal, intimate record of life as it was and they established her as one of the great early twentieth-century documentary photographers.[2] Like Sylvia, she believed that women's lives were rendered intolerable by both outside forces, such as bad housing, inadequate education and health care, and by an inability to organize and manage available resources. Together they began to establish and foster community participation, shared responsibilities and a great camaraderie.

At first the women's appearance was regarded with extreme suspicion by many. They were 'toffs' and didn't belong. Thanks to such huge characters as Nellie Cressall, whose husband George was Lansbury's political agent for thirty-two years, this suspicion did not last long. Nellie had joined the WSPU in 1911 and lived all her life in Poplar; she was a councillor for forty-six years, was elected Mayor in 1943 and made a Freeman of the Borough in 1959. But in 1912 Nellie Cressall was 29 and game for a fight. Author David Mitchell recorded an interview with Nellie in 1963. 'Sylvia was a real friend,' she told him, 'We all loved her. She was a warm human person. Of course, she had a better education than me but she used to say, "Nellie, I may have had the education but you have had the experience." When I tell people of the things she did, they don't believe me. Of course we had a lot to put up with to begin with. We had everything thrown at us. Rotten eggs, tomatoes . . . oh dear. They were the days!'

Indeed they were. Even Sylvia was not prepared for the violence she had to contend with: the fish heads, the paper bombs soaked in urine and the bruises caused by rowdies on the rampage. Undaunted, and always protected by a growing bodyguard of friends, she carried on until eventually the trouble died away and more and more women, and men, flocked to hear her speak. Nellie said, 'people came to respect us. After a while you could hear a pin drop at our meetings.'

2. Val Williams, *Women Photographers*, Virago, 1986.

Then, on 11 November 1912 came the bombshell: the hugely popular MP George Lansbury resigned and sought re-election on the one issue, that of Votes for Women:

> The women of our country live hard, laborious lives. Down here where I have lived almost all my years, I have grown to understand in some small way what poverty and destitution mean to the women. We men have wanted to use our votes to improve the social conditions. I want that our mothers, our wives and our sisters should be allowed to join us in this fight.

His policy was that of Emmeline and Christabel's: to attack the government on every issue until it introduced a measure for women's suffrage. He received no backing from the Labour party but was supported by both the WSPU and the NUWSS. Sylvia alone thought he had made a mistake.

However, she threw herself into Lansbury's election campaign and just as she was in the throes of orchestrating a massive rally in Victoria Park, Christabel despatched one of the headquarters officials to take over and mastermind the campaign in her place. The ground was cut from under Sylvia's feet by an insensitive, inefficient young woman with social pretensions and no knowledge of the East End. Rather than cause unnecessary friction, however, Sylvia decided to follow Emmeline Pethick-Lawrence's dignified example. She moved, without protest, to a different district, out of the firing line, and persuaded her team to support the new organizer.

On 26 November, the day of the election, there was torrential rain and far too few vehicles to get electors to the poll, a situation not helped by the WSPU organizer refusing to accept orders from men. Not nearly enough effort had been made on the streets to canvass or to locate registered electors who had moved out of the constituency. As a result, the unthinkable happened – Lansbury lost. Never ones to back a loser, Christabel and Emmeline Pankhurst decided immediately to withdraw from the East End. George Lansbury had joined the growing list of dispensables. They planned to start a new terror campaign of fire bombs and window smashing, before they both disappeared to spend Christmas in Paris.

Headquarters now ordained that the WSPU shops in Bow, Bethnal Green, Poplar and Limehouse should be closed. But to prevent the East End campaign ending in a defeat, Sylvia sucessfully urged her mother and sister to allow her to arrange a working-class deputation to meet Lloyd George. They agreed reluctantly but extended Sylvia's plan to make it a national event. On 23 January 1913 the East End deputation of twenty and over a thousand other women, led by Mrs Flora Drummond, marched to the Treasury. On the same day, the Speaker ruled that the Women's Suffrage amendment would so alter the proposed Reform Bill that it could not be proceeded with and would have to be reintroduced in a new form.

Without more ado, Christabel launched a full-scale arson campaign – 'Burning to Vote' – and Sylvia was finally forced into acknowledging that there would be an inevitable break with her family. She saw their violence as 'negative courage' and called it a 'holy blaze' of self-denial. She began to work with Lansbury, provocatively writing articles for his newspaper, the *Herald*. Ignoring a cardinal WSPU ruling, she also appeared on platforms to speak alongside men!

But there was a huge rallying of support for Lansbury and speeches from many well known figures such as Josiah Wedgwood. However, the now obvious rift in the movement was causing a worrying polarization. Henry Nevinson and a number of other former supporters were pulling back from the WSPU.

Immediately Sylvia and Zelie decided to look for new premises to replace 198 Bow Road. 'The sun shone like a red ball in the misty, whitey-grey sky. Market stalls covered with cheerful pink and yellow rhubarb, cabbages, oranges and all sorts of other interesting things lined both sides of the narrow Roman Road,' she wrote. They bought buns at the baker's and ate them as they walked along, until they reached number 321, the only premises in the road available to rent, a bug-ridden former second-hand clothes shop. There was a parlour behind, a tiny scullery/kitchen and three small rooms upstairs; the flooring was full of holes and the shop window was broken, but to the two girls it all represented the beginning of a dream.

Friends rallied; they cleaned and swept and polished and brought furniture and fittings, for by this time the WSPU had withdrawn funds from Sylvia. They planned a lending library, an immediate jumble sale to raise money and, in no time, the purple, white and green banner was raised over their new home. 'The Roman Road, as they called it, was busy with kindly people,' Sylvia wrote. 'That morning my heart warmed to them for ever.'

15

East Enders

'We do not intend you should be pleased.'

Emmeline Pankhurst

The events of 1913 all over Britain have etched themselves into the national memory. Women chained themselves to railings, were mauled by the police and crowds, dragged by the hair and trampled underfoot. Prisoners were force-fed, stately homes set ablaze, golf courses destroyed, railway upholstery slashed, flower beds wrecked. The total cost of the arson damage in the course of the year was estimated at £510,150. Elderly ladies applied for gun licences and telephone wires were cut. In Manchester thirteen valuable paintings were attacked and in Kew Gardens the orchid house was smashed and plants destroyed. Lloyd George's new house at Walton-on-the-Hill was blown up and then came the violent death of Emily Wilding Davison. When Emmeline Pankhurst was labelled a 'wicked old woman', she replied, 'we do not intend you should be pleased'.

In the wider world, war threatened and yet the danger hardly seemed to register in a Britain more concerned with militancy at home. As Alan Palmer has said in his book *The East End*, 'It was as though the nerve cells of the body politic were misfiring on all fronts.' There was parliamentary conflict over reform of the House of Lords; there was continuing trouble in Ireland with a Protestant backlash and much industrial unrest. Keir Hardie was extremely worried, and during the summer of 1913 he tried unsuccessfully to run a campaign focusing on the war issue – he even referred again to a 'United States of Europe'.

Still Sylvia made no public denunciation of WSPU and its destructive militancy. In fact, she made a few of her own touchingly inept attempts at stone throwing. The evening after the women's deputation to Parliament, she returned home to Linden Gardens, where she was still living, and in the dark gathered a few lumps of concrete. She then went to the House of Commons, where, on the pretext of seeing Keir Hardie, she was admitted to wait in St Stephen's Hall. She sat there alone, trying to make up her mind what to do: she did not want to break the stained glass window or any object that had been lovingly made by an artist, but she did want to cause a disturbance. Eventually she picked on a rather dull portrait (it was of the new Speaker), even then hoping that she could break the glass without damaging the picture itself. Vandalism did not come easily to her. She self-consciously threw the missile, which bounced off the picture and broke in smithereens on the floor, leaving the work of art intact behind its unbroken glass. Even the police, who rushed out to remove Sylvia, were hugely amused by her failure as she sat waiting for Keir Hardie to arrive. He came, also smiling broadly, and Sylvia was released without charge.

The following Tuesday a peaceful protest in the pouring rain was attacked by the police and Mrs Drummond was knocked unconscious into the mud. Sylvia was arrested and, 'spurred by an intolerable sense of outrage and disgust at the police brutality', she swept an inkpot from the recorder's desk in the charge room and put her inky palm print on the Superintendent's face 'not to hurt him but to mark him'. Sylvia was amused by newspaper headlines shrieking 'The Black Hand'. She was sentenced to fourteen days or a 40s fine, which the WSPU paid as part of their new policy to keep as many women out of prison and as active as possible.

At the end of May, Sylvia formed the East London Federation of the WSPU. Unlike its parent body, it was to be democratic, with an elected leader and organizer. Men were also welcome – a decision at sharp variance with her mother's policy. There were to be twice weekly meetings in the afternoon and in the evening to make it possible for as many people as possible to attend. Sylvia knew that to make her organization work efficiently, she must start an immediate training programme. She employed Miss Rose to give elocution lessons and train public speakers, and some of the local men, such as Lansbury and his son, were invited in for heckling practice.

She also recognized the urgent need for funds. In February the ever supportive Henry Harben donated £50 a year for three years to the Federation and was to prove a consistently generous benefactor in the future. However, it was Norah Smyth, elected Treasurer, who contributed the most. In fact, the greater part of her father's legacy would be willingly drip-fed into the movement.[1] She propped up most of Sylvia's East End activities, including the launch of a newspaper in 1914.

---

1. When she died in Ireland in 1962, Norah bequeathed £100 annually free of legacy duty to 'Estelle Sylvia Pankhurst'.

On 14 February – only a week after Sylvia, Zelie and Norah had opened their new premises at 321 Roman Road – Sylvia held a meeting at Bromley by Bow Town Hall. Stones were thrown and she was arrested. Again the WSPU paid her fine. The following Monday in an icy, bitter wind Sylvia climbed onto a cart outside a local council school and spoke to the crowd of shivering women, clutching shawls and coats around themselves for warmth. Zelie, a bright amusing speaker, attracted an even bigger audience, while Sylvia, 'numbed by the cold', sat beside her. Then she, too, spoke, appealing to the women to be prepared to make the sacrifice of imprisonment, even though this could cause suffering. As she turned to walk away, on impulse she threw a stone at an undertaker's window, whereupon the crowd of men and women went wild. Willie Lansbury, shouting 'Votes for Women', was arrested, as were Sylvia and several others. She, Willie and Zelie were sentenced to two months hard labour with no option this time of a fine.

Since a new Rule had been introduced permitting prisoners to wear their own clothes, the fur coat, which had stood Sylvia in such good stead on that freezing train journey across America, came into its own again. They were not allowed writing materials but instead were given a slate. This time she also smuggled in paper and pencils under her skirt.

She immediately went on hunger and thirst strike, permitting herself only a daily mouthwash, being careful not to swallow the water. She was not tempted at all by the chicken, fruit and Brands Essence placed, as she described it, like a still-life group, on the table in her cell. On the third day, on being told she would be fed by force, she panicked but would not give in and then began the twice-daily nightmare ritual of the steel gag, the rubber tube, the vomiting and the agony. She would lie on the bed, head down, struggling to vomit the food that had been poured into her. The flesh around her eyes and the eyeballs themselves became more and more painful. The sight of Zelie Emerson, also on hunger strike, horrified her when the two were allowed to meet in the prison yard some time later, and Sylvia felt guilty that she was the cause of Zelie's imprisonment.

She wrote to Keir Hardie but the letter was returned, insufficiently addressed. He was still in her thoughts. 'I felt once that a dear friend was beside me in the cell and afterwards there smote upon me sometimes that this dear friend was dead.' She also wrote a letter to her mother for publication in the press to counteract the authorities' claim that she was well and a model prisoner. 'I am fighting, fighting, fighting. I have four, five and six wardresses every day, as well as two doctors . . . I am afraid they may be saying that we don't resist. Yet my shoulders are bruised with struggling while they hold the tube into my throat.'[2]

At first Sylvia kept a diary, but as the weeks passed, she found 'the events it chronicled were too hateful to dwell on'. So, during her many imprisonments over the years, she turned to poetry as the 'most concentrated form of expression', and wrote enough verse to produce an anthology, *Writ on a Cold Slate*. This is not great poetry. It is not even very good poetry, yet some of it reflects the sensitive troubled spirit beneath the mask of the militant:

Unto the Birds

Unto the birds, much bread, much bread we fling,
For heavy grief forbids that we should eat:
So is this prison girt about with song,
With music recompensed our heedless alms;

But blackbird's finest trilling on his flute
And sweetest twittering of magic throats
Hath power alone to sharpen sorrow's tooth
A poignant birth unto sad memory bring:

For all the birds are singing to their loves,
And every note finds echo here within,
Where loving hearts their parted loves desire,
Mourning the smart of absence long endured.

On Monday, 10 March, King George V recorded in his diary: 'At 1.30 pm, drove in State to the House of Lords to open Parliament. I wore my crown as many people wished it. It had not been worn for the opening of Parliament for over 60 years. There were very few peers present which did not look well. In the Mall on the way to Westminster 5 Suffragettes ran out with a petition but didn't get near the coach . . .'.[3]

Sylvia was still in prison when, on 25 March, Home Secretary Reginald McKenna's infamous Bill was introduced: 'Prisoners' (Temporary Discharge for Ill Health') – dubbed the 'Cat and Mouse' Bill by the Suffragettes. This bill

2. Letter to Emmeline Pankhurst, 18 March 1913, WSPU Collection, Museum of London.
3. Royal Archives, Windsor, King George V's Diary.

enabled the authorities to release seriously weakened hunger strikers on a special licence that specified the date of their re-arrest. There were many in Parliament who thought that the women should be left to starve themselves, but the Prime Minister was anxious about the possibility of mass martyrdom being carried out. The King, too, revealed much anxiety. On 29 March his private secretary wrote to Mr McKenna from Windsor Castle:

> His Majesty quite recognises that the accounts written by women of their sufferings in prison are probably much exaggerated, if not actually untrue, but unfortunately the public see and believe these stories.
>
> The King is glad that your Bill will, to a great extent, do away with the need for 'forcible feeding' and His Majesty trusts that, without publishing the fact, this unpleasant duty will only be resorted to in extreme cases, such as that quoted by you of women convicted of taking or attempting to take Human life and when there is every reason to believe the offence would be repeated on their release.
>
> Are there many cases in which by means of 'Forcible Feeding' the prisoners are able to complete the full term of their sentence?
>
> The King's point is that . . . if the women's health breaks down through their starving themselves they will fail to arouse that sympathy which is evinced towards them when they claim 'Forcible Feeding' as the cause.[4]

The Home Secretary replied on 31 March 1913: 'You ask me whether there are many cases in which by forcible feeding prisoners are able to complete the full term of their sentence. Since the beginning of the year six prisoners have been released after forcible feeding' Of these, only three had completed their sentence. The three who had not completed their sentence were Sylvia Pankhurst, who served five weeks out of the eight she was sentenced to; Lilian Lenton, who was suffering from pleurisy; and May Billinghurst, who was a paraplegic.[5]

The truth of what had been happening to Sylvia inside Holloway had been hushed up. For Sylvia, faint, sick, her head swimming, her eyes like 'cups of blood', her voice 'high-pitched and strange', had decided that starvation was not enough and she began to walk . . . she walked on through the night, round and round her cell, staggering, falling against the walls, her legs swollen and

4. Royal Archives, Windsor, PS/GV/0459/3.
5. Royal Archives, Windsor, PS/GV/0459/4.

sore, on and on for twenty-eight hours. The walking relieved the constipation that she, like all hunger strikers, had suffered. When the Prison doctor eventually arrived, he arranged that she should be released in two days' time on condition that she drank two cups of milk each day.

Meanwhile, Zelie, who had attempted suicide, was feverish and asking for Sylvia, who, shocked at her condition, resolved to return to her own hunger strike. This time there was no attempt to force-feed her, and on Good Friday, Sylvia was released and returned, first to her empty studio in Linden Gardens and then to the Pembridge Gardens Nursing Home. Nurse Pine did not recognize her, so distorted were her features, and when a distraught Keir Hardie arrived a few hours later, Sylvia was distressed to see his hair was unkempt and his face haggard with anxiety. She blamed herself for his condition: 'I have caused you this grief, O tender heart!' The nursing home was soon to be named affectionately 'Mouse Castle', for it was to the tender 'bulldog' care of Nurse Pine that the 'Mice' were to come for rest and recovery after release under the Cat and Mouse Act.

Sylvia's article in the *Daily Mail* turned the tide of public opinion. There was growing revulsion not only against forcible feeding (wardresses were being paid an extra wage for the additional strain on them and a number resigned), but also the Act itself. Keir Hardie spoke in Parliament, saying, 'The endurance and heroism these women are showing in prison, equals, if it does not excel, anything we have witnessed on the field of battle . . .'. He was by no means alone.

George Bernard Shaw was prolific and vociferous in his disgust. 'If you take a woman and torture her you torture me,' he wrote. The *Medical Times* declared, 'Rather than be a party to such an outrage we would resign the most lucrative appointment ever held by a member of the "noble" profession'. All this was reported with gusto in *The Suffragette*, which increased its size due to the excess of news.

Emmeline Pankhurst was sentenced to three years penal servitude on 3 April for conspiring with others to place explosives with intent to destroy. She had accepted responsibility for the blowing up of Lloyd George's house. Once in prison she embarked on a hunger strike, and although she was not force-fed, and the Cat and Mouse Act was not yet law, she was released on special licence on 12 April. The authorities tried to re-arrest her after fifteen days but she was still too ill and went to stay with Ethel Smyth at Hook Green in Surrey; she never fully recovered her health.

Prison for the women (and the suffrage-supporting men) of the East End was a truly horrific experience and not one on which to embark lightly. Jobs were lost and children were left to the care of neighbours. They were often vilified by critics, who were cruelly unsympathetic and did not understand the idealism that motivated the campaigners. Always aware of the problems facing her members in prison, Sylvia established a fund to help their families.

The women made good use of their time to develop new friendships and to plan and organize future events. Those outside held rallies and 6-mile solidarity marches to Holloway and even to Brixton, where Willie Lansbury was incarcerated, often returning home exhausted in the small hours. This was to be the pattern henceforth – arrest, starvation, release and re-arrest. Sylvia herself went on hunger strike nine times in the last six months of that year.

Sylvia was well enough by 25 May to take part in a mass rally in nearby Victoria Park. Thousands of boughs had been decorated with paper almond blossom and these, with the Trade Union banners, the children in white, the gay colours of the WSPU and other suffrage societies and the 'bright red caps of Liberty', made a colourful show amid the tawdriness of the East End streets. It was the beginning of a massive East End surge of enthusiasm in which the Trades Union movement and other political and suffrage organizations joined forces. When the police tried to rent rooms in the Bow Road, in order to keep an eye on her activities, they were told there were 'no rooms available'.

There were many ways in which Sylvia was now gradually moving the East London Federation further and further from the WSPU. With Christabel in exile, the WSPU was becoming more secretive and isolated, whereas Sylvia relied totally on the willing support and protection of her local workers. She had become one of them. Like her sister, but in her own world and in her own way, the democratic Sylvia was now also enjoying the limelight.

Then came the black day of 4 June 1913. The King wrote in his diary:

We all left for Epsom at 12.40 to see the Derby. The police say it was the largest crowd that has ever been there, the road was blocked and it took us some time to get on the course. It was a most disastrous Derby . . . I ran Anmer . . . just as the horses were coming round Tattenham Corner a Suffragette [Miss Davison] dashed out and tried to catch Anmer's bridle. Of course she was knocked down and seriously injured and poor Herbert Jones and Anmer were sent flying. Jones, unconscious and badly cut, broken ribs and slight concussion, a most regrettable and scandalous proceeding . . . A most disappointing day . . . Got home 5.15 . . . Tea with May[6] in the garden . . .[7]

6. The King's pet name for Queen Mary.
7. Royal Archives, Windsor, King George V's Diary.

That 'scandalous proceeding' is probably the best remembered of all Suffragette images and resulted in the death of Emily Wilding Davison five days later.

Sylvia, like all the Suffragettes, dressed in white, went with her mother to join the thousands who assembled for the funeral on 14 June. As Emmeline emerged, she was arrested under the 'Cat and Mouse' Act and driven back to prison without protest. True to form, after the funeral Sylvia put pencil to paper in what she said herself was an 'eccentric' manifesto, and sent it to the *Daily Mail*:

> The crowded, trivial race-course and the glaring sun,
> The swift rush out into that horror of the horses' hoofs: a frantic clinging impact.
> Then, unseen, the column of flame that rises up to Heaven as the great heart bursts – the ascending spirit is set free.
> O deed of infinite majesty! Great heart that none could ever know!
> Mean, sordid things they write of her in printed sheets whose objects fill our minds with petty things . . .

The editor of the *Daily Mail* planned to publish her effort, but because it was in pencil on scrappy paper, he was not sure it was authentic. By the time he had confirmed authorship, she had decided against publication.

Towards the end of June, Sylvia had invited the Men's Federation for Women's Suffrage and the recently formed Free Speech Defence League to join the East End women in a Trafalgar Square Rally. Among the Defence League's speakers were Keir Hardie, Josiah Wedgwood and Frank Smith. The gathering got out of hand and the crowd rushed down Whitehall to Downing Street. As a result, a few days later two detectives handed Sylvia a piece of paper through the window of her Linden Gardens studio. It was a summons, issued under a rarely used statute of Edward III, referring to Sylvia as 'a disturber of the peace of our Lord the King'.

In no time at all she was back in Holloway, the now essential bag of papers and pencils hidden under her skirt, ready for the torrent of articles and letters she proposed to write. Already weakened by the earlier hunger and thirst strikes, Sylvia's renewed efforts at starvation and relentless walking made her ill very quickly. She was determined to be released in order to attend a rally in Bromley Public Hall. Under the 'Cat and Mouse' Act her constant fainting fits made it impossible for the authorities to keep her in prison and so she was taken by two wardresses to the tiny home of Mr and Mrs Payne, shoemakers of 28 Ford Road. The Paynes moved their double bed downstairs into the front parlour, tied up the doorknocker and even stopped work in order to give her some peace. But the detectives waiting outside the house provoked a disturbance by Sylvia's supporters. As there was constant noise, Mrs Payne took her to an even smaller room upstairs and this became her home for several months between frequent stays in prison.

In *The Suffragette Movement* she describes, with real concern, not for herself but for the Paynes, the bedroom that was now hers. 'Mrs Payne told me that as a young bride she hung her bed with pink curtains but plunged those curtains into a bucket of water the night of her marriage on account of the bugs she was horrified to find crawling over them. When I lit my candle on sleepless nights, I would see a dozen or more of them on the wall, though disinfectants were always burnt in the room in my absence.' Sylvia's convalescence at the Paynes brought a constant flow of visitors, including even the Bishop of London. She was showered with gifts and flowers and there were dozens of letters asking her to deal with problems of landlords and tenants, government departments, insurance societies and trades unions.

The contrast now between Sylvia's life and that of Christabel, who was still living in Paris with her pomeranian named Fay, a present from Emmeline, could not have been greater. Christabel, more and more right-wing, wrote from Deauville to Henry Harben on 1 August, saying that, 'since the Labour party entered the House of Commons it has made every possible mistake and has done nothing at all that was wise and effective. If our country can be governed only by riot and violence I AM GAME for that sort of thing. But I mean to have a try at the other thing first – when the vote is won!'

During the summer the East London Federation grew in number so that more and more police were directed to attend Sylvia's meetings. Many of the women adopted the tactics of the early days: disguise. They dressed up in wigs, veils and all kinds of outrageous costumes, although Sylvia herself felt this was cowardly and usually preferred full-frontal honesty. The 21 July meeting at Bromley Public Hall in Bow was one such theatrical occasion.

Sylvia's licence under the Cat and Mouse Act had already expired and, ill as she was, she agreed to hide her identity under a long dark coat with a high collar and a small hat pulled down over her eyes. Once on the platform she threw off the coat to the cheers of all those present and spoke with passion of the 'chains of poverty'. As she jumped down to talk to the audience, her guards turned a hose on the police, 'flushing' them out into the road while Sylvia escaped down an alley and hid in a disused stable. It was 4.00 in the morning before help came in the form of Willie and Edgar Lansbury driving a cart piled high with wood. Sylvia hid under a blanket but detectives were everywhere. The Lansbury boys unloaded their wood, tied Sylvia into a sack, put her on the cart and surrounded her by more sackloads of logs. She was driven for what seemed like hours out to Epping Forest, where George Lansbury's sister-in-law Bessie Brine gave her shelter.

There were other exciting occasions when Sylvia agreed to a disguise. On 27 July wearing a wig, a shepherd's plaid coat and skirt, her front stuffed with newspapers and a transparent veil, she was driven to Trafalgar Square to the largest crowd she had ever seen. 'There was a strange, deep, growling sound in the crowd about me I had never heard before: the sound of angry men.' Soon Sylvia was back in Holloway. 'I was at first so horrified by the return there I felt I could have knocked my head against the wall.'

Nevinson declared: 'the barbarity of the "Cat and Mouse Act" has struck very deep into the mind of the ordinary man and woman . . . A great deal also is due to Miss Sylvia Pankhurst's action in throwing herself upon the genuine chivalry and good sense of the workers in the East End. I think that was a stroke of genius.' There was now a new element developing amongst Sylvia's supporters. They were eager to respond in kind to some of the police brutality and were arriving at meetings equipped with sticks and batons. More dangerous was the East End's very own weapon, a 'Saturday night'. This was a tarred rope, twisted, knotted and sometimes weighted with lead. The local press was rewarded with spectacular headline stories and seemingly endless column inches: 'Wild Scenes in the East End', 'Threat of Gunpowder and Violence', 'Socialist-Suffragette Riots'.

Sylvia's health had been seriously undermined by the hunger striking, so friends urged her to take a holiday – not a word she understood. She and Norah decided to go to Finland to meet the first women elected to a modern Parliament, as well as visiting Sweden, Norway and Denmark. They were given an enthusiastic welcome everywhere but were most impressed by the social services in Denmark. 'Admirable Denmark seemed to me the happiest, most fraternal and, therefore, noblest country in the world!

There was to be a 'Welcome Home' meeting at Bow Baths Hall on 13 October to which Sylvia and Norah went in a mood of euphoric anticipation and unrealistic idealism: 'we would re-create the East End . . . sweep poverty and slums from out the land'. As they sat on the platform there was an agitated cry from the audience of 'Jump, Sylvia, jump!' There was a rush from behind as detectives tried to grab Sylvia. A battle royal ensued as she was passed from person to person, constantly changing hats to confuse her pursuers. She escaped, steered by the celebrated East End prize-fighter 'Kosher' Hunt, into the pouring rain, where he lent her his scarf as additional disguise and they disappeared in the dark. Zelie Emerson was knocked unconscious in the fracas and her skull fractured.

Nothing daunted Sylvia, and despite recurring pains, she decided to keep an engagement to speak the following night at Poplar Town Hall. She again, if reluctantly, agreed to a disguise, and dressed in poor clothes with a mock baby in her arms, she travelled with some friends on the top of a bus. But the police were one stop ahead. As she dismounted she was stopped by two officers, arrested and it was back to prison. Weakened as she was, Sylvia began another nine days of hunger and thirst strike but this time on release was no longer able to walk. So she attended meetings on a stretcher.

With Sylvia's apparently limitless compassion, her anxiety for the escalating Irish problem was now also occupying her thoughts. In an attempt to tackle the appalling working conditions of both Catholic and Protestant areas of Ireland, James Larkin, a fiery, spell-binding orator, was advancing the cause of the Irish Transport and General Workers' Union formed by James Connolly. Employers, taking fright, declared a lock-out of Union members, including women. There was a riot and the police, famed for their brutality, used truncheons on men, women and children. People were killed and Larkin arrested. The lock-out victims pleaded in vain for help from the British government and in the end were starved into submission. The *Daily Herald* led a nationwide campaign and many children were brought over from Dublin to English homes. The Pethick-Lawrences cared for several in their Surrey cottage. Despite the fact that Sylvia's 'Cat and Mouse' licence had expired and she knew she would probably be arrested, she agreed to speak at Lansbury's mass rally in support of the victims at the Albert Hall on 1 November.

That decision was to lead to the final break in the already fractured Pankhurst family. A furious Christabel, who now considered her sister to be breaking every rule in the WSPU book, issued a statement from Paris declaring that Sylvia had gone to the meeting as an independent and not as a part of the WSPU. Not surprisingly, Sylvia sent a rejoinder in fighting spirit to all WSPU branches on 19 November, dealing with 'this little storm in a tea cup'. She complained that, since the WSPU was short of speakers, she should have been invited to speak, especially since publicity and funds were desperately needed. 'There was a time when the WSPU held far more meetings than any other society. That is not the case today.' She wrote: 'People are asking whether I or the East London Federation of the WSPU have formed any kind of alliance with The Daily Herald League. The answer is quite simply:

"no we have not".' This statement in itself caused her some trouble, for she had to make amends to her men supporters in the East End for appearing ungracious for their help.

Annie Kenney thereupon sent a circular from her sick bed on 25 November attacking Sylvia's gloomy picture of the state of the WSPU, and Christabel, incensed, wrote to her sister, 'It is essential for the public to understand that you are working independently of us. As you have complete confidence in your policy and way of doing things, this should suit you perfectly.' The rift was about to become public. Nor did Adela escape. She had completed training at Studely Agricultural College in February and found work as head gardener at Rode Manor, Somerset, but was still lonely and unhappy tucked away in the countryside. A letter from Annie Kenney in November, urging her to promise never to speak in England again, must have been a cruel blow, which, she suspected, had been aimed by Christabel. Certainly Emmeline and Christabel were worried by Sylvia's increasing independence and feared that she and Adela might join forces in a competitive organization.

There appears to have been very little contact with Keir Hardie this time, only the occasional, rather wistful mention in Sylvia's writings. It would seem that the self-confidence she had gained on her foreign travels had developed Sylvia's self-reliance. Hardie himself was ageing and weary: Fenner Brockway suggested in his autobiography that Hardie could perhaps have been tiring of the Pankhursts' unending quest for martyrdom and even that Sylvia's emotional demands had become a burden. It seems more likely that the circumstances of their lives had changed and that she was no longer content to sit at anyone's feet, not even Hardie's, although her socialist and pacifist ideals had been nurtured in his company. But she was at last forging her own path.

The time for those romantic evenings, plotting by the fire in Nevill's Court or walking across Richmond Park together planning a brave new world, had simply passed. Sylvia was more mature and part of a blossoming socialist world of her own, whereas Hardie, she noted sadly, had even given up wearing his red tie and was dressed in sombre grey. His meetings were often heckled: 'it made me sad,' she confessed. Indeed, in the early autumn Hardie had gone to see her recuperating in bed: 'In spite of his gentleness, it was almost a quarrel – on my part not his. I saw myself now in the position towards him in which I had so often seen my mother: he trying to help her, she flouting his efforts. I did not want him to help me to get free or even to try.' When her mother had also paid a visit and expressed a wish to avoid meeting Hardie, Sylvia said with some sadness, 'he will not come again'

Caroline Benn believes that, 'he had given her more than himself – he had given her a cause of her own. All the women who passed through Hardie's life were profoundly affected by his political beliefs.' Sylvia found a way to unite socialism and feminism, and when the women's vote was finally won, it was Christabel and Emmeline who were left 'wandering'. Their moment had passed. Sylvia was poised for greater things.

16

War on all Fronts

'I tell you quite frankly that I have listened with the greatest interest to . . . a very moderate and well-reasoned presentation of your case and I will give it . . . very careful and mature consideration . . . on one point, I am glad to say I am in complete agreement with you . . . if you are going to give the franchise to women, you must give it to them on the same terms that you do to men . . . It is no good tinkering with a thing of this kind . . . If the change has to come we must face it boldly and make it thoroughgoing and democratic in its basis.'

Asquith's reply to Sylvia following the ELFS deputation on 12 June 1914

Christabel makes no mention of the final parting of the Pankhurst ways in her autobiography, no reference at all to what must have been the two most poignant and painful of family meetings in Paris, early in January 1914.

Sylvia was in Holloway between 4 and 10 January and, shortly after release, decided she had to respond to the summonses she had been receiving from her sister. She was reluctant to leave the country for fear of arrest and because she had so many commitments now in the East End. Besides, as she said: 'I realised that, like so many others, I was to be given the "conge".'[1] But a truculent Christabel was not to be ignored and so, travelling with Norah for support and to represent the members, Sylvia left from Harwich in a private cabin, still feeling miserably ill after her prison experiences. They found that Emmeline, too, was far from well, and it appears that Christabel, pomeranian on lap, did all the talking. Norah, who was a loyal supporter of the WSPU but had nevertheless chosen to move with Sylvia into the East End, remained silent. 'Like me, she desired to avoid a breach. Dogged in her fidelities and by temperament, unable to express herself under emotion . . .'.

There seemed no end to Sylvia's misdemeanours according to Christabel: she had spoken at Lansbury's pro-Larkin meeting – contrary to WSPU policy; she

1. The sack.

worked with Lansbury – the WSPU 'did not want to be mixed up with him'; she had a democratic constitution – the WSPU did not agree with that; the working women's movement was of no value; Sylvia's friendship with Lansbury and Henry Harben was unwelcome; the East London Federation was diverting funds that might be given to the WSPU (it is true that Harben was supporting both). Sylvia had her own ideas and they were not needed. 'We want all our women to take their instructions and walk in step like an army,' Christabel declared.

'Oppressed by a sense of tragedy, grieved by her ruthlessness,' Sylvia made no reply. They drove in the Bois de Boulogne, Christabel with her dog on her arm, but Sylvia was in no mood to benefit from the pleasures of Paris; she was suffering from fatigue and headaches, and she could see that her mother was pale and emaciated. In the afternoon the conversation turned bitter and aggressive. Norah Smyth knew that donations due to the East London Federation had already found their way to Lincolns Inn. She challenged Christabel, who questioned the need of such a 'simple' organization as theirs for money. Emmeline, now clearly distressed, tried to ameliorate the situation by offering some supporting funds to Sylvia – an idea firmly rejected by Christabel. 'Oh no,' she said, 'we can't have that. We must have a clean break.' And so it was that the East London Federation was expelled from the WSPU.

Sylvia was in a daze, barely hearing Christabel's words. Images of their childhood, the early days at Green Hayes and in Russell Square, were rushing through her mind as the words of their father echoed around the room: 'you are the four pillars of my house'. Emmeline must have recalled those words with equal pain, but Christabel showed no such emotion.

On her return to London it seems that Sylvia invited Adela to join her in the East End movement. According to Adela, interestingly (if her account is to be relied on) Sylvia told her that in fact it was she who had cut herself off from the WSPU and not vice versa. Adela had been travelling on the Continent with a family friend as a companion-governess, a job Mrs Pankhurst considered demeaning and therefore put a stop to. Even so, Adela did not want to do anything to hurt her mother and consequently refused Sylvia's suggestion.

It was not long before Adela herself made the painful journey to Paris and, like Sylvia, experienced rejection. Being a committed socialist, she had already been forbidden (by Annie Kenney) to speak in England, but her story is best told in her own words:

I saw mother and Christabel in Paris . . . mother was against me. She seemed to think I was a great failure. I was ashamed to tell her how hard things were and curiously, perhaps, I did not explain that I had an offer of a post at Chester the following March to teach gardening in a boys' school. Mother seemed to think I had not tried to get work and wanted to come into the movement as Christabel's rival.

As it was, Adela was subjected to a torrent of long-harboured complaints from Christabel, although they seem to have been of a peculiarly petty and personal nature. Of course, Adela's ideals were, at this stage, far closer to those of Sylvia than was comfortable for Emmeline and Christabel, who were afraid that the two girls together might establish a rival organization. She did not tell her about Sylvia's attempt to recruit her, nor about her refusal. 'Had I done so she and Christabel would probably have thought better about me,' she said.

All those childhood grudges, nursed over the years of isolation and hostility, emerged that day in Paris. Adela seems to have somewhat unfairly blamed Sylvia for all her ills, a bitterness she carried to the end of her life. At the age of only 28 Adela was utterly demolished; there was no fight left in her. 'It appeared to me quite right that my indiscretions should banish me from my country,' she wrote. It was suggested that Adela would fare better in Australia:

I was very miserable but down in the bottom of my heart, hope was stirring. I felt that I was not such a fool or a knave as I had been made out and that in another country I should find my feet and happiness. Nothing would have induced me to enter a fight with Sylvia and the rest of the family and my mother's action in getting me out of the way was best for myself and all concerned. She gave me what money she could spare – it was very little and I often wondered what she thought I would do in Australia when it was spent.

I was young and she was old. Our points of view could not be the same. Tolerance was certainly not to be learned in the school in which she had been trained. If she had been tolerant and broadminded she could not have been leader of the Suffragettes. She had nearly forgotten me as a daughter . . . and I must confess I had largely forgotten her as a mother . . . It was part of the price paid by us for votes for British women . . .

Emmeline, for her part, wrote to Ethel Smyth afterwards, 'I have pangs of maternal weakness but I harden my heart.' On 2 February 1914 Adela sailed, alone, on the Geelong for Canberra. She did not see her mother or sisters again.

There was considerable irritation amongst East London members when Sylvia told them of the expulsion. They resented their ejection from the WSPU. However, when it was proposed to change the name of the East

London Federation to the East London Federation of Suffragettes, after yet another bitter exchange of letters, Emmeline wrote, with some justification: 'As for the name, Christabel and I do not approve of the one you suggest because the name "Suffragettes" would be altogether misleading to the public. The WSPU and "The Suffragettes" have become interchangeable terms.' She said that if Sylvia insisted on the 'East London Federation of Suffragettes' – the ELFS – she would not carry reports of her activities in *The Suffragette*. She then suggested a number of alternatives, such as the East London Federation for the Vote, East London Women's Franchise Federation or East London Working Women's Union for the Vote. None of these appealed to the women in Bow and they decided to defy Emmeline and become the ELFS, adding bright red for liberty to the WSPU colours of purple, white and green.

With independence declared, the ELFS decided to launch a newspaper. The WSPU journal *The Suffragette* and the Pethick-Lawrence's paper *Votes for Women* were devoted only to a single campaign and their circulation was declining. The name chosen by the ELFS was the *Woman's Dreadnought*.[2] The irony was not lost on her that the rivalry between Germany and Britain focused on building bigger and better battleships – now known colloquially as dreadnoughts. It was not Sylvia's favourite name but she accepted the majority vote. The paper, which was to focus on a wide range of women's interest issues, was to pay for itself by advertisements (and donations).

Launching a newspaper is an all-consuming business and finding a publisher is not easy. J.E. Francis at the Athenaeum Press, a good friend to the Suffragettes, wrote advisedly to Sylvia on 13 February 1914:

Personally I am not really anxious to print your paper because it will mean I shall have to read every word of it . . . but I have got the idea that your paper ought to come out and if I can help the issue of necessary information and, at the same time, give work to some very splendid people I must not be deterred by the trouble it will give myself. No doubt the end will be that we shall quarrel and you will take the paper away somewhere else because I cannot make you see my point of view about something you want inserted and I cannot see your point of view as to the necessity of its going in and so insist on it being taken out.

What foresight – for they ran into trouble in the first issue, when Sylvia included a statement by Ethel Moorhead, the first Scottish prisoner to be force-fed. It was omitted by Mr Francis because, he argued, the government

---

2. HMS *Dreadnought* was the world's largest, fastest battleship, launched in February 1906.

had not been given time to reply. Sylvia immediately removed the *Dreadnought* to an East End printer, although her friendship with Mr Francis survived and he undertook the printing again some years later.

Despite Zelie Emerson's best efforts, shopkeepers were reluctant to take advertising space and in the end only the manufacturers of Neave's Food and Lipton's Cocoa signed a three-month contract. The paper was to be sold for one halfpenny for the first four days after publication and then distributed free door to door. The first eight-page issue appeared on 8 March 1914: the *Dreadnought* then ran until July 1924. Sylvia always encouraged her East Enders to contribute – she valued their ideas and views and did her best to edit their contributions sensitively, in order not to destroy their vitality and originality. The paper was their voice.

For Sylvia, the commitment of the newspaper and the campaign as a whole prevented her from attempting to earn a living from painting, and even writing became more difficult. There was now no longer the possibility of denying the family feud and the press made the most of Sylvia's expulsion. She had always adopted the WSPU motto of 'Deeds not Words' and had never voiced her private criticism of the way the campaign was conducted. Now she was on her own and discretion was hardly an option.

There is a delightful exchange of letters between Norah Smyth and the *New York Times*. The paper was eager for a full-blooded, 1000-word attack by Sylvia on the WSPU, and for her to claim that: 'the WSPU is disorganised and crippled financially, that the Cat and Mouse Bill has practically crushed the militant movement, and any other points she may desire'. A week later the editor, Ernest Marshall, returned the article, since 'it does not contain the material we requested and consequently is of no use to us'.

Sylvia certainly ploughed back whatever journalistic earnings came her way, but it was Norah who, over the years, gave most of her inheritance to the ELFS and their many projects. She was a remarkable woman, intelligent, shy, efficient, remembered by friends in later life, when she lived in Malta, as a much loved, tender-hearted eccentric with a collection of stray cats called Tristan and Isolde, Thisbe and Pyramon, Oedipuss and Midas. She had one blue eye and one brown, wore her hair cropped short, in the fashion of the day, and men's brogues several sizes too big. It was Sylvia's good fortune that she gathered men and women of Norah's calibre around her. Nellie Cressall used to say, 'It's all your money we're using,' and Norah would reply, 'I don't mind, it's in a good cause.' Henry Harben was a tower of strength, too, regularly lending money to help with the acquisition or restoration of premises.

When Emmeline returned to England on 10 February, she and Sylvia embarked on a parallel series of public speaking appearances. These often ended in prison, but although they were each in and out of Holloway at the same time, they never met. As Martin Pugh notes, 'Sylvia . . . had begun to eclipse her mother by the sheer spectacle of her clashes with the police.' One of these involved being carried in procession shoulder high on a collapsed wheelchair. While in prison, Sylvia had planned to lead the ELFS in procession to Westminster Abbey for the service on Mothering Sunday, 22 March. Released on 14 March, she wrote to the Dean of Westminster explaining their intention and asking him to include a reference to votes for women in the service. Sylvia's agnosticism did not affect her sense of theatre.

There was consternation in Bow because Sylvia was known to be extremely weak and members were naturally worried that she could not cope with the strain of such a journey. It is about 6 miles from Bow to Westminster. They borrowed a spinal chair for her from the Cripples' Institute but in the crush of people, it buckled. Not to be deterred, Sylvia was hoisted, still sitting, symbolically saint-like, above the crowd and carried, shoulder-high, to the Abbey with the rebel priest, the Reverend C.A. Wills, leading the way. Again, symbolically, the Abbey gates were shut and the marchers, who now numbered several thousand, were told there was no room for them. So Mr Wills conducted his own service outside and Sylvia, high on adrenalin, reported, 'all pain had left me'. But on the way home in a hired ambulance, once the excitement was over, she was violently sick.

Sylvia used her nine imprisonments between February and June 1914 to create an imaginative programme for the future of the ELFS. Her long-term vision was for a re-housed East End in centrally heated homes, with a communal nursery and playground for the children. In the shorter term she planned a no-vote, no-rent strike but was sympathetic to the natural fear of East Enders who could consequently lose their homes. She realized that in fact only a crisis would provoke such drastic action; she did not know how imminent that crisis was.

Meanwhile, in what appears to have been a desperate last stand to defend her now shaky power-base, Christabel wrote a series of extraordinary articles, which were then produced as a book, *The Great Scourge*. The 'scourge' was venereal disease, from which, she claimed, 80 per cent of British men suffered. 'Therefore marriage is best avoided. Votes for Women – Chastity for Men!' was her new message; it also marked the beginning of her interest in religion.

Sylvia received an invitation to speak in Budapest at Easter, where the Pankhurst name was known and revered. All expenses and a proportion of the proceeds were to be paid, which permitted Sylvia to take Zelie as a companion. Almost on the spur of the moment she decided to call on Christabel as they passed through Paris and arrived, unannounced, at the apartment in the rue de la Grande Armée. Christabel was out, but the maid greeted the visitors with almost hysterical excitement, having seen Sylvia in cinema newsreels. She rushed off to prepare a meal while they waited. Christabel was less enthusiastic, embarrassingly remote and uninterested in their Hungarian trip. Sylvia realized that the fiery, protective Zelie was about to explode, and although they had a long wait before their train was due, they left without eating.

Both Zelie and Sylvia were ill and still suffering from the after-effects of their prison experiences. They barely coped with the arduous journey, supporting each other as best they could. 'Though I was temporarily the weaker the afflictions of my companion were the graver,' Sylvia wrote. Her recollections of that journey are as detailed and sensitive as those of her travels in America, although there is additional warmth in her writing. She clearly loved the countryside and its people. Easter Sunday found Zelie and Sylvia absorbing the atmosphere of the incense and the bells in the 'gorgeous' bronze and gold basilica, where they listened to the preacher declaiming against socialism. Then they travelled with friends on a sightseeing tour of the city, enjoying the colour, the gaiety and the fashions. In a newly developed showcase suburb for 30,000 people, Sylvia saw how her vision for the East End of London could be realized and was overwhelmed there by the state provision for orphaned and destitute children. On the other hand, the women's prison was worse than Holloway:

> So dejected they looked and one was so hopelessly sorrowful that I was constrained to take her hand, miserably wishing that I had the power to help her. She burst into shuddering sobs. I guided her to a bench, then saw that all the others were weeping too . . . They seized my hands, trying to kiss them; even the girl in the bed stretched out her arms. Distressed that I had occasioned their tears I pressed their hands, poor children but would not let them touch mine with their lips; their humility grieved and embarrassed me. As we left them, the suffrage ladies told me they would think I had scorned their kisses. I knew of nothing to dispel that thought save to blow kisses to them from the door.

A large audience gathered for Sylvia's meeting in the great hall of the Vigado. She told them of the struggle by British women for the vote and was warmly praised for the 'incredible greatness' of the hunger strikers in their heroic fight 'for human freedom'.

From Budapest the couple went on to Vienna, where they were filmed and feted, taken to see *Die Walkure* from a box at the Opera House and out to walk in the peace of the Vienna Woods. They gathered violets among the beeches, where Sylvia said she felt like a caged wild thing, liberated among the trees. 'Poor town-bred children; what joys you miss!'

While Sylvia was away, the ILP hosted a major celebration of its 21st birthday, which was attended by Lillie and during which Hardie gave her an extraordinary and unexpected accolade. Waiting for the applause to subside, he looked back to the foundation of the ILP: 'Never, even in those days, did she offer one word of reproof. Many a bitter tear she shed but one of the proud boasts of my life is to be able to say that if she has suffered much in health and spirit, never has she reproached me for what I have done for the cause I loved.'

Arriving back in Bow after the European visit, Sylvia was extremely worried by Zelie's appearance, 'her face nervously strained, her figure shrunk'. The campaigns were taking their toll. However, there was a positive development: before leaving for Europe, Sylvia had taken a walk in dense fog one morning and come across a large empty house, 400 Old Ford Road. Previously it had been a school, then a factory and had a hall capable of seating about 300, which was connected to the main house by a smaller flat-roofed hall.

With yet more financial support from Henry Harben and the usual practical help from the community, the women set to work. A supportive all-male group had sprung up, known as The Rebels Social and Political Union. They helped, and between them all the building was painted, decorated and restored to make the HQ of the ELFS and a home for Norah, Sylvia and the Paynes. Amid much bustle and excitement the ELFS organized a library, a choir, lectures, concerts and a 'Junior Suffragettes Club'. As the 'Women's Hall' it became a focus and a home for anyone in need. The house warming was on 5 May and the next day Zelie Emerson, very reluctantly, set off back to America. Sylvia had been advised by doctors that Zelie must return if she was to recover from her fractured skull and force-feeding. But it took many hours of painful, distressing persuasion by Sylvia to win her agreement.

Roughly a year after the parting Zelie wrote to her from America enclosing a poem that indicated there may have been something more than a platonic friendship:

Dear Sylvia, I have not heard from you so I conclude that you do not wish to see me. However I would like to know what was the cause for your not wanting me to speak for us any more . . .

I know that I am a 'self righteous little prig' but would like to know what else I am to you . . .

Of course you know that nothing that has happened or may happen between us can ever alter my feeling toward you and perhaps some day . . . I may be of service to you and the cause for that is after all the only thing that really matters . . .

> To Sylvia Pankhurst
>
> You did not understand, and in your eyes
> I saw a vague surprise,
> As if my voice came from some distant sphere,
> Too far for you to hear;
> Alas! In other days it was not so
> Those days of long ago
>
> II
> Time was when all my being was thrown wide
> All veils were drawn aside
> That you might enter anywhere at will
> Now all is hushed and still
> Save for a sound recurring more and more
> The shutting of a door

As ever. Yours Zelie Emerson.
Thanks for the hair.

The political tension on both home and foreign fronts was becoming increasingly alarming, although for the people in the East End the likelihood of war in Europe still seemed remote and strangely unreal. Hardie was doing his best to 'alert the still slumbering millions of the danger of drifting into war'.

In Ireland, despite improvements to be brought about by the proposed Home Rule Bill, the enmity between Catholics and Protestants was as bitter as ever. Both sides had established private armies. Civil war loomed. Any hopes that women held of winning the vote were dashed in the midst of all this. A deputation from Belfast went to see Sir Edward Canson, leader of the Ulster Unionists, and sat on his doorstep through an entire weekend until he agreed to meet them. They were disappointed. Sir Edward refused to introduce the issue of the promised Votes for Ulster Women. The result was the first major uprising of Ulster Suffragettes. Bombs exploded and buildings were set on fire, and when the leaders were arrested and charged with possession of fire-arms, they demanded to know why Sir Edward and his colleagues had not been arrested too. They were as guilty of violence as the women.

In Europe, while the naval race was escalating, Britain formed a buffer alliance known as the Triple Entente. Austria, Turkey, Bulgaria and the Balkans were all tussling with conflicting aims and ambitions of their own and edging closer towards Germany. Consequently, at home, as Sylvia said, 'Changes the Gladstonian era would have deemed remarkable were passing through Parliament with scant public notice.' The Parliament Act, which removed the Lords' ultimate right to veto legislation, was passed in the Commons; the Trades Union Act and the disestablishment of the Welsh Church now seemed trivial.

Christabel, still commanding her troops from Paris, was writing strident letters to Emmeline Pethick-Lawrence, who had told her that her place should be in London. Christabel replied, 'You know anti-militancy does affect the reasoning faculty adversely. People who are most rational and logical and enlightened when their political movements are at stake, suddenly lose their bearings when weak. It is the weakness of the pro-suffragists that is the enemy now.' That spring she had launched an unprecedented campaign of destruction. In the first seven months of 1914 three Scottish castles were destroyed in one night, the Carnegie Library in Birmingham was burnt, the Rokeby Venus was slashed, as was a portrait of Millais in London's National Portrait Gallery. Stately homes all over the British Isles were attacked and, among many other incidents, railway stations, piers, sports pavilions and haystacks were damaged. A bomb was exploded in Westminster Abbey and £2,000 worth of flood damage was done to the great Albert Hall organ. Churchmen referred to 'unparalleled wickedness' and 'infamous crimes' and many women were themselves injured in the disturbances.

Sylvia, still refusing to use arson or attack property or works of art, was active as ever in her own way. She organized a huge May Day event in Victoria Park. In the centre of a group of twenty women chained to each other, she arrived at the Park where banners and maypoles were being erected. But the police charged, hitting out with truncheons and eventually smashing the padlocked chains. Sylvia was flung on to the floor of a taxi, followed by four officers who leapt in swearing, pinching and arm-twisting. This time in Holloway she determined that the next deputation to Asquith must be an elected group of working people from the East End in order to prove that the demand for the vote was indeed both democratic and of the masses.

Freed on 30 May, she wrote to the Prime Minister asking him to receive a deputation elected by open rallies to be held in the East End. The rallies would also vote on the demand they preferred: without exception, they unanimously selected 'a vote for every woman over 21'.

He refused. She wrote again, explaining that a large proportion of the women of the East End who were enduring terrible hardships were 'impatient to take a constitutional part in moulding the conditions under which they have to live'. She told him she regarded the deputation of such importance that if he refused to meet it, she would not only refuse food and water in Holloway when, most likely, she was re-arrested, she would also continue her strike outside the House of Commons when she was released. Asquith again refused. When Sylvia told the last rally meeting of Asquith's refusal and of her intention to carry out the threat, women were in tears.

On the evening of 10 June, 'The whole district was aroused; the roadway thronged. Wills asked to be allowed to say a prayer from the window. We knew he was jeopardising his career and respected his courage. I looked out on the throng . . . men with bared heads and the women with streaming tears.' Sylvia was clearly too weak to walk to Westminster, so was carried on a stretcher by four bearers, including H.W. Nevinson. Not long after the procession had started, police charged, Sylvia was thrown to the ground and within minutes she was back in Holloway. The marchers re-formed and continued to Parliament Square without her. The elected deputation of nine women and three men was finally allowed inside the House. They were told that the Prime Minister was away but would be given their message. The women made speeches in the forbidden ground of Parliament Square and no one was arrested.

On 11 June the Commons debated the hunger strikes and Home Secretary Reginald McKenna referred to 'a phenomenon absolutely without precedent in our history'. He decided that patient and determined action would be best and that he would consider criminal charges against the WSPU subscribers and so intimidate them into capitulation. Asquith continued to refuse the East Enders their audience. Norah Smyth, fearing Asquith would let Sylvia die, wrote to Emmeline, begging her to link the WSPU efforts to those of the ELFS. Emmeline replied, 'Your action is not in conformity with WSPU policy and tell Sylvia I advise her, when she comes out of prison, to go home and let her friends take care of her.'

On 18 June, Sylvia was released, weak and in pain after her latest hunger strike. It was already dusk when she persuaded Norah to drive her immediately to the House of Commons, where a small group of women was waiting. Josiah

Wedgwood and Keir Hardie were there too, kind and caring and clearly troubled at her condition. Keir tried to contact the Prime Minister, and when he returned it was only to confirm that as she was blacklisted for having thrown her missile at the Speaker's picture, she must write to him apologizing for having 'broken the rules of the House'.

She agreed but then insisted that her friends lay her on the ground, near the statue of Oliver Cromwell where, she said, she would stay without eating or drinking until she died or Mr Asquith agreed to see the East End deputation. Nevinson described the scene later. 'I stood beside her, very helpless, while she lay on the steps, apparently dying, and the police, perhaps in pity, hesitated to drive her away. At last, to my infinite relief Keir Hardie came out of the House and on hearing from me what the situation was stood with me.' George Lansbury joined them and the three men went immediately to see the Prime Minister, returning jubilant with the news that Asquith had relented. He agreed to see six of the delegates on the following Saturday, 20 June.

'Everyone was laughing and talking around me.' Was this the turning of the tide? Next day Sylvia prepared a statement. She felt this was an opportunity for the people from Bow to speak for themselves. Those who were the elected representatives were led by Julia Scurr, whose husband John later became an MP. There was stout, old Mrs Savoy, the brush maker, 'always jolly despite her dropsy and palpitations', who George Lansbury described as 'the best woman in Old Ford'; motherly, anxious Mrs Payne; Mrs Bird, mother of six, living on her husband's wage of £1.5.0 weekly; Mrs Watkins; and frail little Mrs Parsons. They told their harrowing stories to a startled and softening Asquith. He was surprisingly impressed and praised the way in which they were conducting their campaign with clarity and without resort to 'criminal methods'. He said, 'I think it is a very moderate and well-reasoned presentation of your case and I will give it, you may be quite sure, very careful and mature consideration.' He also declared, 'if you are going to give the franchise to women, you must give it to them on the same terms that you do to men ... That is, make it a democratic measure ... If the change has to come, we must face it boldly, and make it thoroughgoing and democratic in its basis.'

This was the nearest Sylvia had ever come to a vote of confidence, and the press also agreed that women's suffrage could not long be delayed. The women from the East End had achieved a breakthrough on the strength of their presentation, but, as they all agreed, it was Sylvia who had brought them to this moment.

With a General Election likely before the end of the year, Sylvia and Prime

Minister Asquith were in general harmony on the best way to approach the question of suffrage – and it was not Emmeline or Christabel's way.

George Lansbury then arranged a breakfast meeting between Sylvia, himself and Lloyd George in the Commons. Money-conscious as ever, she took the lengthy bus trip from Bow to Parliament rather than choose the extravagance of a cab. By the time she arrived, still unwell, she was extremely tired, the light behind Lloyd George hurt her eyes and she immediately feared that the meeting was doomed. Besides, she noted, Lloyd George was far too quick a thinker for Lansbury.

He told them that he would indeed put his weight behind a Reform Bill, which would include women's enfranchisement and an offer to resign if he failed. His backing would be conditional on the end of militancy. Sylvia admitted later that she should perhaps have asked for a written guarantee, but instead she made a serious tactical error. She said that she doubted Christabel would agree to a truce, short of a government measure. He replied curtly that he would debate the matter only with Christabel herself.

George Lansbury interpreted the meeting rather more positively than Sylvia, who feared no certain promises had, in fact, been given, and he communicated his enthusiastic excitement immediately to Christabel. She responded, just as Sylvia had anticipated. No truce. So Sylvia wrote to her sister, offering to visit Paris and relay her own impression of the meeting. The reply was a telegram from Christabel to Norah: 'tell your friend not to come'. Christabel was becoming irritated by her younger sister's increased influence with MPs and the respect with which she was apparently now being treated.

The following weekend in late July, Sylvia and Norah went down to Penshurst in Kent, near her favourite Cinder Hill, where they booked into the local hotel under assumed names. But Keir Hardie blundered by sending a telegram to 'Pankhurst', thus exposing their cover and causing the innkeeper much anxiety. He begged the two women to remove their ELFS badges: his landlord, Lord de Lisle, would be angry if he gave them shelter, as Suffragettes had recently attacked his home, Penshurst Place. Hardie eventually joined Sylvia and Norah and, after much discussion, agreed to urge that Adult Manhood and Womanhood Suffrage should be the Labour Party's main plank at the coming election. Everything appeared to be coming together very well.

It is arguable that, had it not been for the war, Sylvia, the Pankhurst who through a combination of militant courageous action and a belief in democracy and debate, would have at long last brought the women's movement closer to success than it had ever been. But it was not to be.

On 22 July, Emmeline, weak and exhausted, escaped across the Channel to join Christabel in Brittany. On 26 July, Sylvia and the ELFS members went out for a picnic among the hornbeams and beeches of Epping Forest. On 28 July, Winston Churchill, then First Lord of the Admiralty, wrote to Clementine:[3] 'My darling One and beautiful. Everything trends towards catastrophe and collapse . . . I am interested, geared up and happy. Is it not horrible to be built like that? . . . I wondered whether those stupid Kings and Emperors cd not assemble together and revivify Kingship by saving the nations from hell, but we all drift on in a kind of dull cataleptic trance. As if it was someone else's operation!' At the end of July, Sylvia left for Ireland to investigate the troubles there.

A month earlier, on 28 June 1914, Archduke Ferdinand, heir to the Austro-Hungarian throne had been assassinated, with his wife, in Sarajevo by a Serbian secret society known as the Black Hand. The Serbs, Slav by race, were allied to Russia and historically friendly with France. Austria's ally was Germany. Britain was still wavering in her loyalties, since the King was inconveniently cousin to Kaiser Wilhelm of Germany, the Russian Tsar and the Austrian Emperor, but was increasingly anxious about German ambitions.

The murder of Archduke Franz Ferdinand had provided the spark to light a fuse but it was barely noticed in a British press more occupied with domestic events in Ireland. Austria had declared war on Serbia in June. Russia was then automatically drawn in. Finally, on 3 August when Germany invaded neutral, 'gallant little' Belgium as part of their designs on France, Britain was left with no option. Such a small country as Belgium had to be protected.

On 3 August in the House of Commons, Keir Hardie, who was already being attacked for his pacifist views, spoke bitterly against the war. He warned of the terrible suffering it would bring to the poor. Caroline Benn describes how while he spoke, he felt 'a cold, cold wind behind his back'. It was the sound of the National Anthem being quietly sung across all parties.

And so it was that on 4 August 1914 Britain declared war on Germany.

---

3. Mary Soames (ed.), *Speaking for Themselves*, Doubleday, 1998.

17

Our Sylvia

'I was writing at home one evening. On the silence arose an ominous grinding . . . growing in volume . . . throbbing, pulsating, filling the air with its sound . . . An air raid! . . .

'Mrs Payne was on my threshold, her face ineffably tender. "Miss Pankhurst come down to us!" Half smiling, she reached out her arms to me. "Let us keep together." . . .

'"No use to worry; only a few houses will be struck among the thousands," I rallied her gently, feeling detached from it all – and far away. The thought of the bombs crashing down on the densely populated city was appalling – yet for our household I had no least shade of apprehension – and for myself Life had no great claim. I was only a member of the salvage corps, saving and succouring as I might amid this wreckage.'

Sylvia Pankhurst on the first Zeppelin raid, 31 May 1915

While Keir Hardie was being attacked and vilified as a traitor and a coward (to the point of needing protection from the public), Emmeline and Christabel were agonizing in Brittany over the future of the WSPU and Sylvia had returned to Bow. There she was to orchestrate her own war against war and to establish her own personal welfare state – to do, in effect, what she felt the government should be doing. At first her focus was on the East End she had grown to love, but as the war progressed, she widened her horizons to promote the restructuring and reform of society as a whole. Under the banner of the ELFS she also continued her tireless campaign for universal franchise.

At the outbreak of war in August 1914 the emaciated, exhausted Emmeline with Ethel Smyth and Christabel spent hours deliberating what course the WSPU should take. It was in France that they had first heard the declaration of war. At home many Suffragettes were quietly hopeful that international events would put a stop to violence and that they would no longer be required to go on the rampage. Christabel herself judged that she could now withdraw from the franchise fight without loss of face, change horses and become, instead, a national figurehead for patriotism.

She made a brief visit to England on 8 September and, dressed in dramatic pale green silk against a backdrop of dark green velvet, spoke at the London Opera House. She made no mention of Votes for Women to the puzzled audience but spoke now as an authority on war. The time fighting for the vote might have been better spent fighting the Germans, she claimed. There was a new, strangely un-Pankhurst religious note to her message. In France she had begun to study the Bible and she told readers of *The Suffragette*, on 7 August, that the war was God's vengeance on those who had held women in subjection.

A little later Christabel and Emmeline announced that they planned to return to England to travel the country, speaking in music halls, cinemas and civic centres. They hoped to whip up patriotic fervour and urge young men to answer the call to arms, 'Your Country Needs You', while handing out white feathers to those who did not. Annie Kenney was sent to tour America to rally support. The WSPU role was, they all agreed, to lead the war effort.

Sylvia wrote impulsively to her mother to protest. The reply was 'I am ashamed to know where you and Adela stand.' Sylvia recorded: 'I thought of my father's peace crusade of the seventies, his unswerving life-long advocacy of Peace and internationalism, in which for nineteen years she had supported him; her stand with us, her children, against the Boer War – all this negated, a vast rift lay between our past and her present intention.'

Meantime, Hardie was moving further and further away from the Labour party and its jingoistic paper, the *Daily Citizen*. He had found a new, unpredictable ally in George Bernard Shaw who, Sylvia felt, was often capricious and a 'great jester', and with whom she was to lock horns on a wide range of issues over the next thirty years.

In July advertisements in the East End newspapers had been inviting holidaymakers to take an August Bank Holiday trip to Boulogne for 11/6d return. Within three weeks of the declaration 120,000 men took that journey. So many of them did not return. Before long, a requisitioned bus proclaiming 'To Berlin and Back – free' was running between the recruiting office next to Poplar Recreation Ground, up the East India Dock Road and on to the Tower of London. There was a groundswell of anti-German feeling that spilled over to anyone with a foreign sounding name. The kennels of animal welfare societies filled with abandoned dachshunds. Five thousand Belgian Jewish refugees were settled in Spitalfields but were not welcome. Anti-German hysteria was inevitable and the crowds of angry people sought vengeance on innocent shopkeepers – even women were beaten up. At first, the bitter social discontent of the pre-war years was forgotten in sentimental jingoism, fuelled by rousing patriotic songs, the poetry of Rupert Brooke 'from some corner of a foreign field'. War was popular. At least it was in August 1914.

Sylvia described how lights were dimmed for the blackout – few East Enders could afford the heavier curtains purchased by richer families and most relied on a single candle or lowered gaslamp. Baroness Williams (Shirley Williams, former 'old' Labour cabinet minister and co-founder of the Liberal Democrats) has written in her preface to the new edition of Sylvia's book (see page 231) *The Home Front*, 'There were two home fronts in First World War Britain, and they were very different – the home front of middle-class England and the other which ran through the dingy terraces of the working class. They shared the suffering of absent and lost loved ones but whereas daily life for the middle classes changed little, for the women struggling in munitions factories and coping with huge families in slum houses with an outside lavatory and no hot water, life was hell.' It was, she says, 'a society of such brutish class division, so callous in the administration of its partial and biased laws, that one is amazed not only that we today share with it the same country, but that we also share with it the same century'.

Sylvia immediately set herself to writing hundreds of letters and articles, leading deputations and protest marches. The words 'hurried', 'rushed' and 'ran' occur on every page of *The Home Front*, as she threw herself, with her usual zest, night and day, into righting all wrongs. In addition to all this she edited and wrote many of the features in the *Woman's Dreadnought*, which was increasing its circulation. 'I rested only when incapable of working. Recreation outside my work never occurred to me.'

Determined to expose government hypocrisies and injustices, she blazed, 'Are you prepared to go on tamely starving, as though you and your children did not matter. The men in power have plunged us into war for their commercial interests. They pass bills in the interests of financiers. What will they do for you?' Hardie, too, continued to attack those making money out of the war: he denounced the Relief Act, which did not help the poor whose poverty was not caused by the war, but he was surrounded on all sides by triumphal militarism.

Sylvia's own passionate convictions lost the ELFS many members, for women were understandably uncertain where their duty lay. By siding with Sylvia were they abandoning their men? Sitting at home with Norah Smyth and Mrs Payne, Sylvia found that even they, her closest friends, were confused and unsure of their own feelings. Norah, who had been a supporter of the war, was anxiously seeking reassurance from Sylvia for her 'dishevelled brain'. As time went on, however, and the tragic letters began to arrive home describing the agony of trench life, membership rose again and new branches were opened in other parts of London.

In those early years, Sylvia managed to win admiration from the most surprising places. The anti-suffrage, anti-socialist *Evening Times* wrote of the work of the ELFS: 'Once again the suffragettes are showing that, whatever may be their faults in other directions, they are organisers of rare genius.' In London, as the initial patriotic zeal faded, reality set in.

For women of means, the war offered undreamed of opportunities. With their men away at the Front, they learned to drive. They formed support organizations to care for soldiers' wives, refugees, and sick children. Women ran libraries and joined the police or the ambulance corps. The Women's Institute was founded in 1915 by Lady Denman, who as a member of the Women's Liberal Association was a non-militant suffragist. The Institute's original purpose was to assist the war effort with food production in rural areas, but later it widened its horizons to provide educational support in citizenship and public affairs for newly enfranchised rural women voters. But of them all, only Sylvia's ELFS still, defiantly, flew the franchise flag.

Conditions had certainly been bad before war was declared, but as prices began to rise, so too did a sense of panic. Families of eight, nine and ten children were left without any means of support at all and threatened with eviction. Sylvia's own account of the escalating distress is harrowing:

How could one face a starving family with nothing to offer save milk for the baby? The wife of an unemployed stevedore fainted on her doorstep . . . there was a woman with six children under thirteen and twins of two months being fed on boiled bread there being no other food in the house . . . the wife of a greaser, who had disappeared when his ship was commandeered, had been four days without food for her six children . . .

Men were taken from their homes at a few hours' notice and set off without knowledge of their destination or when they would return. On the wall near Sylvia's house hung a banner which spoke for them all. 'Please Landlord don't be offended/ Don't come for the rent till the war is ended'

Those first two weeks of August were swallowed up in a maelstrom of unco-ordinated national activity. There was so much going on yet so little was achieved. The War Office had issued notices in which separation allowances were listed: 1/1d daily for the wives of privates, corporals and sergeants plus a 3/6d weekly allowance for London living. The child allowance was 2d a day for boys until the age of 14 and for girls until the age of 16. Often the allowances were late or never materialized. With rent at around 6s a week, sugar 4d a lb and margarine 10d a lb, women all over the country were forced to sell their furniture and even their clothes. There was terrible confusion.

On 28 August the wartime Coalition Government led by Asquith passed the Defence of the Realm Act (D.O.R.A.). This nullified all existing constitutional safeguards for civil liberties; offences included the spreading of 'reports likely to cause disaffection or alarm'. Power was given to the police to search a suspect's house at any time. Needless to say, Sylvia regarded this as an erosion of liberty. She opposed attempts to revive the Contagious Diseases regulation, which made it compulsory for women suspected as prostitutes to be inspected for venereal disease. She also opposed, as being the first step towards conscription, the National Registration Act.

On 17 August, Sylvia, having been appointed to the Poplar Committee, attended its first meeting presided over by the Mayor. She was bursting with ideas for the Committee, whose aim was to help local people. They were simple ideas such as regular rubbish clearance (both to prevent the spread of disease and provide employment), low-cost restaurants, house building on vacant land, and encouraging the unemployed to harvest food in the country. Despite the war, she wanted to use the opportunity to achieve her longstanding ideal: 'to wipe out poverty, to transform the dreary wastes of the slums to a pleasance of happy well-being. I had grown up with the dream of it.'

She was dismayed by the bourgeois, somewhat dilatory character of her Committee colleagues. The membership consisted largely of thickset, middle-aged men leavened by a few women, including Susan Lawrence who eventually became an MP and called Sylvia 'delightfully noisy', Mrs Julia Scurr of the ELFS and Mrs Attlee, newly married to Clement Attlee who became Labour Prime Minister after World War II. They had just settled in comfortably suburban Woodford Green, on the edge of Sylvia's favourite Epping Forest. Sylvia commented, rather amusingly in view of her own background, 'One would have thought her a middle class fish out of water without any affinities here in Poplar; but probably she was shy.'

There was a great deal of discussion, only to result in an adjournment to 24 August with nothing planned. Sylvia was not prepared to wait. She realized that urgent, practical measures must be taken. She managed to attract huge support but some criticism, too, for her sometimes thoughtless lack of gratitude. She was determined that those who had been left behind in the East End to face the hardship should maintain their independence and dignity.

First she set up a milk distribution centre in 400 Old Ford Road. But the babies were often too ill to digest their feed. Since mothers were often frantic with worry, Sylvia also established a clinic there, where doctors were available, without charge, to advise those whose children were poorly. One of the doctors was Barbara Tchaykovsky, who had run the White Cross League for the child victims of the dock strike in May 1912. She had been an active member of the WSPU until Emmeline and Christabel's belligerence so appalled her that she left and joined Sylvia's Federation.

It was quite incredible that by 31 August 1914 Sylvia had opened her first Cost Price restaurant in the Old Ford Road premises. It was a miracle of loaves and fishes proportions, for during 1915 she and her team served about 400 meals a day and gave help to 1000 mothers and babies at the clinic.

From conception to opening, the conversion of the premises took only a few days, thanks to the superhuman efforts of Willie Lansbury, who was now running his father's timber yard. He gave wood for the furniture, made by local men from the Rebels' Social and Political Union. They hired gas stoves and boilers from a nearby company and china and glass was mostly donated by enthusiastic families. Chicken carcasses, allotment produce and bread, all were donated. Money poured in and before long organizations in many other areas copied the scheme.

The opening day was festive. Sylvia, Norah and all the organizers ate there. Sylvia had intended to use the restaurant daily herself, but the cook, Mrs Ennis Richmond, wife of a country clergyman and a self-declared 'food reformist', had a penchant for dried beans. These had a drastic effect on Sylvia's fragile digestion and she clutched a hot water bottle to suppress the pain.

Sylvia was not alone in her culinary concern. She had never been a food connoisseur – in fact, Annie Kenney's memories of the daily fare in Chelsea were hardly flattering. But the women of Bow also thought Mrs Richmond's 'food reform' stance was outrageous. Imagine putting unpeeled potatoes into a soup! Sylvia turned to Keir Hardie – himself no gastronome – to ask his advice, as she had so often done: 'Shall I permit the expert to improve the people against their will?' He answered 'yes', and when Sylvia argued with him he grunted, 'have we fallen so low that we must discuss potato skins?'

'I'll never forget those dinners,' Nellie Cressall recalled. 'They were made of meat pudding, greens and potatoes. They had it with a slice of spotted dog all for 1 penny. It did not pay of course. But I think many a life was saved by the sacrifice and service of the people who carried on all through the war <u>and after</u>.'

That a small organization with so little experience managed such a feat on such a tiny budget was a credit to Sylvia's ability. She had inherited the

Pankhurst talent for inspiring and persuading anyone and everyone to help her in whatever she wanted to do. She swept them along with her enthusiasm. In later years Harry Pollitt, who was to become the Secretary General of the British Communist Party, said of Sylvia: 'she had the remarkable gift of extracting the last ounce of energy as well as the last penny from everyone with whom she came in contact to help with the work and activities she directed from Old Ford Road. She was loved in Poplar and though I have often heard that she was very difficult to get on with, I never found it so.'

Sometimes her schemes were too ambitious and over-stretched even her own organizational capabilities. However, behind her there were capable women like Norah holding the reins and, importantly as it turned out later, keeping the books. Norah also took her camera wherever she went and her remarkable archive of photographs is a unique inside story of life on the home front.

In August, Sylvia wrote to Queen Mary criticizing the conditions in Queen Mary's Workshops. These had been established in Her Majesty's name, to give work to unemployed women but at abysmal rates of pay. She called them 'Queen Mary's sweatshops'. The Toy Factory was Sylvia's answer to the problem. Just off Roman Road she found a house with a small workshop in the garden and there, in October, opened her co-operative, employing fifty-nine people at 5d a hour or £1 a week. No one made a profit. Alongside the toymaking, Sylvia also opened a small nursery with the help of Lady Sybil Smith, daughter of Lord Antrim. Irritated by the social round of Mayfair, she gave up four days a week to care for the East End babies while their mothers were at work in the factory. She presented them with a superb, pristine dolls' house from her own children's nursery.

War or no war, mothers still wanted to give presents to their children. German toys were no longer being imported and there was a gap in the market that Sylvia aimed to fill. One of the women who came to help her was her old friend from the Art College days, Amy K. Browning, and for Sylvia this toymaking reminded her of the creative world she had lost; it was an outlet for her own imaginative skills. If one of the women designed a suitable toy, it was purchased by the factory and a royalty paid on sales.

Perhaps unwisely, Sylvia took pity on a young Polish woman, Regina Hercbergova, who had been sent to her by Keir Hardie. He assured Sylvia that she had experience of management in Switzerland and wanted Sylvia to give her a job. It seems Miss Hercbergova had no idea how to keep the books and so Sylvia's uncle, businessman Herbert Goulden, spent some time instructing her and before long she became factory manager.

She was demonstrative and theatrically affectionate to Sylvia, who found herself in the embarrassing position of spending more and more time finishing off, or even remaking, shoddy toys that had slipped the manageress's notice. Sylvia's standard was high. But Miss Hercbergova blossomed and as she did, she began to demand economies in the running of the venture, increasing her own wages while reducing those of the staff. 'She seemed thirsty as a tigress for her priorities,' said Sylvia. There was, eventually, a hard-earned lesson that 'those who try to pay a decent wage run the risk of finding cheaper commodities sweeping theirs from the market'.

Despite the obvious day-to-day social benefit of the scheme, its commercial base was shaky. Sylvia had difficulty in finding benefactors; the project had less appeal than baby milk and her wealthy friends judged that the factory should have been self-supporting from the outset. Once again, when funds failed it was the ever-generous Norah who saved the day. No one realized just how much she had invested in her friend's dreams until in 1933, after publication of *The Home Front*, Sylvia was sued by Regina Hercbergova for libel. Norah was required to supply evidence and her generosity became clear.

Sylvia had experimented first with carved wooden toys, such as she had seen in Austria on holiday with Emmeline Pethick-Lawrence. They were made, somewhat provocatively, by Herr Niederhofer, a German woodworker from the Lansbury yard. He was an excellent craftsman and no one reacted against him. In fact, Sylvia was delighted with the happy, easy-going creativity and friendship in the workrooms. It was a haven, sheltering them all from the harshness of life outside. Next, with the help of the art students, Sylvia graduated to the manufacture of stuffed dolls. There were white dolls, black dolls and yellow dolls, and all sold well. Lively monkeys, lambs, saucy terriers all began to occupy the shelves and, before long, other factories followed suit, often, Sylvia complained, producing lower quality goods at even lower prices. There was no end to the innovation. After soft, rag baby dolls, Sylvia tried china dolls, but the sample heads that arrived from the potteries were not good enough. Sylvia took a taxi-load of the toys to Gordon Selfridge, who had recently opened the first American-style departmental store, in Oxford Street.

Barbara Winslow in *Sylvia Pankhurst. Sexual Politics and Political Activism* takes a rather cool, realistic look at Sylvia's East End projects. She believes that they were very small scale and did little, if anything, to ameliorate the community's overwhelming problems of poverty and unemployment. Nor did the women who benefited necessarily join the ELFS or become involved with Sylvia's agitation. This may have been true in the grander scale of things, but on the other hand, hearing the story from those who were present, there seems no doubt at all that the East Enders themselves believed Sylvia's presence among them was a great strength and a force for good.

She and Norah spent their first war Christmas in Scarborough, travelling north by train to see the devastation caused by German warships on 16 December. Standing on the breakwater looking out to sea, it was bitterly cold, the wind howled and people waited and watched, terrified the Germans would land. Boats were being blown up, men washed ashore, some drenched and wounded, some horribly mutilated and dead. The town itself was battered and scarred by shells and shrapnel. It was all too much for Sylvia, and Norah agreed they should leave.

On the way back to London Sylvia suggested, on impulse, that they ought to go across to Paris: 'one ought to know what one can'. And amazingly, despite the war, there was no difficulty in making the journey. In Paris wounded soldiers were being cared for in the Hotel Majestic, converted by Henry Harben into an English war hospital. Harben himself greeted the women, 'effervescent with enthusiasm'. But Sylvia and Norah were again too distressed by the misery they saw, although Harben regaled them with heart-warming stories of wonderful medical successes.

Being in Paris, so near to Emmeline, was too painful for Sylvia. Despite their differences and despite the hurt she wanted to see her mother. She found her, sitting by the fire, with Nurse Pine, obsessed with the war, which totally occupied her conversation. Sylvia had already determined not to enter into argument and sat listening, speechless. Norah told Emmeline of their visit to Scarborough, which released a tirade of angry criticism that the British coastline should be defended when every man was needed to fight in Europe. 'She seemed a very Maenad of the War with her flashing eyes . . . We were distant from each other as though a thousand leagues had intervened . . . A sad anti-climax to a life's struggles . . . I was glad to get away exhausted by sorrow.'

On their return to Bow in the New Year, Sylvia organized several parties for children. Actors, musicians and singers entertained around the Christmas tree and the number of donated presents was so great that every child had an armful of toys to take home.

The weather of New Year 1915 was grim. In February, Sylvia with Mrs Harben and George Lansbury formed the League of Rights for Soldiers' and Sailors' Wives and Relatives. They agitated for pensions for widows and dependents and allowances for wives left at home. For several years they held meetings all over the country and, according to George Lansbury, the government formed a new organization, which met most of their demands but was run by politicians 'on the make'. He said: 'Sylvia Pankhurst worked day and night, rushing from town to town, from one Government office to another . . . the War Office must have been considerably worried by her attentions. It is certain, however, that many thousands of women and children owe her, and the rest of the committee, thanks for securing something approaching decent treatment . . .'.

Sylvia had suggested that Lansbury's wife Bessie would become the honorary secretary but was saddened that although she accepted, she was unable to take a very active role: 'she was far too much overwhelmed, depressed by her housework, her excessively large family and the longstanding varicose ulcers . . . Indeed she was one of the women who made women of my sort Suffragettes.'

As starvation faced many of the East Enders, Sylvia discovered that huge quantities of food relief from the Commonwealth were being diverted to the army and to commercial companies rather than being distributed directly to the poor. The Mayor of Poplar was himself quietly cutting down the work of the Poplar Committee and recruitment increased as hunger forced men into the army.

Later, when Sylvia discovered that supplies of bacon and sugar, no longer available in the East End, could be found 'up West' and that wealthy ladies were feeding milk to their dogs, she and Norah organized yet another deputation. They went with thirty ELFS members to Harrods and the Army and Navy Stores to stock up. They then trooped off to the House of Commons to see the Prime Minister. He was understandably anxious as the ladies dumped all their food parcels on his desk. Were they bombs? Sylvia assured him that they weren't, but if he didn't organize food for the starving East Enders, she would return with a 300-strong deputation, and if there was still no joy, with 3000. It worked. Relief began to trickle through to Poplar immediately.

As a fund raising effort for the Toy Factory, Lady Sybil had arranged many drawing room events in the houses of the well-meaning rich. With a deep sense of dread and foreboding, Sylvia agreed to attend one of these occasions in March at the Maidenhead home of Nancy Astor.[1] She and Lady Sybil were met off the train by Mrs Astor in a large motor car. On the journey to the Astor mansion Sylvia listened, in embarrassed silence, as Mrs Astor discoursed volubly on the 'slackers' who were ducking their share of war service. She had just read a marvellous book, she said, which advised her that

1. Nancy Astor (1879–1964) was the American wife of wealthy Waldorf Astor MP. He died in 1919 and Nancy took his seat, to become the first woman Member of Parliament in Great Britain.

to indulge in luxury was 'to increase the poor man's burden'. So she fixed them all with a gimlet eye and shouted defiantly, 'I am going to be austere. I am not going to increase the poor man's burden.' As they overtook a young horseman, Mrs Astor stuck her head through the window and shrieked to him at the top of her voice, 'why aren't you in khaki?'

A roaring fire welcomed them (as did the servants) in the entrance hall, but Mrs Astor was suddenly called away to support her sister who had just received news, by telegram, that a close friend had been killed at the front. Sylvia admitted, somewhat sheepishly, that she was sorry for the reason but glad that it had relieved her of Mrs Astor's company. 'I wished myself a thousand miles away.'

Sylvia and Lady Sybil talked to the saddened company, telling them of the suffering of the East End women and their efforts in the Toy Factory. They talked so much that Lady Sybil even forgot to take tea or any of the delicacies laid out on the table. It was proving an illuminating experience for the two friends. 'Many people enjoy having their hearts touched,' Sylvia wrote afterwards, 'then pass to the next sensation quite unchanged.'

In the evening the men appeared in their starched fronts, Mrs Astor and her sisters in black silk with white ruffles. Over a sumptuous dinner Mrs Astor declared her proposed austerity and then later, to Sylvia's unconcealed disgust, the women filed out, leaving the men to take port by the fire. 'I had forgotten that such foolish customs still obtained.' There was a moment of solitary panic when Sylvia realized that Lady Sybil had vanished and she was alone, sinking into the sofa, with a group of women eager to know what war work she was engaged in. 'Nothing. I answered, with passion. I am not connected with the War.'

There followed a musical evening, church next day (to which Sylvia did not go), a massive lunch and a visit to the hospital for wounded soldiers in the grounds, (but the matron would not admit them). Sylvia escaped early with Lady Sybil, taking with her the hard-earned £15 and a donation from Mrs Astor for their fund.

In April, to bring together the clinic and nursery, Sylvia had found a disused pub, The Gunmakers' Arms, at 438 Old Ford Road. Within a fortnight she converted the premises, renamed them The Mothers' Arms and opened a truly progressive nursery school. Its brochure, tender and compassionate in tone, outlined a new approach to childhood well ahead of its time, which must have been startling to people whose hard lives left little room for more than the most basic needs of their children.

The main bar had become the reception room, where medicines, new laid eggs from the country and invalid foods were to be stored; in the deep drawers

Sylvia planned to keep layettes and maternity clothes sent from all over the world. The old bar parlour was the doctors' surgery. On the first floor the day nursery walls were painted white with blue floors and there were cots for afternoon resting and low level tables and chairs for easy play. On arrival babies were be bathed (most people had no hot water or even bathrooms) in the former taproom and changed into non-uniform, nursery clothes to protect their own precious garments. There were to be walks in nearby Victoria Park in the morning. Upstairs a Montessori school catered for children from two and a half to five years and above this was a flat roof surrounded by high railings, where the children could play or rest in fine weather. Both the City of London Corporation and the Ministries of Health and Education supported this enterprise financially.

During the evening of 31 May 1915, LZ38 – the first Zeppelin[2] to reach England – arrived over Bow. Norah Smyth was on the flat roof of the house in Old Ford Road, defiant until falling shrapnel forced her inside. There were crashes, more crashes and again more crashes; 'the very earth shook,' reported Sylvia. Seven people, including a child, were killed and thirty-five injured.

Next day hundreds of well-dressed tourists arrived, some from abroad, holidaymaking in the summer sun, others in smart cars or taxis from the West End. All were eager to look at the damage and, hopefully, perhaps see a bomb. Passengers on the top of passing buses craned curiously to see the damage.

Towns such as Chatham, Margate, Folkestone and Southend, in south-east England, were all at risk during the war and bombs were dropped as far north as Yorkshire and even Edinburgh. But because so many people lived densely packed in the overcrowded narrow streets near London Docks, they were in continual fear. There was nowhere else in Britain so constantly exposed to the threat of imminent death.

2. Named after its designer, Count Zeppelin, who ran an aircraft works at Friedrichschafen on Lake Constance.

18

Dear Sylphia

'He was our man.'

W.C. Anderson MP, ILP

Sylvia felt deeply the pain of those around her and was always ready to try to ease, personally, the suffering of anyone who needed her. One of those who never forgot 'our Sylvia' was the mother of her first 'War Baby'. Sylvia described the shock of finding herself, with no training, helping in the delivery of a little boy in an upstairs slum. The doctor was young, tough and unsympathetic; the mother, who was lame, was hysterically insisting that she was not pregnant – it was a tumour, she wailed. 'I ain't done nothing.' The doctor swore and shook her until Sylvia, distressed, asked, 'May I sit by her? Perhaps she would be less afraid of me? I obeyed his directions as he gave them, gazing with anxiety which bordered on horror at the birth thus sordidly enacted . . .'.

Eventually, Sylvia was sent off to fetch boiling water and returned to find the baby's head had emerged: 'There was a struggle. It seemed the infant would be strangled . . . I turned away in dread . . . "That was a nasty one . . . got twisted somehow." The doctor spoke cheerily . . . he passed it to me . . . 'wash it well; use plenty of soap' . . . I was consumed by anxiety . . . At last when mother and child were safely tucked down in clean sheets, I could go, my mind in turmoil, terrible and strange . . .'.

But it did not end there. Sylvia returned several times to see the baby and arranged for daily nursing and food from The Mothers' Arms. The father was a soldier named Bodger, but unless the two were married, the mother was not eligible for an allowance. So Sylvia tracked him down, persuaded him to marry the mother, found a ring and a willing vicar and, with Norah Smyth, organized a modest reception. 'It is doubtful whether I have committed a mortal sin in helping to tie those two together permanently. She will get her separation allowance but now they will produce more children,' she said.

The welfare of children and the protection of mothers was to become one of Sylvia's great preoccupations as she grew older. She left an unpublished draft article entitled, 'Versus Law. Is Legal Marriage a Success?' In it she comments: 'It is a startling but true thought that if there were no legal marriage there would be no illegitimate children.' She goes on to demand better treatment of the single parent of either sex and especially of all children, whatever their birth status.

In tandem with her day-to-day concern for the East End, Sylvia was actively involved with the international women's peace movement, which was defiantly organizing conferences between the warring countries. Sylvia found herself in the position of a mother whose duty appeared to be to leave her 'children' in the care of others while she took on the burden of the wider issues. It was not unlike the situation that had faced her own mother, all those years before, when she founded the WSPU.

Sylvia had agreed to attend a major peace congress in The Hague, which Millicent Fawcett condemned as 'akin to treason'. Women from Austria, Holland, Germany, Russia and Belgium were being permitted to attend. Emmeline Pethick-Lawrence was leading a delegation from America, where she and her husband had become involved in a campaign to lobby for a negotiated peace.

Knowing that the British delegation would certainly be refused travel permits, Sylvia drafted a set of resolutions to be sent to the congress. She showed them to Keir Hardie for his observations. Such meetings were becoming rare, 'so burdened was I by the volume and stress of our work'. He was enthusiastic, encouraging Sylvia to propose that the congress form a committee to consider her ideas. Even so, she was miserably anxious about his declining health.

As a result of the gathering at The Hague, a permanent organization was formed, of which the British arm, The Women's International League, first met in autumn 1915, Sylvia being elected to the committee. However, she soon felt that its moderate, conciliatory tone, 'carrying no fiery cross', was not for her and that she would do better to achieve what she could more directly at home.

Despite his frailty, Keir Hardie seemed able to rally for public speaking, although concerned observers noted that he was prone to fall asleep. In Norwich at a demonstration over the iniquitous conditions workers were required to endure in the production of weapons for private armament firms, he remonstrated, 'In time of war one would have thought the rich classes would grovel on their knees before the poor who are doing so much to pile up their wealth. Instead the men who are working eighty four hours a week are being libelled, maligned, insulted . . .'.

In April, Hardie booked into a health spa near Caterham in Surrey. Sylvia saw him briefly; she had been worried about him all year, and one day, in his absence, she even advertised for a woman to care for him. But Hardie would have none of it. He was also in touch with the Pethick-Lawrences who, like Sylvia, were anxious for their old friend and had sent him some books to read. He wrote to Frederick: 'I heartily thank you and Mrs Lawrence for your two readable books which I have just received from you. They have the rare quality of being readable and of appealing to the more emotional side of a man's being. My wife and daughter are here and are receiving a good bit of benefit from their visit, more in proportion than I have got. Kindest regards to you both . . .'. Also that April *The Suffragette* reappeared after a gap of eight months, renamed *Britannia*. Its leading article declared that it was a thousand times more the duty of women to fight the Kaiser for the sake of liberty than it had been to fight anti-suffrage governments in the past.

The truth about events in Europe was being filtered home through a smokescreen of censorship. For instance, during the Battle of the Somme in 1916 the *Daily Mirror* declared exultantly in a five-page article, 'The General Situation is Favourable'. There were reports of 3500 German prisoners being taken and, jubilantly, 'our losses have been very light'. In fact, on the first day of the battle an unbelievable 20,000 British soldiers died. Long lists of the dead began to appear in the local press and, gradually, it became apparent that whole battalions of 'pals' who had volunteered together were being wiped out.

In May, to Hardie's despair, Labour joined the coalition government. As a result he decided to give up Nevill's Court and retire from Parliament. Sylvia was one of the first to know. She received a letter from Caterham dated 27 May 1915:

Dear Sylvia,

I wish I could respond worthily to your letter of the other day. That is out of the question.

I may be at Nevill's Court on Monday for about two hours – 12 noon till 2 o/c And if you could make it to come and see me then, I shall be delighted.

I have given up Nevill's Court and intend to gift and sell a lot of the stuff that is there. You have, I think, two products of your genius there, one hangs over the fireplace, and the other on the left hand side of the room as you go in. The one over the fireplace I have so closely associated with you that I should not like to part with it. And if you can see your way to allow my nominal ownership to continue I shall regard that with pleasure.

I have a great many letters of yours, especially those from America and a good many others. They are well worth preserving and I should like to return them to you. I could let you have the whole of those now at Nevill's Court, and you could use your discretion as to which are worthy of being kept and published and which should be destroyed. But I must leave the matter entirely in your hands. I have not ['now' inserted] the capacity for dealing with such a matter.

There is much in what you say about the War and the state of my health. As Aye. K

The letter was written by Frank Smith but the word 'now' and the very shaky signature were added by Hardie. Sylvia assumed he was moving into a clinic where he could be cared for. But no, he was going home to Cumnock – and Lillie.

When Sylvia arrived with sinking heart at Nevill's Court, Hardie was already there, his voice gruff. She realized that he was sharing with her the end of his working life and his awareness of approaching death. She could not accept it, holding back her tears. He had even forgotten that he had asked to keep the painting she had done for him at Penshurst – it was a picture of a child who Hardie said resembled Sylvia. He tried to persuade her to choose a keepsake from the familiar clutter in his room but Sylvia, unable to grasp the reality of the situation, could not bring herself to take so final a step. 'We were tongue-tied as never before,' she admitted. 'I struggling dumbly, desperately to maintain my slender self-control that I might not distress him, might not add to the suffering obviously consuming him.' Then Frank Smith arrived and there followed an awkward, disjointed exchange. 'Keir, in his agony . . . seemed to loom over us like some great tragic ruin.' When Frank Smith was out of the room, Sylvia seized the opportunity to say goodbye, to feel him near her and to hear his voice for the last time. He simply said: 'you have been very brave'.

On 28 July a postcard arrived from Caterham. It was tragic and in his own hand. 'Dear Sylphia. In about a week I expect to be gone from here with no more mind control than when I came. Love.' He had forgotten how to spell her name. The truth was that Hardie was sinking; he was developing strange moods and paranoia about those around him as well as a fearful temper – added to which he was determined to sleep with Lillie, who would have none of it. The family had a terrible time.

Cruelly, Emmeline's paper *Britannia* chose this moment to publish a cartoon of Hardie reproduced from *Punch*. It showed the Kaiser presenting him with a bag of money above the caption 'Also, the Nobel prize though tardy, I now confer on Keir von Hardie.' Greatly upset, Sylvia wrote to her mother saying she had seen it and hoping she would print no more such things, as Hardie was dying. Emmeline did not reply.

In London, Hardie was still in Sylvia's mind and heart. She had a dream of him playing with a puppy and decided to go down to Bethnal Green market and find a suitable old English sheep dog, 'the most human of dogs', to send him as a pet. Instead she fell in love with a fat little black retriever that snuggled up to her on her knee as she took it home on the bus. Sadly, Frank Smith had to tell her that Hardie was much too ill to care for it and besides, the family had been forced to send their own dog away because Hardie had taken a dislike to it. It would be better to wait for a while. That news was, for Sylvia, like the bell tolling for Hardie, who had always adored animals. She kept the puppy and called him Donald after Hardie's favourite pit pony, but all the women in the restaurant and the ELFS office called him Jimmie – Hardie's pet name as a child.

Conscription was now being threatened and on Sunday, 26 September, Sylvia took part in a joint demonstration by socialists, some suffragists and trades unionists in Trafalgar Square. Emmeline Pethick-Lawrence was there, as were Charlotte Despard and Henry Hyndman. Sylvia had already spoken when she noticed newsboys moving among the huge crowds. At first she could not see what their placards were saying and then suddenly came the news she had been dreading so long.

'Keir Hardie dead.'

Right: George Lansbury, farm colony pioneer and Labour leader from 1930, on his allotment.

Below: Sylvia in the fur coat she bought for her American tour, with Norah Smyth and the adoring Zelie Emerson, 1912.

'Our Sylvia' addressing East-Enders after painting her Bow Road shop front 'in letters of gold',
1912.

Mrs Pankhurst leaving on a speaking tour,
1910.

Christabel in Paris in 1913 reading *The
Suffragette*, which she edited from exile.

The Cost Price Restaurant, Old Ford Row, Bow.

Hard work at the Toy Factory.

Sylvia and Willie Gallagher (in bow tie) at a meeting in Moscow during the Second Congress of the Third International, 1920.

One of Sylvia's political posters, 'Aren't They Worth Defending?', 1918.

Red Cottage, Sylvia and Silvio's first home in Woodford.

The fourth pillar. Motherhood. Sylvia with baby Richard 1928.

Above: 1934. *l to r*: Corio, Judge Petrescu, Sylvia, Mrs Petrescu. In front of Arcadiu and Richard.

Right: A note written by Richard on the back of the Romanian holiday snap.

Dear Dudu,
This is the picture of you and me.
From Richard Keir Pethick Pankhurst.
Best Wishes To Dudu Petrescu

POSTER PARADE AT THE HOUSE OF COMMONS, WESTMINSTER:
Left to Right: Mrs. M. A. Cotton, Sylvia Pankhurst, Mrs. Tedros, Mme. Anderson, and Mrs. Kerrie.

Top: Campaigning for Ethiopian indepen-dence, 1946.

Above: Sylvia with Emperor Haile Selassie snapped on a box brownie camera by Richard, in the grounds of the Emperor's Bath home, c.1937.

Right: The 'poisonous rag'. Sylvia's newspaper, the *New Times and Ethiopia News*, 1938.

Top: Sylvia, handbag bulging as ever, with the Emperor, in Ethiopia.

Above: The Pankhurst family. *Back row l to r:* Konjit Seyoum, Alula Pankhurst with Helena Alula Pankhurst, David Loakes. *Front row l to r:* Alex Loakes, Rita Pankhurst, Henoq Alula Pankhurst, Dr Richard Pankhurst, Laura Pankhurst.

– 19 –

Revolutionary

'What a loss is ours. I don't think anyone, among the many thousands who mourn for him, knew, understood or loved him better than you and I.'

Frank Smith to Sylvia, 26 September 1915

Inevitably, the death of Keir Hardie was to take Sylvia to yet another crossroads in her life. She was still only 33. Surrounded once again and comforted at this time by some of her old pacifist friends – the Pethick-Lawrences, George Lansbury and Fenner Brockway – she was, as the war continued, to turn her face eastwards.

But sitting, head between her knees, at the foot of Nelson's Column as the newspaper boys yelled the headlines on that September day, she was dazed, disbelieving and lost. She was now, in one sense, herself a 'war widow', for it was undoubtedly the war that had finally claimed her love. Her mind and emotions in turmoil, she went home to try and write a eulogy for the *Woman's Dreadnought*.

Sylvia's 2500-word obituary for Hardie tells us as much about the woman as about the man. Her notes remain, in pencil as usual, shaky, incoherent and uncontrolled, with sometimes only a few words or one line on a page, ripped out and put aside:

Keir Hardie has been the greatest human being of our time . . .

Fate fitly named this man, who was braver and more steadfast than the general human kind; Keir (Rock) was his mother's name, Hardie, his father's. He was a child of nature, akin to the Scotch moors. His father was a fisherman, and he too had the weather-fashioned look of those who follow the calling of the sea. He was built for great strength, his head more grandly carved than any other; his deep-set eyes like sunshine distilled, as we see it through the waters of a pool in the brown earth . . .

As the years passed, the great brow was seamed with thought and the intense griefs of one who feels sorrow more deeply than others may, but keeps the hurts fast locked within. But he had always the heart of the child near to God, and the child's eager fresh outlook on things beautiful and new . . .

Idle gossip discussed his dress. What should one say of it, but that it was part of him? His clothes became him well, because they did not hide the man within . . .

One wondered always at the wealth of things he knew. He seemed ever ready to unravel any mechanical or chemical problem, or to explain and give the history of any theory of religion, philosophy, or politics, but on the rare occasion when he had not grasped the gist of a matter he always said so definitely. He was often silent and would sit listening to others, but he had the talker's gift and expressed himself clearly and vividly . . .

But all these gifts were but as the carpeting grass and flowers on the great mountain side of his life's work . . .

The first joyous revelation of his life was religious. He wished that all might live according to the Sermon on the Mount. When he first heard of Socialism he shrank from it as material, but as he grasped the fullness of its ideal he realised that it could make Christ's teaching practical . . . eventually he came to look upon State Socialism as the necessary prelude to a free Communism . . .

The first Labour Member of Parliament, he was for years absolutely alone . . .

It is possible that he was never so lonely and disheartened in those years of preparation, as sometimes after what seemed to the outward world an extraordinarily sudden measure of success had crowned his efforts in 1895–6 . . . Then, at last, he must have learnt that he was no ordinary Labour Member, as those others were, but the herald of a coming age. The knowledge must have pained him, for he did not want to be the leader of inferiors, but the comrade of men as true and steadfast as himself . . .

One of the outstanding features of his years of absolute isolation as the sole Labour Member was his fight for the unemployed . . . Walter Crane drew him carrying the unemployed workman on his back into the Houses of Parliament . . .

Had Keir Hardie lived in a communistic world, he would have been a great writer, painter or musician . . .

No body of people . . . ever appealed to him in vain . . . The people of India adored him . . . At home . . . none had more reason to be grateful to him than the little band of women who broke out of the ILP to fight for their enfranchisement . . .

He made the Labour movement a coherent political force . . .

No Member of Parliament was so persistent as he in sifting cases of hardship . . . He was revered by the labour movement of every country . . .

He was ever keenly conscious of other people's sorrows. A mining or railway disaster was to him always a sharp personal grief. The War came to his sensitive soul as a hideous nightmare of horror . . . He had hoped that the strength of the growing socialist movement would make this War impossible. Undoubtedly his grief hastened the ending of his life . . .

George Bernard Shaw had also been asked to contribute an article, which he did, although he said that Sylvia's effort was far better than his. He wrote, somewhat more concisely, with typical irony:

I really do not see what Hardie could do but die. Could we expect him to hang on and sit there among the poor slaves who imagined themselves Socialists until the touchstone of war found them out and exposed them for what they are? That the workers themselves – the Labour party he had so painfully dragged into existence – should snatch still more eagerly at the war to surrender those liberties and escape back into servility, crying 'you may trust your masters: they will treat you well' . . . This was what broke the will to live in Keir Hardie.

His bitterness was almost more than Sylvia could bear.

It was Katherine Glasier who revealed to her the secret of Keir Hardie's illegitimacy. The first chapter of his unfinished autobiography had been found at Cumnock and in this he referred to his birth being branded by a 'bar sinister'. His 'beautiful silence' moved Sylvia to write in her own book, 'Waves of thought were rending me, grief for the sadness of life, amaze at its poignant drama. Novels, romances, what is the need of them? Not one is so strange, so poignant as the true romance of life.'

What happened to the puppy Sylvia had bought for Hardie? She had not the heart to send him away and so she and Norah gave him a home. That Christmas, the second of the war, Sylvia and Norah took Jim to Merthyr to 'renew . . . the communion of memory' with Hardie. They enjoyed long mountain walks, meeting old friends and listening to children singing the words Hardie had written for the Welsh anthem. Shutting her eyes, she recalled his visit to Merthyr one Easter when a scurry of children rushed to meet him and he was 'brought to a standstill by the clasp of a toddler's arms about his leg'.

Sylvia never forgot the children. When she and Norah returned to Bow, she was determined to inject some light on the East End scene and give them a traditional party, something happy that they would be able to remember of their overshadowed young lives. Nine hundred children came to be given presents by Father Christmas (Norah Smyth), and George Lansbury and a friend presented a puppet show. GBS was invited to judge an essay competition for the child who best described the party. He did so in his usual style:

> Miss Molly Beer . . .
> *In account with* G. Bernard Shaw
> Correcting two mistakes in grammar 1d
> Striking out two apostrophes put before 's' when there was nothing belonging ½d
> Completing the word 'affectionately' as it was written 'affec' 1d
> Counting 22 kisses for Miss Pankhurst 1½d.
> I award Miss Beer a special prize of 3d. for laziness. She was in such a hurry to get into bed that she wrote the shortest essay . . . so she has only 1d to pay.

In the spring a pageant was planned in co-operation with the local residents. The children were garlanded with primroses and flowers, dressed as 'The Spirit of the Spring', 'The Spirit of the Woods' and 'The Spirit of Peace'. Three-year-olds wore the red caps of liberty, 16-year-old Rose Pengelly played the pan pipes and danced, 'delicious, little creature'. She should have performed again the following Saturday, but at work in the factory her hand was crushed by machinery, she fainted and then, according to Sylvia, because her employer would not pay for a cab, she walked to the station and took a train to the London Hospital where she had her thumb and two fingers amputated.

So what next? There was much to be done. In March 1916 Sylvia decided that the time had come to change the name of her organization and so the ELFS became the Workers' Suffrage Federation (WSF). The government had announced a full commitment to adult suffrage after the war and the new name, in Sylvia's mind, marked a change of emphasis from a reforming to a revolutionary movement. The change was democratically agreed and minuted (as were all the ELFS decisions), and over the following year the WSF began to attract new members of a more political character, although it lost some of its original supporters on the way.

At a conference of Suffragettes in Caxton Hall in 1916, Sylvia once again ran against the tide. Most were in favour of accepting limited suffrage for women on a property-based qualification. Sylvia spoke forcefully, as she had always done, in favour of universal suffrage for men and women. This would give the vote, at last, to the soldiers who had fought so courageously and been disenfranchised because they had lost their residential qualifications. The meeting voted against Sylvia, apart from Emmeline Pethick-Lawrence, whose Women's International League was still in step with her friend. Pragmatic and sensitive as she could be when dealing with the troubles of individual people, Sylvia could become intransigent and unyielding when she sensed she was under fire on issues that were her life's blood.

Angrily, she hit out at 'comfortable middle-class women', who she felt were self-serving. But this was her perpetual dilemma. These were the very people who had been financially supporting her East End social work. Maud Arncliff Sennett complained bitterly: 'I thought it a poor return to make for those kind-hearted comfortable middle class women whose money was going to support her organisation and officers in the East End, to say nothing of those splendid gifts I have seen on her platform at the Christmas proceedings.' Norah Smyth, in charge of the WSF purse strings, was worried that Sylvia's outspoken behaviour would lose them much needed income. Indeed it did.

Towards the end of the year the finances of the WSF were in increasing trouble. The Toy Factory in particular continued to lose money. Mrs Hercbergova seems to have been working autonomously and had, by this time, transformed the factory from Sylvia's ideal of a co-operative into a profit-making enterprise. She refused increased wages for the workers, although she gave regular pay rises to herself. She turned the factory into the kind of sweatshop that was anathema to Sylvia. Norah Smyth noted in her diary that by 1920 to keep the factory going she had sold her shares, her oak table for £6.10s and 'the rest of my jewellery for £9.10s.0d, then took it, with a cheque I cashed to Mrs H. Felt quite worn out!'

When Sylvia, years later, published the whole sorry story in *The Home Front*, Mrs Hercbergova sued her for libel, by which time Norah was living in Italy. Sylvia, of course, being Sylvia, had few financial records and wrote to her old friend for help. The resulting diary excerpts and correspondence, which Norah had filed, give a very personal, vivid account of the stormy life in the toy factory, of Mrs Hercbergova's truculent tantrums and the chaos: 'the girls used to sing and play and there was no discipline at all'.

A member of the factory staff recorded that 'Miss Smyth used to go in the mornings, very often at 9 o'clock and give hints as to how the toys should be shaped ... Mrs Hercbergova always lived in very good style ... Miss Hercbergova never came in before 10 o'clock but was often not seen till lunch or later.' It seems that eventually, in 1921, when Sylvia was in prison for sedition, Mrs Hercbergova took over and threw her off the committee – a fact not mentioned in Sylvia's own writings.

Disaster followed disaster in the war. The sinking of the *Lusitania*, the retreat
from Gallipoli, Jutland, the Battle of the Somme and on and on. At home, in
Bow, the office was daily visited by the disabled and their families begging the
WSF to help them. Letters from the men overseas were pouring in, too.
Mothers, girlfriends and wives brought them to share with Sylvia. There were
heartwarming letters and tragic letters, each one used as ammunition against
the authorities by Sylvia and her team to try and bring about improvements.

The Home Front is heavily illustrated with examples of individual stories,
hardship and heroism, which Sylvia clearly guarded and treasured, for it was
not until fourteen years after the Armistice that she finally wrote it all down.
These were stories which, being sometimes almost too tragic to bear, were
instrumental in motivating her to continue grappling with the wider issues. For
instance, she tells of the day she was asked to visit the bereaved parents of a
Jewish boy, their only son Aby, who had enlisted at the age of 18 without their
consent. They were prostrate and incoherent in their grief, but their daughter
produced a pile of tattered letters for Sylvia to read. They were affectionate
letters, so apologetic for the agony he had caused his mother and father,
describing, in an almost detached, matter-of-fact-way, that his pay was 4/2d for
two weeks, which he spent on bread, and asking them for a photograph of his
mother and to pray for him.

Then came the official notice dated 15 January 1916 that Aby was in
hospital, suffering from wounds and shock, having been involved in a mine
explosion. They also received a reassuring letter from Aby, clearly concealing
the truth. 'Dear mother . . . We get plenty of food in the hospital . . . I know
it will break your heart this, but don't get upset about it. I will be all right, but
I would very much like to see you.'

He left hospital on 19 January. He wrote many such letters, uncomplaining
and begging them not to worry. He wrote 'I am sending this photo of one of
the officers who was killed . . . He was very good to us . . . Please frame it for
a keepsake . . .'. On 23 February Aby wrote again to his mother:

> Dear Mother . . . we were in the trenches and I was ill, so I went out and they
> took me to prison and I am in a bit of trouble now, and won't get any money
> for a long time. I will have to go in front of a Court. I will try my best to get out
> of it, so don't worry. But, dear Mother, try to send some money, not very
> much, but try your best. I will let you know in my next how I get on . . .

There was no 'next'. Dated 8 April 1916 the following official document
arrived at Aby's home:

Sir,

I am directed to inform you that a report has been received from the War Office to the effect that No . . . 11th Battn. Middlesex Regiment, G.S., was sentenced after trial by court martial to suffer death by being shot for desertion, and the sentence was duly executed on 20 March 1916.

There were many such horrific stories.

Sylvia dared to publish these letters in the *Dreadnought* and began courageously to gather more information about other executions on the front. It appeared that there were many. There were also first-hand accounts of terrible brutality among the men – punishment, crucifixions and torture. At home the conscientious objectors fared little better, fed on bread and water, kicked, beaten and kept in dark punishment cells. The official figures were that the total number of death sentences from August 1914 to December 1919 was 3076, of which only 343 were carried out.

The *Dreadnought* was increasing in stature and circulation but it was also under police and Home Office surveillance. It was, arguably, one of the most important anti-war, non-sectarian socialist papers in Britain. Even the forthright Shaw became a subscriber. Sylvia was as brave in print as in speech, and many of the articles she featured could have been accounted treasonable. The offices of the newspaper were raided after Sylvia wrote a column urging the armed forces to refuse to fight, but on this occasion no action was taken. However, in October and November 1917 two issues were suppressed.

Political historian Mary Davis says, 'there were two distinguishing features of the paper which make it stand out from the rest[1] – features which were and remained the abiding hallmark of Sylvia's politics throughout her adult life. One, of course, was the long-standing commitment to women's rights, which had been the starting point of her activism in the East End. The other was much more unusual for the time – an understanding of imperialism and its association with the poisonous ideology of racism. To these two must be added something more intangible, but no less important – the freshness and readability of the paper. It was well designed and laid out with effective use of illustrations, cartoons and pictures.'

A graphic illustration of Sylvia's journalistic courage came with the Irish Easter rising against the British Government in 1916. Padraic Pearse and James Connolly were executed for treason alongside the thirteen other rebel leaders who signed the proclamation of a Republic on Easter Monday. Three

---

1. There were many socialist papers and broadsheets at the time.

thousand people were interned but soon released. Eleven civilians were killed by British forces

This abortive rebellion was covered for the *Dreadnought* in an enterprising coup, by an 18-year-old journalist and WSF member, Patricia Lynch. She bravely smuggled herself into Dublin as the sister of an equally brave, sympathetic army officer and was the first to write about events there, defying the news blackout and somehow avoiding arrest. She wrote:

> In O'Connell street and along Eden Quay the dust was still thick upon the ground, the air was heavy with burning and dense clouds of smoke obscured the ruins . . . Could the Germans do worse to us? . . . they tell us to pity the Belgians . . . it's us that needs pitying, I'm thinking.' The affair at the Post office aroused great horror. 'To turn machine guns on them and they running away.'
>
> One woman spoke to me. She was elderly, dressed in black, her eyes red with weeping and she stumbled against me. Her only son, a Sinn Feiner, had been killed in the fighting . . . 'As much ammunition was being used for one sniper as would wipe out a German regiment' she said, adding bitterly 'But then the English don't hate the Germans the way they hate us.'

Risking a charge of incitement, Sylvia published her report on 13 May 1916. That edition sold out and established Sylvia's own reputation as an enterprising and far-sighted editor. She recalled her feelings many years later in *The Home Front*:

> To me the death of James Connolly was more grievous than any because his rebellion struck deeper than mere nationalism. It is a truism that countries held under an alien dominance remain politically stagnant and, to a large extent are culturally repressed. Recognition of this made me a supporter of Irish nationalism. Yet after national self-government had been attained, the social problems with which we in England were wrestling, would still be present in Ireland . . . Some of the Irish deceived themselves with dreams . . . Were English rule but removed – they asserted – happy fraternity without social strife would readily establish itself. I was under no such illusions. I saw Ireland as she was; backward, politically, industrially, culturally. Connolly was of another order than these dreamers . . . He had buttressed experience by economic study. Though he had thrown in his lot with the Sinn Fein patriots, he remained an internationalist. By far the ablest personality in the Irish Labour movement . . . I knew that the Easter Monday rebellion was the first blow in an intensified struggle which would end in Irish self-government, a necessary

step in Irish evolution . . . Yet Connolly was needed so seriously for the after-building; him, at least, it seemed Fate should have spared.[2]

During 1917 the WSPU ceased to exist and in its place Christabel launched the jingoistic 'Women's Party', dedicated to the subordination of all issues to that of the war effort.

But Sylvia never gave up the franchise fight. Gradually her disenchantment with the British system of party politics was shaping her long-term view. The role women were playing in the war made it impossible now for them to be denied the vote when it was all over. They had won their spurs. After the years of anguish and struggle came the realization that the end was in sight, and the government began drawing up a Franchise Bill.

But Sylvia was not at all jubilant. She wrote to the *Call* (the British Socialist Party newspaper) explaining clearly why socialists could not support the proposed bill:

1 A woman is not to vote until 30 years of age, though the adult age is 21.
2 A woman is on a property basis when enfranchised
3 A woman loses both her Parliamentary and local government vote if she or her husband accept Poor Law Relief; her husband retaining his Parliamentary and losing his local government vote if he accepts Poor Law relief.
4 A woman loses her local government vote if she ceases to live with her husband, i.e. if he deserts her she loses her vote but he retains his.
5 Conscientious Objectors to military service are to be disenfranchised.

It was clear that Sylvia's attention was now turning ever more towards Russia. There the people were increasingly restless about the appalling losses their country was suffering, and desperate for peace. Two million people had died in 1915 alone and starvation now loomed. In February 1917 it was the angry women workers in St Petersburg (Petrograd) who finally took to the streets, followed immediately by the entire population of the city, and despite an initial attempt by the army to stop the rebellion, the soldiers too defied the Tsar and laid down their arms.

On March 16 the Tsar had signed the form of abdication, which ended, 'May the Lord God help Russia.' A provisional government was established, consisting of bankers, bureaucrats and professionals, led by Alexander

2. *The Home Front*, ch.XL.

Kerensky, who did nothing to extricate Russia from the war, although there was still considerable fear in London that this would happen. Emmeline Pankhurst, backed by the government, immediately decided to go on a fact-finding visit to Moscow, where she met Kerensky and urged him not to give up the fight.

After a turbulent summer, the final act in the Russian Revolution came on 7 November 1917, when the Bolsheviks overthrew the provisional government and the Communist Party, led by Lenin, seized power. Lenin soon opened his negotiations with the Germans and spoke of his hope for a 'democratic peace', but the British government was 'disgusted' by what it saw as the Russian betrayal. It was feared that with Russia out of the way, many more German soldiers would become available to fight in France. British workers were equally war-weary and there was a real possibility that the revolutionary fire might sweep Europe.

Sylvia, however, saw it all as a sign of hope for the future. The Russian Revolution released her once and for all from the family fight, for which she had been willing to die. The vote – for men and for women – became a meaningless issue, as she turned against the entire concept of parliamentary government. From being a suffragist and a feminist she was now a revolutionary, ready to unite the workers of the world – and as such she was a marked woman.

Sylvia changed the name of her organization again, this time to The Workers' Socialist Federation, with the motto 'For International Socialism' and the avowed intention of overthrowing capitalism. The *Workers' Dreadnought*, as her paper was now called, carried articles by many leading communists, writers and thinkers, including the work of Karl Marx and some translations of speeches by Lenin.

One of its new contributors was an Italian anarchist socialist. His name was Silvio Corio and he was to stand beside her, professionally and personally, for more than thirty years.

20

Silvio and Sylvia

'Comrade Sylvia Pankhurst represents the interests of hundreds upon hundreds of millions of people that are oppressed by the British and other capitalists. That is why she is subjected to a White terror . . . has been deprived of liberty etc.'

Lenin, 1920

Silvio Corio's entrance into Sylvia's life was surprisingly low-key; he slips in through the office door and is first seen writing an article for the *Dreadnought* in 1918.

Due to events in Russia, Sylvia was now being swept along on a new tidal wave of idealism. Like many communists, she saw the 1917 revolution as a door opening the way for freedom from capitalism for many European countries, including Italy. Presumably it was this that initially drew them together.

Sylvia's partnership with Corio was to provide her with emotional security. Outwardly, at least, it had none of the passion of her youthful love affair with Hardie. Her friends were puzzled: they sometimes found Corio difficult and volatile. Nellie Cressall even thought he was 'repulsive'. On the other hand, Mrs Ashman, whose husband worked as a handyman for Sylvia when eventually she moved from Bow to Woodford, remembered him as 'very much a gentleman', and over the years most visitors to their home were impressed by his unassuming kindliness.

Buried amongst the Pankhurst archives there is yet another tantalizing letter. This time it is from Silvio. It is twelve pages long, undated as usual, but probably written in the early 1920s, hinting at more passionate feelings for Sylvia, feelings reminiscent of the Keir Hardie days of walks in Richmond Park. The greater part of the letter is a witty apology to Sylvia after they had quarrelled over the management of the *Workers' Dreadnought* and in particular her dislike of his use of a pseudonym. It begins:

Apologia Pro 'S' being a Fragmentary Essay on Politics: Technicalities; Editorial rights and despotism; the alphabet, its value and importance; names and anonimity; to which is appended a moral: a contrition: a disclaimer: and, in addition to: a few grammatical and ungrammatical errors together with: some useful and candid remarks on various happenings of daily life: by 'An illustrious author'.

He speaks, tongue in cheek, of their argument and plays with the similarity of their names. 'Have mercy on me!' he pleads, 'display not upon my weak intellect the flexious [sic] lines of thy body . . .'. Then on page 12 he addresses himself to Sylvia personally:

Dearest, Now two lines to you. To have rung up the Lab Ex [sic] for me is one of those small acts of great kindness and generosity that you alone are capable of doing and I am obliged to you . . .

It seems it is a long time since I have seen you . . .

Yes I am afraid we shall have to wait for the spring before we go once more to Richmond Park. Richmond Park, now that I know you seems to me Paradise itself. How strange that but few hours should cut so deep in one's mind. Tonight, every night I am sad. I miss you. You do not know how much. As ever S.[1]

Whatever it was that drew them together, it worked for over thirty years.

Sylvia had been so happy in Italy in her artistic heyday as a student, drawing and painting in Venice and then later on holiday with Emmeline Pethick-Lawrence. It seems reasonable to assume that alongside their shared political convictions, Corio may also have revived for her the lingering memory of those long-lost delights.

Silvio Corio was born in Turin in 1877, the son of Luigi and Chiara Domenica. In his youth his fight for trades unionism in a very illiberal Italy led to exile in Paris. There he trained as a printer and then became a journalist until the Italian government demanded his expulsion from France. In 1900 he came to England, paying his way as a waiter, a printer and as correspondent for *Avanti*, the Italian socialist newspaper. According to Sylvia, he also befriended and advised Italian refugees and anarchists, such as Enrico Malatesta who had been a visitor to the Pankhurst house in the Russell Square days.

1. Pankhurst Papers.

Corio was a skilled typographer, intellectually lively, an excellent writer and researcher and moreover was free to travel round Europe gathering news – talents Sylvia recognized and decided to draw into her team. He ran a small printing company, the Agenda Press, at 19 Wine Court, off Fleet Street. There, amongst other more heavy-weight periodicals, he published the seemingly out-of-character *Soho Gazette*, which covered fashion, gossip and exhortations to revive the spirit of Soho until, like Sylvia's *Workers' Dreadnought*, it finally ceased publication in 1924.

Norah Smyth, in particular, was irritated by the intrusion of this male newcomer into their tight-knit female group, especially when he took over the running of the *Dreadnought* office and eventually whisked away her friend to the rural delights of Woodford Green.

Stocky and prematurely bald, Corio was of no particular concern to the authorities by the time Sylvia met him. He had three children: one, a son by an unknown mistress, and two by Italian socialist Clelia Alignani – a son, Percy, and Beatrice Roxanne (known as Rocky). The relationship with Clelia had been stormy and erratic, but by the time Corio and Sylvia met, he seemed ready to settle and provide the strength and support she needed, allowing her the freedom to become ever more active. He admitted he had been bored with Clelia. With Sylvia boredom was not an option. Percy and Rocky did not see a great deal of their father but were close to their mother. However, the family had always kept in touch and later, after their mother died, Sylvia encouraged more contact. There were regular visits and often shared Christmases.

On 7 December 1917 the Representation of the People Bill was finally passed, giving limited franchise to women over 30 who were occupiers or wives of occupiers of land or premises worth not less than £5 annually and to women over 30 who held university degrees. It gave the vote to six times as many women as had been proposed in the various pre-war Conciliation Bills. The breach had been made. In truth, for Sylvia the event for which she had fought and suffered so much was a damp squib. She wrote:

> . . . the pageantry and rejoicing, which in pre-war days would have greeted the victory, were absent when it came . . . the Suffrage movement . . . was a more intelligent and informed movement than that which, gallant as it was, had fought the desperate pre-war fight . . . Awed and humbled by the great catastrophe, and by the huge economic problems it had thrown into naked prominence, the women of the Suffrage movement had learnt that social regeneration is a long and mighty work. The profound divergences of opinion on war and peace had been shown to know no sex.

Meanwhile, Sylvia was again in touch with Adela, who was pursuing much the same left-wing path in Australia that had provoked her mother to complain that she was 'ashamed' of her daughter. She was, Sylvia heard, now the most popular woman in Australia, where the Pankhurst name was nationally celebrated. She was also in the throes of a courtship with Tom Walsh, an exciting, radical rough diamond, fourteen years her senior (she was 32). He was Irish and a devotee of Richard Marsden Pankhurst, whom he had heard speak in favour of Irish Home Rule many years before. They married in 1917, Adela embracing enthusiastically the responsibility of caring for Tom's three young daughters, to be followed by a son and three daughters of her own. Only Sylvia sent good wishes. Tom and Adela planned to merge their political and domestic duties and from then on Adela was to be as uproariously unconventional and energetically controversial as Sylvia – she was in prison six days after the wedding. In a letter to Sylvia on 23 November 1917, she wrote:

Dearest Sylvia,

You will know by this of the great change that has come in my life.

As a matter of fact it has been coming for some time but I wanted to have time to consider. It was a struggle to give up a position in which I could give the whole of my life to the movement but there is only one thing to do, I find, under the circumstances.

You know I would not do this unless I really cared – and I earnestly do. My husband has three little girls who have been motherless for five years and away at school. I knew them before I loved their Father and had grown to be very fond of them.

Hannah, the eldest is nearly 15 and Bessie is 12 and Sallie nearly eleven. They are fine, pretty girls and I am devoted to them. My husband is starting a business with metal which ought to make us fairly well-to-do and I shall go on with my work until I have children of my own, if that ever happens. I hope you will write to me, dearest Sylvia, and that you will come here some day and see me and my husband and children. I am very happy though anxious about the four month gaol which still lie before me unless I am more lucky than I dare hope.

Sylvia was now in touch with, and respected by, many of Europe's leading radicals and revolutionaries. She was involved with a phenomenal number of emerging groups and organizations of political activists. She was British correspondent for the *Communist International* and contributed to the Italian *Avanti* newspaper, whose editor in 1914 had been a scruffy young Italian named Benito Mussolini. In September 1918 she founded the People's Russia Information Bureau (PRIB) with offices above the *Dreadnought* offices in Fleet Street. The following year she co-founded the Hands off Russia Campaign, to protest against British armed support of the anti-Bolsheviks.

During the summer of 1918 the war moved inexorably towards its end and the German command finally agreed to an armistice. By this time 900,000 British troops had died. The Treaty was signed in the Hall of Mirrors at Versailles. Its terms and the way in which the map of Europe was re-drawn could be seen, in hindsight, to pave the way for World War II.

Peace found Sylvia riding high. It is extremely difficult to unravel the events of her life over the next few years in a way that provides a chronological thread. Her Communist crusade, her anti-colonialism, anti-racism and anti-Fascist views took her into a justifiably prominent position on the international stage. She was here, there and everywhere, sometimes, it would appear, all at the same time.

Judging by the pages of the *Dreadnought*, the changes in Sylvia's views reflect a natural progression over the next few years and are not at all the undisciplined changes of course of which she has sometimes been accused. She was always pragmatic. She had come to believe that the roots of the persecution of women lay deep within the capitalist parliamentary system, which exploited all workers, both men and women. It was, therefore, the overthrow of capitalism (and colonialism) that would finally win for women everywhere not only the vote, but also equality.

Sylvia was now unstinting in her efforts for reform at home. She formed an Adult Suffrage Joint Committee to which more than seventy London Labour organizations became affiliated. The aims of the committee were encapsulated in a new slogan, 'Human Suffrage', and included widespread improvements in social welfare and universal adult franchise. With Sylvia at the helm, they lobbied Parliament and in particular Lloyd George persistently.

At the General Election in December 1918 Christabel stood as a candidate for the Women's Party she had founded the previous year – and lost. Like Sylvia, she had worked tirelessly, forging links with captains of industry and promoting an ideology that was taking her further and further to the right. The defeat, which meant the end of her hopes of being the first woman MP, totally demoralized her; she seemed to lose her way and set out on the spiritual journey that she was to follow for the rest of her life: as an evangelical Seventh Day Adventist. For Emmeline, too, the defeat was hard to bear. Yet although the Pankhurst name provided them with ample opportunity to play a major role in public life, both she and Christabel gradually faded into the shadows.

Sylvia alone battled on. She had also been invited by the socialists to stand in the election as a Labour candidate but had refused. She could hardly be elected to an institution that she was now declaring 'doomed'.

In May 1919 Adela had a son, named Richard, and wrote to Sylvia again with happy family news:

> The little girls are writing to you and I hope you won't mind them calling you Auntie. They have no Aunts who are friendly with us and they are so interested in you and what I tell them about your work They are very good children and I think I have made them happy. They adore the little boy but, you see, I have to be careful they do not feel he has more love than they and as you are aunt to him please accept the position to them too . . . I wonder how Mother is? Do try to send me papers – I should love to have any back Dreadnoughts you can give me . . .

By this time the young Harry Pollitt, who would eventually become Secretary General of the British Communist Party, had arrived in London and established himself in the East End. He was a journalist for the *Dreadnought* and a key figure in the River Thames Shop Stewards' Movement, being known locally as 'The Bolshie'.

In May 1920 he wrote an article urging dockers to refuse to load ships with arms scheduled to help the anti-Bolshevik forces. Soon after, in the East India dock a ship called the *Jolly George* was waiting for a cargo of munitions destined for Russia. As a result of the article, dockers refused to load the vessel and sent a deputation to their union, which promised to back strike action. On 10 May newspapers around the world carried the story that the *Jolly George* had been prevented from sailing.

Sylvia's slogan 'Hands off Russia' was soon heard everywhere at noisy meetings in the docks and in Old Ford Road. Harry Pollitt has described Sylvia's activities at this time in his autobiography *Serving my Time*:

> Day after day we were posting up placards, sticky-backs and posters on the dock sides and in various places in the ships and lavatories. Sylvia Pankhurst kept us continuously supplied with copies of Lenin's Appeal to the Working Masses. This was considered by our democratic rulers as a seditious document, so it had to be printed illegally. My landlady in Poplar expressed surprise that my mattress seemed to vary in size from day to day and that I must be a rough sleeper as it was so bumpy. She little knew that inside the mattress we kept our copies of Lenin's appeal and each day took a supply to distribute amongst workers in the docks . . .

Italy was also now a focus of the spreading revolution. It was presumably with the help of Corio's contacts that Sylvia made the first of her journeys, in the tradition of all those indomitable Victorian lady travellers who explored the wildest corners of the world, armed with little more than a handbag, an umbrella and sometimes a Bible.

Sylvia (without the Bible) crossed the Alps on foot. Undercover arrangements had been made for her, first to make a secret and dangerous visit, with Corio, to the Conference of the Italian Socialist Party (PSI) at Bologna during the summer of 1919. It was here that the PSI declared its allegiance to the Communist International. Barbara Winslow explains how Sylvia, 'far from being a lone crack-pot as some of her detractors claim . . . shared identifiable political positions with many in the movement'. She even spoke at the Conference, not only bringing greetings from British workers and welcoming the revolutionary outburst forecast for the next year, but also chiding members for wasting time. 'It is difficult for me to understand how you can possibly make propaganda to win seats in parliament – a body which you mean to abolish in a few months – when you ought to be absorbed in the work of revolutionary preparation.'

But Italy had no Lenin to lead its revolution. Instead, on the sidelines in that same year a small group met in a businessmen's club to form the Milan Fighters' Fascio – the Fascists.[2] Their motto 'Obedience not Discussion' was to prove more potent to an undisciplined Italy.

After the Bologna Conference, Sylvia set off, alone, towards Germany. She climbed the Alps from Italy into Switzerland – an extremely risky project without a visa. With the help of local Swiss socialists she trekked along goat paths over the mountains into Germany and on to Stuttgart. Germany was in a state of post-war chaos and political ferment. Most of the socialists there were in hiding and being persecuted by the authorities.

Sylvia told the story in her unpublished works, *The Red Twilight* and *The Inheritance*. She described meeting up with Norah Smyth and Marxist feminist Clara Zetkin in Zurich and how the three women went first to Frankfurt, where Sylvia established contact with an agent known as 'the eye of Moscow' and was given £500. As ever with the Pankhursts, Sylvia was desperately short of funds for her work and did her best to exploit any friendly contacts she could. The *Dreadnought*, for instance, was now being subsidized by an agent, Theodore Rothstein, who had access to money for groups supporting the Bolsheviks. She and Norah then continued their journey to a Conference in Amsterdam, where

2. Fasces – a bundle of rods and axes – were the Roman symbol of power.

Sylvia proposed an international workers' strike in support of the Soviet Union. Her motion was seconded and passed.

Back in England the whirlwind became a tornado, Sylvia's energy being based solidly now on experience and increasing intellectual stature. She was au fait with all shades of opinion and developing movements and well-read in the opinions of leading activists. The way forward, she believed, lay in the introduction of Russian-style soviets as 'the most democratic form of Government yet established'. She had always based her faith in local community control and had practised this belief during the war in the East End.

In the *Workers' Dreadnought* on 21 February 1920 she wrote: 'The Communist party must keep its doctrine pure . . . its mission is to lead the way without stopping or turning . . . Do not worry about a big communist Party yet; it is better to build a sound one . . .'. During the war the ELFS had argued constantly for local control of food distribution, welfare and relief. She was a lone visionary in her determination to combine her feminism with her communism. Norah Smyth had complained often that the reason the ELFS membership dwindled was simply because most of their supporters could make neither head nor tail of Communism or soviets.

It was not until 1920 that Sylvia first introduced the term 'social soviet' in Britain, although she had been promoting the concept since 1917. Unlike Russian soviets, which were largely factory-based, her proposed social soviets were a practical way to involve the entire working class in the creation of a new kind of organization. This would be based on the areas in which people lived rather than where they worked, and over which workers had control. She saw the soviets as workers' committees, much like branches of the main party. Outlining her vision, she described delegates as 'constantly reporting back and getting instructions from their constituents; whilst members of Parliament are elected for a term of years and only receive anything approaching instructions at election times. Even then, it is the candidate who, in the main, sets forth the programme, the electors merely assenting to or dissenting from the programme as a whole.'[3]

Curiously enough, while Christabel was being fired by a new Christian missionary fervour, Sylvia developed a similarly religious zeal towards the search for political truth. She was at the forefront of Revolutionary Britain. Sylvia and the WSF began to step up their campaign to found social soviets throughout Britain. In March she and Harry Pollitt spoke at a meeting in Bow

3. *Workers' Dreadnought*, 26 January 1918.

Baths, which provoked the wrath of the *East London Advertiser*. 'Welcome to the soviets,' proclaimed the banners. Always Sylvia's message returned to her feminist core: she appealed to women to organize themselves into household soviets of small groups who would know each other and could elect and instruct their representatives.

An article in the *Workers' Dreadnought* in March 1920 was based on her life in Bow but pitched now to a far wider readership, explaining just how the soviet principle could also work for women. She recalled the decision by a group of mothers in Bow to organize a celebration for the children at the end of the war and how the idea of co-operative street parties spread throughout the capital. Everyone was involved, decorations were made, grimy walls painted brightly and individuals with skills such as flower making, sign-writing, sewing or cooking were drawn in, and the children had a wonderful time. 'Just as the women . . . got together to organise peace parties so the working women in Russia co-operate in appointing their delegates to represent them in the soviets. The working women in London and every other part of Britain will do the same very soon.' But it was not to be.

Mary Davis, an admirer of Sylvia, explains: 'acknowledging her enormous achievements as an agitator and organiser . . . whilst she undoubtedly had both sympathy and contact with workers . . . her politics displayed . . . an impatience and a lack of understanding of the historic forms of workers' organisations'.

Sylvia's WSF became the first group in Britain to affiliate with the newly established Third (Communist) International, known as the Comintern. The Comintern was based on revolutionary Marxist principles, and the various left-wing Marxists, such as the British Socialist party, were now under pressure to unite as a single Communist party. But discussions in March 1920 again set Sylvia on a solitary path. Although her WSF was only a tiny minority party within the group, she had her own ideas and firmly rejected any idea of affiliation to the Labour party, which had decided to retain its links with parliament.

On 16 July 1919 there had been the first of a feisty exchange of letters between Sylvia and Lenin. Although he was cautiously critical of her anti-parliamentary stance, Lenin did not underestimate her potential role in the creation of a communist state in Britain. She was much castigated at home for attempting to go it alone, especially as her letter and Lenin's reply, on 28 August, were sent by him for publication in the *Communist International*.[4]

4. Marx Memorial Library.

She had explained her stance with regard to parliamentarianism, which, she felt, was holding back the advance of communism in Britain, and asked for Lenin's opinion. When it arrived it was diplomatic but not what she had expected:

Dear Comrade,

. . . I have no doubt at all that many workers who are among the best, most honest and sincerely revolutionary members of the proletariat are enemies of parliamentarianism and of any participation in Parliament. The older the capitalist culture and bourgeois democracy, in any country, the more understandable this is, since the bourgeoisie in old parliamentary countries has excellently mastered the art of hypocrisy and fooling the people in a thousand ways . . .

What if, in a certain country those who are Communists by their convictions . . . sincere partisans of . . . the Soviet system . . . cannot unite owing to a disagreement over participation in Parliament.

I should consider such a disagreement immaterial at present . . . the question of parliamentarianism is now a partial, secondary question.

I am personally convinced that to renounce participation in parliamentary elections is a mistake on the part of the revolutionary workers of Britain, but better to make that mistake than to delay the formation of a big workers' Communist Party in Britain, out of all the trends and elements listed by you.

. . . We Russians, who have lived through two great revolutions are well aware what importance parliamentarianism can have, and actually does have during a revolutionary period in general and in the very midst of a revolution, in particular . . . Soviet propaganda can, and must, be carried on in and from within, bourgeois parliaments . . .

With Communist greetings Lenin.

Sylvia's letter was inaccurately printed in the British Socialist Party newspaper the *Call* and created a distorted impression of her alleged self-aggrandizement. In particular, it wrongly reported as fact that in June 1919 the WSF had independently set itself up as the official communist party. This was not true and as Sylvia explained to Lenin, although she had agreed to a change of name from the WSF to Communist Party, this name would not be used until attempts to form a united party from the various disparate factions had succeeded. After a great deal of complex in-fighting and disagreements over theory and strategy, the WSF did eventually break away and call its own conference in June 1920.

At this meeting the British Section of the Third International (BSTI) was born – Sylvia's very own Communist Party, the CP (BSTI) – based on non-affiliation to the Labour Party and non-participation in elections. Within three months its membership was 430 and the self-declared official organ was, of course, the *Workers' Dreadnought*. In various letters to the *Call*, this event was called 'fatuous fooling' and 'a tiny and uninfluential gathering'.

So it was that when the Communist Unity Convention was held that summer, Sylvia was excluded. Lenin sent a wireless message to the Congress. It said: 'I consider that the policy of Comrade Sylvia Pankhurst . . . in refusing to collaborate in the amalgamation of the British Socialist Party, Socialist Labour Party and others into a Communist Party, to be wrong.' Sylvia was not at the Conference. She was in Moscow, bearding the lion in his palatial den.

21

The Dread Wasp

'Capitalism is a wrong system of Society, and it has got to be smashed – I would give my life to smash it.'

Sylvia Pankhurst on trial for sedition, 6 November 1920

Undaunted by Home Office confiscation of her passport or the refusal of visas by the embassies of Norway and Finland or the fact that she was under constant surveillance, Sylvia somehow managed to slip out of Britain. With the help of Russian colleagues she embarked on another incredibly hazardous journey, even by today's adventurous standards.

She was determined to get to the Second Congress of the Third International in Moscow in July 1920. She had decided to tackle Lenin in person about their differences. Sylvia told the story of her hair-raising journey in the *Dreadnought*, which by now bore a hammer and sickle emblem and claimed to be 'the Organ of the Communist Party'.

She left from Harwich as a stowaway on a Norwegian freighter to Sweden and then on to Norway, where she had expected to board a 'Soviet steamer'. It was a slight misnomer, for her promised 'steamer' was a battered fishing boat on which she spent 'hours of misery' crossing the Barents Sea to Murmansk. 'The boat, unpainted for many years, was scarcely eight feet across and her gear rusted and weatherworn.' Idealism overcame it all as 'we bounded over the waves, away from Capitalism'.

There was a stench of oil as the little boat pitched and tossed like a mad horse on icy seas, until the captain was forced to seek shelter from the storm in the nearest port. From there to Murmansk and on to St Petersburg where she was impressed by the guard at the Hotel International – a woman who sat, bayonet at the ready, spearing passes given to her by hotel guests. Next day Sylvia took the train for Moscow with a group of kindly comrades who looked after her, gave her their own bedding and found her a sack of hay to serve as a mattress on the bare wooden slats.

Approaching the capital, great forest fires were burning and a smoky haze covered the city. Alighting from the train, she saw 'a great square, a mass of almost motionless people in loose straight clothing, white, grey and dust coloured. Old women sat on the pavement, peddling small, green apples, wild berries and other trifling wares . . . the roads are cobbled, the walls a sunny blend of pink and yellow, the domes of the churches blue, speckled with golden stars . . . The weird St Basil's Cathedral is like a schoolboy's Christmas nightmare and yet it possesses a strange barbaric beauty. The eyes of its architect were put out in order that he might build its like for no other monarch.'

Sylvia booked into the Djelavoi Djor Hotel, blazing with red banners and crowded with droves of delegates from all over the world, many of whom had come equipped with their own food. The British contingent in particular, she said, was inclined to grumble about the rye bread and even the caviar, but was grateful for the daily free supply of cigarettes, cheroots and matches. They soon became tired of sightseeing and spent much of the time in their rooms making tea. Sylvia, being made of different stuff, preferred to explore. 'All this, and even the Conference itself, seemed like a vaporous mist through which one must peer to discover the real life of Soviet Russia.'

Only a few days of the conference remained. The lobby was buzzing with gossip about Lenin's attack on anti-parliamentarians such as the Scottish Marxist shop steward Willie Gallacher and on Sylvia in particular. When she herself arrived, there was even more excitement at the prospect of an open confrontation. Sylvia was greeted with a message from Lenin himself, summoning her to go immediately to the Kremlin where he was waiting to deliver a reprimand to his rebellious 'pupil'. Sylvia did not see the meeting that way at all!

Her initial impression of Lenin was starry-eyed. This indomitable young woman, striding as she was into the heart of European politics, still revealed at times the ingenuous rapture of a little girl:

At first sight one feels as though one has always known him . . . it is not that one has seen so many of his photographs for the photographs are not like him: they represent an altogether heavier, darker and more ponderous man in place of this majestic and mobile being . . . rather short, broadly built, he is quick and nimble in every action just as he is in thought and speech . . . his rather bright complexion looks sandy because it is tanned and freckled by hot sun . . . His bearing is frank and modest, his brown eyes twinkle with kindly amusement . . .

It was as though she could hardly believe that she was there in Moscow, and she was utterly disarmed. The promised bearding never took place and Lenin let her down politely. Sylvia had always been pragmatic and willing to shift her ground, and her instant impressions of Russia gave her a better understanding of the paramount need for unity and acceptance of Lenin's point of view. Perhaps Lenin was right after all. Besides, Sylvia knew only too well that the *Dreadnought* and the WSF were in deep financial trouble. She could see that unless she shifted her position and agreed to support unity, she would not take home the subsidies she so badly needed.

Lenin sat her in the place of honour next to him in the Committee Room, formerly the Tsar's magnificent bedroom, and explained the reasoning behind his letter. She told him, 'Though I am a socialist, I have fought a long time in the suffrage movement and I have seen how important it is to be extreme.' Lenin explained to her how the communists differed from the socialists but stressed how important it was for the two to be affiliated and work together. He urged Sylvia and Gallacher to go back to Britain and join the CPGB. Later Lenin announced to the Conference assembled in the Old Throne Room that the British, and even Sylvia, were now in accord. Delegates jumped to their feet and carried Lenin high on their shoulders singing the Internationale. 'He looked like a happy father among his sons,' she wrote afterwards.

She was taken to the Opera in the Tsar's motor car and given a seat in the former Royal Box and then embarked on an extensive and exhausting tour of the sights. She was a tourist in wonderland but unusually she had no time for art galleries or museums. Trying to satisfy her quest for understanding the lives of ordinary people, she travelled 60 miles to see a metal factory, studied the soviets and the co-operatives, called on a 'House for the Mother and Child' (there was no stigma attached to illegitimacy) and visited model schools and hospitals.

What she neither saw nor appreciated at that time, like many others, was that behind the euphoria of the new ways the oppressive Tsarist regime had simply been replaced by another that was to become even more cruel. The Russian prisons were full of tortured men and women who opposed the Bolsheviks; many were shot. Years later, as an old lady, in a letter to Teresa Billington-Greig she wrote:

I did not join the official party being convinced the policy was unworkable. I believed that Russia, almost a world in itself, could establish socialism within its own borders. For this I was dismissed as a sentimental dreamer, but afterwards that became (ostensibly at least) the official policy. I believed that the correct policy for Russia was to make life happy and prosperous for the mass of people and to avoid atrocities and brutalities both in the interests of the home population and to render socialism attractive to the rest of the world.

Such a task was hard, perhaps too hard but that, I am convinced should have been the aim . . . On the whole the Russians do not seem to have bothered about world public opinion . . . their propaganda . . . converted some but their ruthlessness estranged others. I lost sympathy with their methods but I was, and am, a socialist.

Her return to Britain was even more eventful than her outward journey. Between Moscow and St Petersburg there was a fire on the train and Sylvia described how their eyes streamed and they gasped for breath. She was rescued by Willie Gallacher, who carried her from the burning coach onto the track, in her night clothes, while the carriages were hosed down. At Murmansk she and the other ten returning delegates stood again on the deck of the Norwegian fishing boat, waving goodbye and singing the 'Internationale'. But the sea was still so rough that Sylvia was sick for most of the voyage and it was again Willie Gallacher who played the gentleman. He recalled the nightmare in his memoirs:

We were down in the forward cubby-hole. Sylvia could not stand the confined space and the strong odour that clogs the air in such vessels; she wanted out on deck [sic], and I had to go with her. The seas were dashing across the deck but she wouldn't stay inside. I got a tarpaulin from one of the fishermen, got Sylvia to lie along the hatchway and the beam . . . wedged myself between the hatchway and the beam and held her there all through the night, the sea behaving worse with every passing hour.

The captain then decided to anchor off the northern Norwegian coast and Sylvia was then rowed, with the others, towards some rocks where they slithered and slid ashore to be greeted enthusiastically by local villagers and treated to the best food they had eaten for weeks. 'What a night!' wrote Willie Gallacher. 'Sylvia had come through it very well and though, like the rest of us she had got badly shaken, she wasn't long in getting back to her old lively self with the staff at the station.'

Officials were looking for her when she arrived in Britain but somehow she managed to avoid them yet again, and, as the *Sunday Express* commented, 'completely outwitted the Special Service Branch of New Scotland Yard'. In the golden after-glow of observing Communism in practice, all she could see on her return to Bow were dingy streets and houses, and spindle-legged, under-nourished children. It had been a successful adventure in many ways and certainly one that met with Norah's approval, for Sylvia had returned with promises of considerable Russian finance both then and in the future. Norah Smyth herself made several trips to Sweden to collect this money.

According to a Special Branch report, this money was divided between the debts of Corio's Agenda Press (£1,500), WSF (£500), and the PRIB (£300). In addition, £15 weekly was to be spent on *Dreadnought* staff, £20 weekly on a canvasser, £6 for an agitator in the docks and £10 for the distribution of free literature. In November a further £1,500 arrived, of which £750 was paid to Norah Smyth.

Sylvia was now being ever more closely watched by the authorities and her entire operation assumed a dramatic, cloak and dagger character. Parcels of literature were being passed secretly from person to person, so that in the event of police raids no one would know where they were.

The *Daily Express* on 27 September 1920 headlined, somewhat flippantly, 'Sylvia's World Revolution', with the subtitle, 'Postponed by a Dogfight'. Sylvia had been speaking to a gathering of her Communist Party in a dingy back street hall in Manchester. The article read:

> Hush! The revolution has started. Sylvia Pankhurst has returned from Russia. She has re-appeared in the city of her parents and flung the gauntlet full in the face of capitalism.
>
> Whilst she was doing that this afternoon, there was the most interesting dog fight I have ever seen ... It was a beautiful fight. Even the Communists admitted it. The meeting inside was suspended and ... windows ... were framed with intense faces watching the progress ...
>
> One of the dogs, a black and white terrier, took liberties with one of the most anti-Bolshevist dogs in the district. The two dogs were evidently discussing the Zinovieff theory of the Third International. Oh it was grand! At the climax a woman – anti-Bolshevist and believing in home, family and country – threw a bucket of cold water over the pair and they separated.
>
> What a Sylvia!

Back at the offices of the *Dreadnought* over the last few months a large and jocular personality had arrived from Jamaica. His name was Claude McKay and he was the first black journalist to be employed in Britain. In the midst of her communist fervour Sylvia had not forgotten her commitment to a social system in which race prejudice was unthinkable.

Claude McKay was a self-confessed 'vagabond', a poet who came to England early in 1919 via his travels around America. He discovered the International Club with its 'dogmatists and doctrinaires of radical left ideas; Socialists, Communists, one-big-unionists, trade unionists, soap boxers, poetasters, scribblers, editors of little radical sheets which flourish in London. But foreigners formed the majority of the membership. The Jewish element was the largest . . . these people believed that Marx was the true prophet of the new social order.'

Angered by the *Daily Herald* campaign against French employment of black soldiers in the subjugation of Germany after the war, he wrote to Sylvia as editor of the *Dreadnought*. Not only did she publish his letter, she also invited him to visit her office:

> I found a plain little Queen-Victoria sized woman with plenty of long unruly bronze-like hair. There was no distinction about her clothes, and on the whole she was very undistinguished. But her eyes were fiery, even a little fanatic, with a glint of shrewdness . . . Pankhurst had a personality as picturesque and passionate as any radical in London . . . and in the labor [sic] movement she was always jabbing her hat pin into the hides of the smug and slack labor leaders. Her weekly newspaper might have been called The Dread Wasp.

Before she set out for Moscow, Sylvia had invited McKay to work for her, to find stories in the docks from a black and a white perspective and to read and mark foreign newspapers. His assistant was to be one Comrade Vie. McKay suspected that Comrade Vie was a foreign revolutionary and hints were dropped that he was more important than the impression given by his youthful, bland face.

In September, McKay had been introduced to a young Royal Naval sailor named Springhall. He was lively, intelligent and, even better, a keen reader of the *Dreadnought*. They struck up a friendship and Springhall took to dropping into the *Dreadnought* offices with news items, until one day he arrived with what Claude McKay realized was a piece of dynamite. He decided that the article contained information that was so important he must wait for Sylvia's advice. Her response was instant, and maybe foolhardy, for the intelligence material from Springhall was extraordinary. Fictitious names were used for the author and the battleship he served on, and the *Dreadnought* led on 16 October 1920 with the first of three articles headlined 'Discontent on the Lower Deck'.

It alleged, in revolutionary language, that pay had been reduced, conditions in the Navy had deteriorated since the armistice and that morale was at rock bottom. It urged the men to stand up for their rights: 'Men of the lower deck: Are you going to see your class go under in a fight with the capitalist brutes who made millions out of your sacrifices during the War? . . . You are the Sons of the Working Class and it is your duty to stand by that class and not the class and government which is responsible for the starving of your ex-service brothers.'

This was paramount to incitement to mutiny. It was not the first occasion on which Sylvia had published such material, but this time the authorities had had enough. Within two days the offices of the *Dreadnought* were raided again. When Claude McKay realized that the police had arrived, he hid the original Springhall article down his sock and left 'with a big black grin' to find a toilet, where he shredded the original and flushed it away.

Sylvia was arrested on a charge of sedition. She appeared on 5 November at the Mansion House Police Court, where she treated the assembled company to a dramatic rendering of communist ideology. The magistrate told her she was fortunate not to be charged with treason and sentenced her to six months in the second division. She was given leave to appeal and released on £1000 bail, paid by Norah Smyth, who mortgaged the Agenda Press, of which Sylvia, Norah and Corio were now trustees. The appeal was set for January 1921 in the suitably theatrical setting of the Guildhall in London.

Her passionate performance was worthy of the great Sarah Bernhardt. This little figure, pale, intense and with her hair as usual in disarray, a red carnation in her button hole, held her audience spellbound for an hour and a half as she wrung their hearts (but not the judge's) with the story of her life. With passionate anger she reminded them that she had given up everything, her beloved art, even her family, to pursue her father's mission of rescuing the poor and oppressed from their oppressors. She had herself faced death many times for her beliefs. 'I have gone to war, too,' she exploded, 'and my life will be shortened.' She told of her life in the East End, her second-hand clothes: 'it is wrong that people like you should be comfortable and well-fed, while all around you people are starving'.

With pure and unrestrained emotion she quoted her heroes, Marx and Engels, and read from William Blake, William Morris and Edward Carpenter: 'If I am not level with the lowest I am nothing.' It was outrageous but it came from her soul. It was honest and brave and it failed. The judge, Sir John Bell, upheld the sentence, which, he said, was in no way adequate for the seriousness of her offence.

For once Sylvia was alone with precious little support. Only 300 people turned up at a protest rally in Trafalgar Square, and a letter from her old sparring partner George Bernard Shaw (who was enjoying a huge success in London's West End) was published in the *Workers' Dreadnought*:

> I am very sorry your appeal has not succeeded though, like all sensible people in the movement, I am furious with you for getting into prison quite unnecessarily. Why didn't you make up your mind to keep out of prison instead of persistently breaking into it? The lion will let you put your head into his mouth, because the law says he must; but if you shake your hairpins in his throat, he is only too glad to have an excuse for snapping. However, there is no use scolding you now; so keep up your spirits and look forward to the day of your deliverance.

Conditions in Holloway were no better than they had been in the Suffragette days, and Sylvia was kept in a darkened cell, unable to read or write and forced to tackle arduous cleaning jobs – never her strongest suit. She even carried heavy buckets of coal. Despite all this, the old, compassionate Sylvia was still alive and she worried terribly about her fellow prisoners, although now she saw revolution as the answer to their torment.

Norah Smyth did her best to keep a vigil outside Holloway, where supporters sang the 'Red Flag' (which Shaw described as 'the funeral march of a dead eel') and carried banners saying 'Six Months for Telling the Truth'. Only the Russians sent her letters of encouragement and her story was told in their newspapers for propaganda purposes. Eventually Sylvia became ill and spent some time in the hospital wing, where she was allowed a special diet. By the time she was ready for discharge, she was weak and suffering from acute colitis. She emerged at the prison gates, weak and weeping, on 10 May 1921, to be taken off by Norah Smyth for a celebration breakfast.

Meanwhile, in Australia, Adela had given birth to a daughter who she named Sylvia, and in Italy, Benito Mussolini was elected to parliament.

Sylvia now faced a very different situation from the brief euphoria of her Russian adventure. The Executive Committee of the CP (BSTI), Sylvia's own party, had merged with the Communist Party Great Britain (CPGB), and the *Workers' Dreadnought* ceased to be its official organ. Sylvia was, however, to remain editor, at least for the time being.

They tried to gag the *Dreadnought*, which was the only newspaper in Britain openly reporting controversy within the party. This, said Sylvia, was a sign of healthy development. She furiously denounced the party executive for playing at dictatorship of the proletariat but also being afraid to be revolutionary. Dictatorship, she claimed, was part of a growing process in any movement, but it was a temporary state. She admitted she was saddened that, even in Russia, there were no signs of a withering of dictatorship. They said she must hand over control of the *Dreadnought*. She refused, so they sacked her and Norah resigned in support.

But that was not quite the end of the story. The *Workers' Dreadnought* (still calling itself 'the Organ of the Communist Party' and still edited by Sylvia) continued on its freelance path, castigating the Party for being little more than a puppet of Moscow with no mind of its own. Even Lenin, one of the most powerful men in the world, now came within her sights. His New Economic Policy, which included the encouragement of private trade, was, she felt, transforming him into a politician like any other, re-introducing capitalist ideas and assuring the protection of capitalist companies:

> Lenin. We address you as representative of the Russian Soviet Government and the Russian Communist Party. With deep regret we have observed you hauling down the flag of Communism and abandoning the cause of the emancipation of the workers. With profound sorrow we have watched the development of your policy of making peace with Capitalism and reaction. Why have you done this?

In Poplar the thirty-strong Borough Council, led by George Lansbury and including Nellie Cressall, went to prison rather than levy the crippling rates demanded by the London County Council; their actions became a national scandal. Sylvia told them firmly that they were tackling the problem of poverty from the wrong direction. It would be better to increase the factory owners' rates or, better still, get rid of them and set up soviets. This would be a truly radical example to the country.

But no one listened, and in a desperate attempt to form a pressure group, she set up, with Norah, the Unemployed Workers' Organisation, which, in an undignified and unworthy attempt to make herself heard, besieged the Town Hall. George Lansbury called the police and several people were hurt.

And then, hidden deep in the miles of critical newspaper prose, emerged a name that has such terrible connotations today: Adolf Hitler. Sylvia was the first editor in Britain to foresee the new dangers emerging in Germany and the young Adolf Hitler's rise to power. Hitler, born in 1889, had a very disturbed childhood and when dreams of being an artist failed, turned to house painting. In 1918 he was moved by the Armistice to turn instead to politics and led an armed rising in Munich in 1923. He was sent to prison for five years, where he wrote the first part of *Mein Kampf* and emerged a hero after only twelve months.

Though it would be ten years before Hitler became Chancellor of Germany, Sylvia spotlit the threat occasioned by the confrontation between fascism and communism: the fascism of Hitler's new Nazi party and Benito Mussolini, who had become Il Duce, fascist dictator of Italy, and communism, as inspired by Russia.

For a year she fought on. Her paper, still entertaining and original, was less read by the people for whom it was written: the people she wanted to save were not asking to be saved. They were fed up with fighting and wanted some fun. Fun was seldom on Sylvia's menu.

Despite the poverty that undoubtedly existed, there was an air of gaiety in the 1920s. Skirts were short, flappers were flapping and Chanel in Paris was causing a revolution of her own with flat shoes, short skirts and boyish hair cuts. George Gershwin, Noel Coward and Charlie Chaplin entertained and in London the BBC opened the Savoy Hill studios with a new programme, *Woman's Hour*. David Mitchell claimed that, 'if in 1923 Sylvia had lain starving on a stretcher outside the Houses of Parliament . . . there would have been few hands to lift her . . . She was, in fact, becoming a bore.'

The December 1923 General Election resulted in the formation of a minority Labour government. Ramsay MacDonald became the first Labour Prime Minister; her father's long-ago dream had been fulfilled but Sylvia did not rejoice. Eleven women MPs went to the House of Commons that month. Sylvia commented tartly of Lady Astor, who had become the first woman MP in 1919, 'the place for her is in the home and not the House. The woman professional politican is neither more nor less desirable than the man professional politician.'

The *Workers' Dreadnought* commented on 4 January 1924 that 'Parliamentary Government is a failure; it does not grip the interest of the masses.' In a short space of time that year, faithful Mrs Payne died and Norah wrote a long letter, begging Sylvia to rethink her policies. Then, in July 1924 the *Dreadnought* finally ceased publication.

It was time to move on. Ford Road was empty and meaningless. Sylvia was tired, a rebel apparently without a cause. But not for long. Her mid-life crisis would be short-lived.

22

The Fourth Pillar

'I opened my eyes and saw that my youth had fled. Then I said that I should have a child of my own in whom I should live again.'

Sylvia Pankhurst, *In the Days of my Youth*

Reactionary Woodford Green was, in many ways, a most surprising place for socialist revolutionary, internationalist Sylvia to make her home. In those days there was not a black face for miles and the first synagogue was almost forty years away. On the edge of the glorious forest of Epping, with its ancient, twisted hornbeam trees, magnificent beeches and shady glades, Woodford was an easy weekend escape for oppressed and overcrowded East Enders. Sylvia herself had enjoyed picnics there, and her friend Bessie Lansbury's brother had made it his home. Sylvia had found refuge with his family when hiding from the police and her spirit responded to the rural surroundings.

Pretty, white weather-boarded houses still fringed Woodford's huge village green where cricket had been played since 1735. In the late eighteenth and early nineteenth centuries more affluent business and professional men built themselves substantial villas in large gardens. Local social historian and author Josephine Boyle says: 'Gradually, in the early twentieth century, as the middle-classes expanded, more and more young Londoners made their homes in this oasis.' Clement Attlee and his wife were amongst them. They bought a house on the much sought-after new Monkham's Estate, and the future leader of the Labour party and eventual Prime Minister could later be seen on a Saturday morning lifting his new baby Martin in his pram over the stile on to the Green.

The arrival of the railway to Woodford in 1856 had already created a social barrier that as the developers moved in was becoming well and truly entrenched. The working classes now lived mostly 'on the other side of the line', down streets with names like Prospect Road. They shopped at the Co-op and went to the nearby secondary modern school. The commuting middle-classes lived in tree-lined Prince's Avenue and Snakes Lane, shopped at Sainsburys and sent their sons to Bancroft's Grammar School. The Woodford County High School for Girls opened in 1919.

By the time Sylvia moved in, Woodford had become decidedly 'desirable' and, stranger still, Winston Churchill, her old adversary, was its Constitutional and Anti-Socialist MP. However, Sylvia's first toehold in this village-turned-suburb was entirely in character. She and Norah found a ramshackle, rat-infested, semi-detached weather-boarded cottage, known euphemistically as Vyne Cottage. She changed its name immediately to Red Cottage. Overlooking the Green, it was set back from the main road at Woodford Wells between London and Epping. Her old friend Henry Harben helped out with the purchase price. Sylvia's initial intention was to devote herself to writing the books for which she had had no time in her politically active years.

Some accounts say that she moved to Woodford with Norah and that their plan was to run left-wing study groups. But the place was tiny; there was hardly room for three and it seems more likely that, if Norah shared it with Sylvia initially, she moved out when Silvio moved in. Sylvia may even have lived there alone for a few months.

It is easy to feel sad for Norah, displaced by a man after so many years of unstinting devotion to Sylvia and the cause. She commented ruefully on the friendship with Silvio that Sylvia needed a sharper brain than hers: 'mine was not intellectual enough, partly because she had the effect of stultifying what little I had, partly because I was always overworked and never had time or energy to think'.

One half of the cottage, with two bedrooms, was the home of the Powter family. Leslie Powter was born in 1921 and lived there with his two brothers, sister and parents. His father had grown up in the cottage. Whether they were Sylvia's tenants is unclear. 'It was an absolute slum,' Mr Powter recalls. 'We had a cold water tap and bathed in a tin bath; there was no electricity and a toilet up the garden. Eventually we were given a council house.' Mrs Powter grew flowers, especially dahlias, to sell to passers-by, and when Sylvia moved in she decided to follow Mrs Powter's example by serving tea and cakes in the garden. When life was too much or Silvio had lost his temper, she would 'trot round' for a cup of tea – Mrs Powter's shoulder was a comfort to cry on.

'Red Cottage' teas were advertised in the *Worker's Dreadnought*. Customers also came from the nearby Horse and Well public house, as well as lorry drivers and passengers and crews from the various buses, which had their terminus opposite. As she had always done, Sylvia drew on a circle of willing helpers from Bow. She was still well loved, her charisma had not dimmed with age and friends flocked around, happy to be with her.

Annie Barnes was one of those old faithfuls who came down from the East End at weekends. Sylvia couldn't cook, so someone had to make the cakes. Annie, who had first thought Silvio the gardener, recorded an interview with writer Brian Harrison in 1974 in which she described how Sylvia was once caught *boiling* a rasher of bacon. Norah O'Connell (later Mrs Walshe) recalled in a letter to David Mitchell in 1964: 'I thought Sylvia was a wonderful person . . . so brave but she did demand service from everyone and some of her friends became tired of it. It was a curious household, so untidy and casual . . .'.

In January 1924 Lenin, dying in Moscow, had proclaimed his likely successor Josef Stalin as 'unbearable'. In Rome the Italian socialist deputy Giacomo Matteotti ended an outspoken speech criticizing Mussolini, with the words 'and now get ready for my death'. Shortly afterwards he was assassinated. These events flashed a warning light for the far-seeing Sylvia. Democracy appeared to her to be increasingly under threat from the emerging dictators. She began making notes for a new book, *The Red Twilight*, which was to chronicle the demise of communism and what she viewed as the ominous fascist lust for power.

During this unusually chaotic but creative period in her life, Sylvia embarked on yet another mammoth project. Her 638-page book *India and the Earthly Paradise* was published in Bombay in 1926 but has never appeared in Britain. Sylvia's fascination with India had been long established. Walter Crane, her mentor in the art school days, had visited the subcontinent and produced and illustrated a travel book in 1907. The same year, Keir Hardie had undertaken a sensationally successful tour of India, during which he told her that he was being 'worshipped'.

Sylvia herself had never been there and has been criticized for superficiality and failing to grasp the complexities of Indian life. But the book is meticulously researched. Certainly Sylvia spent hours, day after day, in the British Museum reading room, and was helped by William Wedgwood-Benn, appointed Secretary of State for India in 1929, and her old friend Frederick Pethick-Lawrence, who was eventually to assume that post.

Social historian and active member of the Sylvia Pankhurst Memorial Committee, Mary Davis also believes the book deserves attention as one of the very few British anti-racist and anti-imperialist attempts to analyze Indian culture, traditions and history. Never did she adopt the 'haughty superiority of the conquering race,' she says.

This was followed in 1927 by *Delphos or the Future of the International Language*, an introduction to Interlingua, written during 1926. Silvio Corio spoke Interlingua, an international language rather like the better known Esperanto, and Sylvia was convinced that it paved a way to better understanding.

The General Strike took place in 1926. Sylvia cared for a stream of miners' children in the cramped accommodation at Red Cottage, but her active involvement was comparatively low-key compared with the earlier years. Her health was not good and she found campaigning a strain. In the autumn her mother was invited to stand as a Conservative parliamentary candidate in Whitechapel, although an election was not due until 1929. This could have been seen as the last and most dramatic snub to Sylvia, for Emmeline, now almost 70 years old, began speaking and proselytizing Conservatism in the East End heartland Sylvia had come to regard as her own emotional home. In the spring of 1927 Emmeline even moved into furnished lodgings over a barber's shop in Wapping in order to be closer to the campaign. It was a strangely unwise decision; she had no chance of success.

In 1926 Sylvia had confided to her old friend Charlotte Drake that she was expecting a baby; but it was only wishful thinking. However, in April 1927 she telephoned Mrs Drake again. This time there was no mistake, she 'could feel the baby kicking'. Mrs Drake bought her a ring to protect her respectability when they went to see the midwife together, where she confirmed what Sylvia wanted so badly to hear. At the age of 45 she was pregnant.

Euphoric, she was desperate to share her happiness and repair the breach between herself and her mother. The gulf between the two had become ever wider over the years as Emmeline's life took some bizarre and unpredictable turns. During the war her views and those of Sylvia could not have been further apart. Emmeline was an imperialist, monarchist and anti-bolshevist. To the amazement and dismay of her friends, she had adopted four orphan babies, one of whom she eventually handed over to Christabel, while the others were largely left to the care of the long-suffering Nurse Pine. The girls and Nurse Pine had led a strange life, travelling with Emmeline for six years wherever she went, lecturing in Canada, Bermuda and America, until eventually they all went to the South of France, where Emmeline opened a teashop in Antibes. When this failed, she returned, impoverished as ever, to live with her sister in London. One by one the children were found alternative homes and vanished from the story.

Emmeline was staying with friends at Chipping Ongar in Essex when she heard the terrible news of Sylvia's expected baby, whereupon she is said to have taken to her bed and wept for days. However, Sylvia still longed to heal the hurt that both she and her mother had suffered and during the pregnancy called to see her while she was back in London. It was hopeless. Emmeline's sense of propriety had been devastated beyond repair by her daughter's behaviour, and Sylvia's aunt told friends that when she arrived, Emmeline retreated to her room, refusing to see 'that scarlet woman'.

When Annie Barnes asked Sylvia why she would not marry Silvio, she justified her actions on the grounds that were they to be married, they would be deported and shot as anti-fascists. It was a theatrical response but not entirely unjustified, since in those days women lost their British nationality on marriage to a foreigner.

Kindly Mrs Drake offered to see Sylvia through the birth at her own home, but Emmeline Pethick-Lawrence and Lady Sybil Smith wisely thought it would be safer for her to stay in a nursing home. Sylvia was booked into Fitzjohn's Avenue in Hampstead for her confinement. After a miserable pregnancy and a difficult labour during snowstorms and blizzards, she gave birth to Richard Keir Pethick Pankhurst on 4 December 1927.

Sylvia, lonely and allowed no visitors in the nursing home, felt compelled to try, yet again, to appeal to her mother. But her letter was intercepted and never reached its destination. She also wrote to Emmeline Pethick-Lawrence: 'Yes, dear friend, he is a fine, healthy, beautiful child, perfect in every way and yet I am told that if I had not come here when I did I should not have brought him out alive.' In the New Year mother and son went to recover at the Pethick-Lawrence home.

Talking to Reynold's *Illustrated News* after the birth, Sylvia spoke movingly about her new status and the controversy surrounding it. 'My son is the child of a happy union of affection and long friendship of two people who care for each other. His father is not a wealthy man but he is a man of fine character. I do not believe it is eugenic or fair to children that they should be brought into the world except as a natural result of affection between their parents. I do not seek publicity but want to share the joys of motherhood with my darling.'

Her own mother, now aged 69, was failing in health, although she was still commanding rapturous audiences. When on 29 March 1928 she was present in the House of Commons to witness the final debate on equal franchise for women, she was too weak to climb the stairs to the public gallery. On 14 June she died. The Franchise Bill, for which she had devoted her life, had been passed a month earlier and became known as 'the flapper vote'. Women were at last entitled to vote on equal terms with men.

There were those who blamed grief over Sylvia's outrageous behaviour for

Emmeline's death, but it is much more likely that years of imprisonment and hunger striking had simply taken their toll. Emmeline Pankhurst's funeral, at St John's Church, Smith Square, was an appropriately theatrical affair, reminiscent of the great Suffragette parades she had masterminded. Everyone was there, including Sylvia with Richard in his pram. The jockey of the King's horse under which Emily Davison had died was present with a wreath 'to do honour to the memory of Mrs Pankhurst and Miss Emily Davison'. There were flags and flowers and the newspapers were filled with pages of biographical outpourings. Christabel was red-eyed and Sylvia, overcome and fainting, had to be supported. But it was too late for tears. There was no chance now of finding the mother she had lost. She was herself a mother and determinedly looking forward to a very different kind of relationship with her son. She was defiantly proud of Richard, and it was not long before the scandal of his birth to the son of the man Sylvia described as her 'soul mate' whom she had known and loved for ten years was international news.

While Sylvia was away, Silvio had booked a local handyman, Mr Ashman, to help him build a shack in the garden of Red Cottage. It came in sections and was erected very slowly, Silvio on the floors and the younger Mr Ashman on the roof. The plan was for Sylvia to have a bolt-hole when writing, although eventually the hut became an anti-war museum.

Piecing together clues buried in the Pankhurst collection, it seems that Sylvia borrowed money for the building from Emmeline Pethick-Lawrence, with whom she was still closely in touch. It also appears that Silvio, who was no better at managing money than Sylvia, had overspent, and there are some distraught notes to Emmeline Pethick-Lawrence. Sylvia is clearly beside herself with distress at a misunderstanding between them, partly for fear that Emmeline might withdraw her badly needed financial support. Sylvia's only possible means of financing her family was by writing, and this was a daunting prospect with a tiny baby. The finished letter is lost but the drafts are revealing:

Dearest Emmeline, When I got your letter I felt all my world had crashed down and that worst of all I had lost your love and that my poor little Richard would suffer terribly for only I know the attention to him would have to be set aside for hours at a time if I were without help.

But more than that the awful thing that you think I have deceived you. Well dear the old Sylvia cried and said she must not even take . . .

You are right to say you were astounded. You are right and yet I was almost as much in the dark. I was in another world somehow in the nursing home and at Farnham . . .

Clearly the problems were ironed out, for Sylvia and Emmeline Pethick-Lawrence sustained regular and warm contact until Emmeline's death in 1954.

Sylvia then embarked on several articles about her mother, leading up to the unveiling of a statue in her memory in Victoria Tower Gardens, near the Houses of Parliament. Before writing she seems to have sought Mrs Pethick-Lawrence's advice about certain aspects of Mrs Pankhurst's life, to which Emmeline replied:

> Dearest Sylvia . . . with regard to the matter on which you ask my opinion. I consider that you have done the better thing in leaving the subject untouched . . . From what I know I think your mother's financial affairs would not be easy to explain. I regard your mother dispassionately (as you do) as a most interesting human problem. She was undoubtedly a great force and like Napoleon who, in some respects she resembled, has been used to effect . . . I believe that she conceived her objective in the spirit of enthusiasm. In the end it obsessed her like a passion . . . she threw scruples, affections, honour, loyalty and her own principles to the wind. The movement developed her powers – ALL her powers – for good and for evil. Cruelty, ruthlessness – as you say – I should add betrayal . . . she was capable of beautiful tenderness, magnificent sense, justice and self sacrifice. These things in the course of the struggle became changed . . . she sacrificed her very soul. That is how I look at it. I hope to see you and Richard in the New Year. Much love.

In another letter she said, 'she was great in her littleness, human in her greatness, superb at moments of crisis . . .'.

Sylvia was the only Pankhurst daughter present at the unveiling, by Stanley Baldwin, of the statue on 6 March 1930. Even she had not been officially invited and was not on the platform. She sat with Richard, in the audience. Christabel was in America and Adela in Australia. But some 500 Suffragettes kept her company. Journalist Henry Brailsford wrote a eulogy. But it was Sylvia's own words that once again tugged the heartstrings. Writing in the *Star* on 'My Mother', she insisted that she would be remembered as '*the* Suffragette', not for any of the right-wing roles she later played. 'We do not make beams from the hollow, decaying trunk of the fallen oak. We use the upsoaring tree in the full vigour of its sap.'

Adela had written to her mother when Emmeline was dying and the letter pleased her greatly. Adela said she and Tom had come to believe that class warfare, labour against capital, was a dangerous idea and that they intended to found a movement for industrial peace. This they did in 1929. The aim of the

Australian Women's Guild of Empire was to combat communism, to establish industrial co-operation and peace, to uphold Christian ideals, safeguard the family and to deepen the appreciation of the value of British citizenship and Australian membership of the British Empire.

Sylvia was now to devote herself to the childhood of young Richard. He was to be her next and happiest cause; her fourth 'pillar'. Despite Silvio's constant attention and willingness to cook and shop and take over the domestic routine at which Sylvia was totally inept, life was not easy.

Sylvia, almost alone among the Pankhursts, seems to have enjoyed long-lasting friendships. Henry Harben, for instance, wrote to her at about this time. He was living in the Boulevard Malherbes in Paris and it appears that Sylvia had written to ask if he could find work for a young friend in need. He replied 'in sincere friendship and admiration', thanking her for the 'delightful letter':

> . . . it is not only your activities that interest me but the true proposition in which you set your motherhood, the optimism born of goodness and natural joy . . . Ah! How few of our women nowadays are like that! Here in Paris nearly every woman one knows (not only the smart people either) are outwardly dressed far too expensively for their husbands' means and inwardly damaged by repeated abortions; no ideals; no foyer; no God but pleasure and no religion but self . . . Your letter came like a breeze of sunny air – I was so glad and happy to receive it . . . and I wish you in the future the realisation of all that your letter sketches . . . if I can in any way contribute to helping you through your darker moments you may rely on me so far as my poor capacities go . . .

By 1928 Sylvia had a contract from Longman to write the book that became her best known work, *The Suffragette Movement*.

Between 1928 and 1930, a period of phenomenal literary output and motherly concern, Mrs Walshe, her friend from the East End, was in regular touch. The letters Sylvia wrote to her are now in the David Mitchell Collection in the Museum of London:

18 October 1928

From Red Cottage

Dear Mrs Walshe. Many thanks for the little garments for Richard; they are most useful and comfortable . . . I am glad your boy is doing well, you deserve it. Richard is making big efforts to talk . . .

By the next time she wrote, the family had moved. According to Mr Powter, the council had condemned Red Cottage for residential purposes and he and his family were re-housed. Sylvia, though she still owned the property, moved out to a three-storeyed rambling house with a large garden known as 'West Dene' in Charteris Road, on the right side of the railway line. It was just out of sight of the new, eminently respectable Monkham's Estate, but looking west towards London there were still fields, smallholdings and farms. It was a paradise for a small boy to grow up in. Sylvia wrote again in early 1929:

From West Dene, Charteris Road

Dear Mrs Walshe,

I told you, I think, I had a contract to write a book. I am in despair about my writing. Richard wakes early and keeps me on the go till eleven or so. If I can get him to sleep from then till 1p.m. it is the best I can hope for frequently – today he woke whenever I put him down and unless I put him to sleep in my arms he won't sleep at all . . . afternoon he won't sleep except if he had not slept the morning. If I do make him sleep I have more trouble at bed time. If I get him to sleep at 6p.m. I am lucky; it is more likely to be 7.30 and I have to sing to him and rock him to accomplish it . . . Some days I have managed to work between 11.30–12.30, when I have my meal and again from 8–11p.m. and once or twice from 12p.m.–1 a.m. but I can't keep that up . . . The solution is to get someone to take care of Richard part of the time regularly, so that I can count on it . . . Richard's father has been ill with sciatica so I can't count on him to help me with the boy; indeed when he is at home I get less done than when he is out! I don't want to hand my little boy over to anyone – I know how important it is he should be rightly handled . . . I think it is too much to hope that you could do it for me, even for four or five afternoons a week? . . . Actually I find myself so irritable and jaded that when I sit down to write I am often unable to find a sentence . . . yet in the old days words used to pour out without difficulty . . .

During 1930 two-year-old Richard was unwell and anxiety caused the over-protective Sylvia to collapse. She and the little boy were invited to stay with her former Suffragette friend Joan Hodgson at Eggington in Bedfordshire. While they were there, Richard became worse and the doctors insisted on a tonsil operation. Author Simon Houfe, whose grandfather, the classical architect Sir Alfred Richardson, was a friend of the family, has described their encounter with Sylvia at the time. Mrs Hodgson, at the end of her tether, didn't know how to cope with the hysterical mother who had been parted from her child. She was also fielding a barrage of questions from her own inquisitive children on the whereabouts of Richard's mystery father!

Eventually, the operation over, Mrs Hodgson telephoned Sir Alfred and invited herself, with Sylvia and the recuperating Richard, for the day:

> My grandfather responded immediately, insisted they should come at once and determined to give them a wonderful visit . . .
>
> Sylvia came over in a three-wheeler . . . she looked at the pictures and clocks, sat in the sedan chair, examined the lock of Nelson's hair, heard my grandfather read and saw him sketch . . . while the little boy played and piped under the table following with his fingers the patterns of the rich Persian carpet . . . with enormous compassion and skill he steered this shattered woman with the horsy face and projecting teeth through a whole afternoon of hope . . . when the party finally met in the cobbled courtyard before the return to Eggington there was something approaching a smile on that wan, grey face.

In July 1930 when Sylvia wrote again to Mrs Walshe inviting her to visit Woodford, she was making efforts to start a small Montessori School at West Dene. 'Most days I make a point of being free from 4pm to 6pm when Richard goes to bed . . . I seem to be terribly rushed and in arrears and I find it difficult to keep even that time free but I try to make a point of it. We are trying to start a Montessori nursery school . . . Vera Brittain is to be the Hon. Treasurer . . .'. By October the little school was open and attended by four pupils (including Fenner Brockway's daughter). Sylvia wrote again, 'Richard knows practically all his letters (capitals) and begins to have some ideas of the others and has also the idea of word building. He is very quick and has good command of his limbs.'

These early traumas seem to have settled down and the letters between Emmeline Pethick-Lawrence and Sylvia became less fraught. Emmeline wrote at Christmas in 1930: 'I was charmed with the Christmas cards from Richard. I think it is very remarkable that so young a child should be able to choose cards from so definite an idea and preference . . . All that you tell me about his development is most interesting. I like especially the story both of his feelings and his loving ways . . .'. She goes on to say that she plans to buy several copies of Sylvia's *The Suffragette Movement*, and to urge Sylvia to write her mother's biography – 'if Christabel ever writes her life it will be unutterably dull – "me and mother" stuff.' On Boxing Day 1930 Sylvia wrote again:

Dearest Emmeline,

    The spirit moves me to write to you to say that in spite of plenty of anxieties I feel a flood of happiness today. Daddie [*sic*] and Richard are in the garden. It is warm and sunny.

    Richard has not had so much as a cold this winter! He is bright and well. Instead of having the doctor like last year he was able to make Christmas presents for his friends and dress the tree . . . He stitched over a pencil drawing on paper tacked to the ribbon to make the little calendar banners. Then we tore the paper away and the red ribbon was left. He was greatly pleased.

    He looks straight and tall. His bones are straight and his thoughts are kind. He puts bread and cheese for the mouse and crumbs for the birds and milk for the cat. He brought his money box to me to buy a present for Daddy. He has his own ways and his own character . . . I gaze at him amazed, and say to myself 'where have you come from little man?' He is physically joyous as I never was . . . he loves to 'dance' and jump and climb . . .

    It is a daily marvel this new person – like no one else – himself. One realises the miracle more when one realises one bore him. I look at his father – the boy is not him – not me – new entirely. How have you – so entirely individual – sprung from us? This year when I heard the carol singers I thought so often of waiting for him at Hampstead. How wonderful it all was. How you came to make his happy arrival safe and all that one would desire. So I feel a great flood of gratitude and joy . . .

23

Uncontrollable Events

'Mussolini is a Man of Destiny who has re-created the soul of Italy.'
Viscount Rothermere, proprietor of the *Daily Mail*,
following a visit to Italy, 1 April 1928

Sylvia took motherhood very seriously. For a time she tried to run a little Montessori class in order to give Richard friends to play with. Vera Brittain[1] was one of the sponsors.

By 1931 she was exploring ideas for Richard's education and took him to the progressive boarding school Beacon Hill, run by Bertrand Russell and his wife Dora. The prospectus seemed entirely in keeping with Sylvia's educational ideas:

The three principles on which Beacon Hill is founded are the following:
1. That no knowledge of any sort should be withheld from children and young people.
2. Respect for the individual preferences and peculiarities of the child, both in work and behaviour.
3. Morality and reasoning to arise from the children's actual experience in a democratic group and never of necessity from the authority or convenience of adults.
Sex and Anatomical Training . . . involves, of course, complete frankness on the anatomical and physiological facts of sex, marriage and parenthood and the bodily functions . . . We do not expect our children to speak in hushed tones when they wish to go to the lavatory . . . Boys and girls exercise together, without clothes, when the weather permits . . .

Sylvia was offered a trial period of two months in which she stayed in a bed-sitting room at the school to see how Richard enjoyed the surroundings, but

---

1. Mother of Baroness Shirley Williams.

it is not certain that he did, in the end, become a pupil. It is difficult to see how Sylvia could have parted from the little boy by sending him to a boarding school.

Eventually, in January 1935, Richard joined the 'Salvete' (welcoming class) of a small, private local school, St Aubyns, about twenty minutes' walk from West Dene. There he was known as 'Pancake'. However overstretched with work, Sylvia always walked the little boy to and from school, in his smart maroon and navy blazer and cap with a silver badge. They told stories to each other as they went, stories that even today Richard remembers with amusement. Sylvia had intended to collect them all into a children's story-book entitled *Dogland*. The heroes were the family airedale called Jack and a deer-hound Rip, who got up to all kinds of antics, trampling plants, smashing flower pots and stealing washing from the line. Sadly, the stories never reached the publisher's desk.

Richard's early childhood was secure among the piles of books and mountains of paper created by his parents. The top floor of the house was let and there was usually a resident au pair to help with the cleaning.

Sylvia and Corio bought a goat, which they unimaginatively named 'Goatie', and the family switched to drinking goats' milk. Italian meat-eating Silvio seems to have coped with Sylvia's teetotal vegetarianism by regularly meeting friends for a steak in London. Silvio grew vegetables and still did most of the cooking (Charlotte Drake never forgot the boiled lettuce that made her ill). He taught Richard to play chess but never taught or spoke to him in Italian. So Richard read a lot and was accustomed, as was his mother as a child, to the constant flow of politically energetic callers from all around the world. Sylvia's proud belief – not shared by many parents even today – was that her son's development should not be marred by repression. 'Richard is never told "you must not do that!" He works when he wants to. He is a free baby; he should be a free man.' He could have turned out to be a monster. But he didn't; he was a rather shy, studious boy, but he liked going to the pictures at the cinema in South Woodford with his mother, although she said she couldn't cope with the violence and sometimes took him out before the end. A friend once sent him some toy soldiers for his birthday and to Sylvia's delight he put them away, unused.

Between 1930 and 1935, behind this blissful if dishevelled domesticity, Sylvia's professional life continued, like her overburdened study, to be in its accustomed state of uproar. She was contributing the usual torrent of articles to magazines and newspapers, simultaneously writing four books and doing her best to be a conscientious mother. Richard recalls how as a child he would frequently come down for breakfast to find she was at her at her desk, having worked through the night, yet still she walked with him to school. He admits now that he 'didn't enjoy school all that much' and was, on the whole, more at ease with his parents' grown-up friends rather than his contemporaries.

For Sylvia, relaxation did not exist; holidays were a concept she did not understand and 'time out' was a snatched break with friends or her son, taken only when she was too exhausted to carry on. For Richard, this was the norm; he had known nothing else and, as time passed, he became more and more involved with his parents' activities himself. Not that they were neglectful of his childish needs: Silvio read to him and encouraged his own creativity, there were Christmases with a tree and walks with the dogs in the nearby Knighton Woods.

The first, and most surprising, of the books Sylvia wrote during this period was published in 1930. It was a volume of poems translated from the nineteenth-century romantic Romanian national poet Mihail Eminescu. Sylvia had, since her art school days, nursed an interest in folk art and in particular that of Romania. She had read and was greatly impressed by Eminescu's poetry, which had already appeared in French, Italian and German. So, with the help of a dictionary and Dr I.O. Stefanovic in London, she produced an anthology of heroic verse, powerfully castigating social injustice. 'Eminescu's works are for all time,' she wrote. 'Every line of his verse and prose is a polished jewel.' It was an astonishing feat.

The Romanian scholar N. Iorga wrote the introduction and George Bernard Shaw, with whom she continued to enjoy a love–hate battle of wits, sent her a letter, which she used in facsimile, as a preface: 'Sylvia . . . you are the queerest idiot genius of this age . . . the most ungovernable, self-intoxicated, blindly and daftly, wilful little rapscallion-condottera that ever imposed itself on the infra-red end of the revolutionary spectrum as a leader . . . The translation is astonishing and outrageous. It carried me away.'

From 'Emperor and Proletarian':

> What's justice? See the mighty, behind their fortunes shielding,
> Erect their laws and edicts, to serve them as a foil . . .
> And hold in subjugation your lives of ceaseless toil.

In a more identifiably Sylvia style is 'Why Comest Not?':

> Behold the swallows quit the eaves,
> And fall the yellow walnut leaves,
> The hoar frost doth the vineyard rot
> Why comest not? Why comest not?

Mrs Petrescu described the visit in a women's magazine. The Pankhursts arrived in Constanza a day earlier than expected and at the wrong station. Their suitcases remained on the train so they were stranded on the platform with no luggage and no welcoming party. Nevertheless, Mrs Petrescu wrote of their presence as a 'pilgrimage' and was euphoric about Sylvia: 'her eyes she seemed to have borrowed from the grey of the faraway ocean, from the shores of which she had come to Romania.'

Four years later Sylvia, Corio and six-year-old Richard were invited, with other Eminescu translators, to the unveiling of his statue in Constanza, on the Black Sea.

The family travelled by train through Nazi Germany (rather than Italy, where Silvio would have been arrested). Richard remembers how his mother was in a relaxed mood, having by then completed her various books. He recalls how the police on the train were suspicious because his parents had placed a copy of *The Times* over the light to allow him to sleep. They all fell in love with the countryside of Romania, and Richard was trundled, bored and protesting, around the onion-domed and richly coloured churches. He was much more impressed with the exotic palace guards. There was an inevitable problem over diet: the little boy was used only to goats' milk and the family was vegetarian, both difficult needs in a country such as Romania.

There were also idyllic days: they took trips by horse-drawn bus, Silvio went boating in the park with Richard and, as children do regardless of any language barrier, he made friends with Arcadiu, the eight-year-old son of their host Judge Petrescu. Arcadiu is today a professor in Bucharest and treasures memories and mementoes of that holiday. He says: 'The friendship between Richard and me is one of the best feelings that I have. Sixty-eight years of correspondence interrupted only by the war.'

Needless to say, Sylvia embarked on writing a book about the country, which remained unfinished.

Her second work, *Save the Mothers*, was also published in 1930 and was again meticulously researched. It was an appeal for the reduction of the annual death rate of women in childbirth, which at that time was extremely high. Sylvia emphasized the lack of pre-natal care and instruction, covered the neglect of obstetrics in the training of doctors, proposed a £10 maternity grant and a National Maternity Service for all mothers, married or not. The book paved the way for future writers to explore the subject in greater depth and was very well received in Britain and abroad. Vera Brittain was full of praise when she wrote to Sylvia in October 1930 before reviewing the book in the *Clarion*:

I find it most absorbingly interesting and should like to compel all the world to read and re-read . . . your graphic descriptions of what, in personal terms, pregnancy, childbirth and child-rearing mean to the poor mother I have never seen repeated elsewhere . . . I am particularly glad that you have condemned the regulation which forbids mothers to enter hospital until labour has begun – I have always thought that monstrous. My last labour only took three hours and even so was purposely prolonged by my doctor by means of anaesthetics for the baby's sake; had I been going to Queen Charlotte's my daughter would probably have been born in a cab or on a bus . . .

The third work in this period was her classic, *The Suffragette Movement*. The dedication read: 'To my son Richard Keir Pethick Pankhurst this record of struggle is dedicated in the cherished hope that he may give his service to the collective work of humanity.' Published in 1931, the book has been criticized in recent years for its subjective interpretation of historical events, self-aggrandizement and over-emphasis on the Pankhurst role in the fight for the franchise. It *is* autobiographical, but it is much more than that. Its 600 pages reveal an impressive and sensitive understanding of the political and social upheavals through which Sylvia lived and in which her family undeniably played a leading part; it ends in 1918 and is not a definitive history, being frustratingly short of dates. It is a personal story, a family saga, told, as you would expect, through Sylvia's own artistic eyes, with all the passion, poetry and perception of a woman who was at the heart of it all.

Shaw was unusually flattering. He mentions Sylvia in the preface to *Saint Joan* and spoke of her in a BBC broadcast. 'Miss Sylvia Pankhurst, like so many others in the movement, was tortured. In fact, except for burning, she suffered physical torture which Joan was spared. If you read Miss Pankhurst, you will understand a great deal more about the psychology of Joan.' Prime Minister Ramsay MacDonald eventually accepted a copy of *The Suffragette Movement* for the library at 10 Downing Street, despite, as he explained, a 'shortage of space'. Adela's response was an astonishingly bitter 49-page typed, character assassination of her sister, which rests now in the Australian National Library in Canberra. It is a far more ruthless and unkind onslaught than Sylvia's picture of the Pankhursts merited. Was it perhaps because in Sylvia's efforts to appease her publisher and prune her book, she had omitted most of Adela's part in the story?

Her next book, *The Home Front*, which told 'the story of my life and time during the War years, 1914–1915–1916', was published in 1932 with a dedication to Emmeline Pethick-Lawrence, 'whose generous appreciation encouraged the penning of this record'. Bertrand Russell had declined her invitation to write a preface. On first reading, the text ricochets all over the place as though Sylvia was herself taking random pot-shots at the enemy. It is a series of very personal and highly emotional, sometimes disconnected jottings rather than a structured book. Sylvia never hid her emotions as she recalled the courage and tragedy of those terrible days.

Like so many writers, she complained incessantly about her agent, Frank C. Betts, her various publishers and her editors, and they in turn complained about her. On one occasion, to stimulate their interest, she asked her friend and helper Norah Walshe to write, asking for the date of *The Home Front* publication, on the pretext that she wished to purchase a copy. 'Please don't let them think the author suggested it . . . That would not do,' she said.

The file in the British Library marked 'Sylvia Pankhurst and the Society of Authors' catalogues an amusing exchange of correspondence between Sylvia and her long suffering literary advisers from 1930 to 1935. She was annoyed with Frank Betts for editing her copy and criticizing her style, and wrote to Mr Kilham Roberts of the Society in June 1931, 'Please give me your views as to how I should stand up to my literary agent. I find the charge of bad writing a very nasty one – I should thoroughly dislike having to defend my literary style. It is only the fact that I have written and done many things that enables me to face that at all. On the other hand I find it a mean excuse and I know it would absolutely disarm a young writer – coming from his or her own agent!'

The same month, during Sylvia's stay with Dora and Bertrand Russell, the letters came from Silvio, who had clearly taken over secretarial duties and was fighting her corner, lambasting Betts for altering her copy. There are complaints about editors commissioning articles that were rejected by their successors, complaints that publishers sent copy to the printers without showing her the final proofs, and complaints about an article by someone else that appeared under her name.

The Home Front had a bumpy ride. It was delivered to Hutchinson (late as usual) on 16 February 1932. Not surprisingly, the publishers threatened not to pay Sylvia's advance on royalties because she had concurrently taken out a libel action against them. One of their authors, Cecil Bishop, late of the CID, had written a book claiming that Sylvia had planned to kidnap the Prince of Wales. Walter Hutchinson then decided that her own book could be libellous, so she wrote in despair to the Society, 'I regret having to appeal to you so frequently in legal difficulties. They are not of my seeking. Indeed they are to

me most distressing and destructive of the tranquillity required for my work.'
She won her action and was awarded £300 damages and costs.

When the book was finally published, she was in turn entangled in a legal action that resurrected the memory of twenty years before. Mrs Hercbergova, former manager of the Toy Factory, objected to references in *The Home Front* about her alleged lack of experience and financial capabilities. There was yet another battery of lengthy letters between Sylvia, at her wits' end with worry over Silvio's health, and her solicitors, Carter and Bell. One of these from E.A. Bell ends in exasperation: 'I am very much pressed next week so I ask you to relieve me from further correspondence.'

There was a positive aspect to the case, however, for Sylvia, who of course had kept no supporting records or evidence of any sort, re-established contact with Norah Smyth, then living in Florence. Norah replied with copies of the Toy Factory minutes and excerpts from her own diary, which furnished the solicitors with all the necessary information. She wrote to Sylvia: 'I spent all yesterday morning going through my diaries and certainly it was painful reading: what a hell we went through!' The information revealed in the astonishingly efficient records proved the extent of Norah's generosity and personal sacrifice to Sylvia's campaigns over the years. She had sold her furniture, her jewellery and her shares, and reminded Sylvia, 'I think you might make the point that while H was getting £3 a week you were living on bread and margarine and coffee and working at least 14 hours a day.'

It is clear from these letters between the old friends that both Sylvia and Silvio were unwell, presumably from overwork and worry. Sylvia had headaches and was having all her teeth removed. Silvio was suffering from skin eruptions. Norah advised, 'he ought to take a bath in some very strong disinfectant . . . A doctor's wife had carbuncles all over her back and she cured herself at once with it. The other thing they do is inject a drop of pure carbolic . . . Dr Tumblesome in Great Portland Street told my sister . . . Garlic is very good too, tied on; they cured Tommies in Mesopotamia with it, but they were boils.'

Later, during 1935, there were problems with T. Werner Laurie Ltd, who had commissioned a short 40,000-word biography of her mother. But 'short' was not a word Sylvia understood. She sent them two versions – one was 40,000 as requested but the second, much better, ran to 80,000 words.

In addition to the books there were articles, dozens of them, some published, some not. There were far-sighted essays on topics such as oil, predicting, some fifty years ahead of time, the oil-wars of the future; and there were hundreds of letters to editors on everything from country dancing to mixed-sex meal times at Oxford. They are all stored together amongst the Pankhurst Papers, along with numerous demands from frustrated local firms for unpaid bills. No wonder she had headaches and Silvio was unwell.

By this time Sylvia was also writing of her own disillusion with the Bolshevik movement in Russia, which she felt had departed from its original idealism. There, under Stalin, a cruel dictatorship was emerging. The purges of political opponents had begun with the exile or imprisonment of thousands of people. It was not, however, events in Europe that would give Sylvia's life a new direction and lead her towards a new cause. Her future lay in Africa and to what is considered by many historians her finest hour.

Abyssinia (Ethiopia) was the most ancient independent black country in Africa. It had embraced Christianity long before St Augustine came to Britain and successive civilizations had constructed magnificent temples and cities. Backward as it largely was in 1930, peopled by warring tribes of mixed religions, it was nevertheless a hugely important and emotional symbol for black people around the world.

On 2 November 1930 the 41-year-old Ras Tafari was crowned Emperor Haile Selassie, Elect of God, Conquering Lion of the Tribes of Judah, King of Zion, King of Kings, Emperor of Ethiopia, Chevalier Sans Peur et Sans Reproche and Epitome of True Nobility. Addis Ababa, the capital, thronged with thousands of exotic, spear-carrying tribesmen and foreign dignitaries, including the Duke of Gloucester from Britain. Haile Selassie had achieved many reforms since becoming Regent in 1924, but there was far to go.

In Italy, Benito Mussolini, in his black shirt and white spats, had somehow worked his way through the system to become his country's leader. In the years between 1920 and 1930, he had picked Italy up from the previous chaos of constantly changing governments and prime ministers. By 1924 he was in complete control. To the tourists who still flocked to enjoy the antiquities, he had performed miracles: trains ran on time, the Roman Forum was excavated and there was a huge, ongoing programme of public works. What they did not see (but Sylvia did) was the suppression of free speech and the disappearance of those in opposition to the Blackshirts.

In Britain, Oswald Mosley, who had been Chancellor of the Duchy of Lancaster under Ramsay MacDonald, stormed out of the government and was replaced by the moderate Major Clement Attlee in 1930. Mosley then formed the New Party, 'of vitality and manhood', dedicated to a complete revision of the British Parliament. By 1932 this was known as the British Union of Fascists and was attracting rallies of up to 10,000 people on Sylvia's former 'home ground' in the East End.

Sylvia and Silvio now shared a mission. Sylvia may have had the higher profile and been more widely known, but according to friends who knew them at this time, Silvio was 'a brilliant political observer'. Like Sylvia, he was usually 'several jumps ahead and always accurate in his analysis of latest developments'. Ethiopia was surrounded by Italian colonies blocking her access to the sea. They could see the long-term threat of the land hungry Italian dictator and warned that his increasing power would lead to war.

Many people in Britain appeared ready to accept Mussolini and later even Hitler as modernizing reformers. Churchill had admitted he was 'charmed' by Mussolini. It was also convenient for British and French Governments to ignore the persecutions and torture practised by their regimes. By 1923 Mussolini had become Il Duce. Ambitious and envious of the colonial success of Britain and France in Africa, his thoughts turned to Ethiopia, which he judged available for the taking.

Despite the fact that Ethiopia had been a member of the League of Nations since 1924, the British government was prepared to abrogate its responsibilities and shut its eyes to the country's plight. The Italians were ready to pounce and so it was that Ethiopia, wild, remote and virtually unknown to the British, became significant in world history. But the warrior Sylvia was in no mood for what she saw as vacillation and weakness.

In 1932 she formed the Women's International Matteotti Committee (WIMC), to draw attention to the persecution by the Italian Fascists of Giacomo Matteotti's widow Velia and her children. Her initial aim was to bring them to England. However, the plight of the Matteotti family became for her a symbol of the much wider struggle.

From now until the end of her life, Sylvia devoted her still phenomenal energy to the fight against fascism and in particular to the future of the people of Ethiopia. Some of the old familiar names are to be found supporting her on that committee: Charlotte Drake was there, as was Harriot Stanton Blatch, but there were some new and illustrious additions, such as Dora, wife of Bertrand Russell.

The international petition Sylvia drafted was one of the first and most strongly worded warnings of the dangers of fascism. She stood apart from other commentators in her realization that this was a racist and anti-Semitic ideology. She had fought such tyranny all her life. This was no time to stop. She referred to the 'crowning outrage of a dictatorship excelling in terrorism and oppression'. Those who signed her petition included Bertrand Russell, George Lansbury, Emmeline Pethick-Lawrence, Harold and Frida Laski and Henry

Nevinson. One of those who declined was George Bernard Shaw. The drafting of the WIMC petition resulted in trenchant and often amusing exchanges between Sylvia and her old adversary. He wrote:

> What the memorialists, including your incorrigible pugnacious self, are doing, is making an attack on the fascist regime in Italy, under cover of sympathy with the distressed widow and her orphans. Obviously the effect will be to irritate the Fascists . . . If you want to soften the Fascist Government, you must accept at least that it is a Government and approach it as a friend, and assuming its desire to be just and humane . . .
>
> But if you do not care a rap . . . then go ahead by all means and pile on the agony . . . only you must not expect me to sign it . . . you cannot cure nations – least of all the English Nation – of the vice of lecturing other nations on their moral inferiority. Nor shall I cure you.

Sylvia responded:

> . . . I take exception to your argument about the vice of the English lecturing other nations, for the simple reason that I do not recognise nationality at all in this matter. It is a question of ideas and ideals you know . . . and everyone else knows that I should be just as eager to do this for Mrs Matteotti if she happened to be English or . . . a native of Ireland, India, Egypt or any other nation under British rule.

She then went on, in a very long letter, to explain the nature of fascism:

> . . . a manifestation of capitalism which it creates when it finds itself in difficulties, to protect itself from the rising power of the workers . . . Italian fascism is simply a capitalist dictatorship . . .
>
> Viewing all this . . . I see the Italian situation as one of the phenomena which have developed in this transition period which, in a book I am writing now, I have called 'The Red Twilight.'

She finished by reminding Shaw that were he Italian, he would be one of Mussolini's victims. The reply, on a postcard, was robust. 'No: you can't bully me; and you can't even bully Mussolini . . . I know perfectly (human error excepted) what I am about.' So did Sylvia. With her domestic financial problems almost eclipsing the international storm clouds, she had already astutely auctioned all Shaw's previous correspondence with her.

In October 1932 the WIMC published a broadsheet, *Humanity*, carrying Matteotti's own words on the day of his death in 1924: 'You can kill me but you cannot kill the thought within me.'

There was immediate support from anti-fascist academics and organizations around Europe as Sylvia, launching an onslaught on anyone with influence, embarked on what she was best at: lobbying, ear-bending and correspondence. Once again the letters from E. Sylvia Pankhurst began to arrive, often written in green ink, on paper torn from exercise books. Embassies, politicians and editors – she drove them all to distraction. But there is no doubt that ultimately her efforts were recognized and not in vain.

One of her first major successes, for instance, was the sending of aid by a very devious route to the suffering Italian detainees on the penal island of Ponza. Many of those who had befriended Velia were dying there from conditions such as appendicitis and diphtheria, simply because there were no medical facilities and no surgical instruments.

During the summer of 1933, Sylvia and Silvio planned an International Day of Protest in support of all victims of Italian fascism. The purpose of the event was an attempt to bring the dangers to the notice of a blinkered British public. Sylvia achieved considerable support, especially from overseas. The *Manchester Guardian* ran a feature that quoted her words extensively, and her appeal was also published in Switzerland, America, Spain and Sweden. Although the work of the WIMC continued until 1935, Sylvia's efforts were rewarded in September 1933 when Signora Matteotti was finally released and taken into the care of the church.

By 1934 Germany, under its new Chancellor, Adolph Hitler, was defying the terms of the Treaty of Versailles after World War I by re-arming at an alarming rate and had introduced conscription. At this stage King George V, a very conscientious and well-meaning king, intervened personally to warn the Germans of the danger they were creating. The forthright King George V talked bluntly to the German ambassador about the threat his country posed. He urged that the British Government should not be blinded by the 'apparent sweet reasonableness' of the Germans. His Majesty and Sylvia spoke with one voice.

Then in November 1934 an Italian army attacked an Ethiopian force at Welwel, a post in the Ogaden, 100 kilometres inland. Surrounded as it was by Italian Eritrea and the three Somalias (British, French and Italian), the Ogaden gave land-locked Ethiopia vital trading access to the Red Sea and the Indian Ocean. Any resistance was crushed with planes and tanks. The British public was outraged by this flagrant breach of the League of Nations principles, but the governments of both Britain and France declared themselves neutral. A few concerned supporters in London formed the Abyssinia Association to which, for a short time, Sylvia belonged.

In 1935 Sylvia heard, to her astonishment, that George Bernard Shaw had apparently performed another of his acrobatic tricks and become a member of the International Committee of Writers against Fascism. She wrote, reminding him of all the letters he had sent to her, supporting dictators: 'When Hitler rose to power . . . I pleaded with you that, at last, you would declare against this evil and reactionary movement . . . Well, better late than never; I rejoice that you . . . have seen through the hugest sham ever offered to a credulous world!'

But it was not so. Shaw's somewhat unlikely explanation was that he had accepted nomination to the committee without realizing it was anti-fascist! He withdrew immediately. He then went on to accuse Sylvia of getting it all out of proportion: '. . . when the murder of Matteotti leaves me as unmoved politically as the liquidation of the Czar, you write and tell me that I have changed my opinions, which is exactly what I have not done. If I changed my opinions at every assassination I should have no opinions at all. Give your mind seriously to this, Sylvia, for you are much given to shrieking. For instance, you never approach me except to shriek at me. Don't.'

Ramsay MacDonald retired in 1935, to be succeeded as Prime Minister by Stanley Baldwin, who was to play a sensitive and skilful role during the scandal of the abdication of Edward VIII in 1936. This engrossed the British public rather more than the antics of Mussolini.

On 17 April 1935 the *Woodford Times* had reproduced a letter from Sylvia to her MP, Winston Churchill, urging the imposition of sanctions on Italy. 'Horror has been piled on horror,' she wrote, 'in the atrocious campaign, without any effective step being taken by this Government or the League . . . I ask you to make an effective protest in the House of Commons.' Churchill's response, published on 24 April (but dated 19 April), was in brief, non-committal tone. Not satisfied, Sylvia accused him and everyone else of cowardly dealing with both Mussolini and Hitler. 'Malice, weakness and folly have produced the greatest betrayal of history,' she warned. 'Had fascist aggression in Africa been firmly checked at the start, the world would present a very different picture today.'

Until 1935 the Pankhurst–Corio anti-fascist campaign had been conducted from afar. Silvio, of course, had friends and colleagues in Italy, but they had no personal links with Ethiopia and had never met Haile Selassie. Then events came to a head, dramatically changing the situation.

In October 1935, as threatened, Italian troops invaded Ethiopia. Sylvia and Silvio swung into action. They again called for the League of Nations to introduce sanctions against Italy – an embargo on oil and the closing of the Suez Canal to Italian ships – as a means of preventing the spread of Italian ambition. This was now their war. Sylvia launched a tirade of letters to the press – both left and right wing. She also spoke at many pro-League of Nations meetings denouncing the use of mustard gas, the bombing of International Red Cross hospitals and the failure of the League to enforce realistic sanctions. When all this frenetic action appeared to produce no results, she reverted to her normal line of attack. She started a newspaper. The Ethiopian Legation was unwilling to support her and so Sylvia went ahead independently.

The first issue of the *New Times and Ethiopia News* came out on Sylvia's birthday (5 May 1936), although it bore the date of 9 May. It was published by the Walthamstow Press, then advertising itself as 'the most modern of London suburban printing works'.

Life at West Dene had blown itself into a hurricane. There was now a staff working flat out. Two secretaries took non-stop dictation from Sylvia, while a team of voluntary workers occupied the rest of the house, frantically addressing and stuffing envelopes. More and more colourful personalities from all over the world streamed through the house. The young African leader Jomo Kenyatta, resplendent in his robes, came down on the steam train. Dr Harold Moody, much loved founder of the League of Coloured Peoples and one of the first black doctors in Britain, was also a visitor. Woodford had never known anything like the goings-on in Charteris Road. On one occasion the police were called.

The *New Times* was a very professional, well-produced paper whose stature became greatly respected. Its articles were wide ranging, covering such subjects as 'How Hitler Rose to Power' to 'Africa for the Africans'. It was read not only in Britain but also by black Americans and in the West Indies. Every week Sylvia managed to produce a lengthy editorial, revealing an impressive grasp of events and, almost as a sideline, advertised fund-raising jumble sales and garden parties at Red Cottage. The newspaper was sometimes published in the Emperor's own language, Amharic, and smuggled to the Ethiopian resistance. The first issue declared: 'The cause of Ethiopia cannot be divided from the cause of International justice.'

Significantly, at a public meeting at the Royal Forest Hotel in Chingford on 15 May 1936 Churchill finally attacked the Government's 'zig-zag' policy and in particular Stanley Baldwin's conflicting statements: 'Sanctions mean war' (1934) and 'Sanctions – but without war' (1935). For once, he and Sylvia were of one mind when he expressed outrage at the short-sighted policies of the previous years in relation to the 'sinister and uncontrollable events' in Europe.

24

No Peace in their Time

'The flowers piled high before 10 Downing Street are very fitting for the funeral of British honour.'

Professor Lucas, *New Times and Ethiopia News*

Three days before the Italian troops reached Addis Ababa, Haile Selassie and his family were forced to flee. The Emperor left the capital on 2 May 1936 and sailed in a British warship, first to rest in Jerusalem and later, to Sylvia's disgust, incognito in a private steamer to exile in England. He had, in true Ethiopian royal tradition, been in the thick of the battle and even wielded a machine gun at the head of the Palace Guard, but judged that he would be better able to help his country from the safety of Britain.

The British press was curious and on the whole kind, apart from the *Daily Mail*, the *Morning Post* and the *Observer*, who backed Italy. The public loved the little Emperor (he was only 5ft tall). The *Sunday Referee* ran a lengthy article titled 'The Man of the Week', describing him as 'cosmopolitan, shrewd, tenacious, brave', and observing that, 'He takes money from the Japanese, munitions from the French, advice from the British.' But the establishment was wary and in disarray: to treat their visitor as royalty could upset Italy and drive her even closer to Germany; to show disrespect to the Emperor could be bad for British interests in Africa.

For Sylvia, ever the champion of the underdog, the Emperor, descended as Ethiopian legend claims from King Solomon and the Queen of Sheba, was in need of a champion. He became her personal responsibility. Although she appeared at times in awe and somewhat overwhelmed (the photographs of the two of them show her, unusually, beaming happily), she never really saw him as a monarch on a gilded throne. She told him that she had not rallied to his cause because he was an Emperor but because his cause was just. Paramount to her was the future of the people he represented and consequently the future of Africa and so the world.

Sylvia was far ahead of the times. Haile Selassie was, after all, black. Most people in Britain still considered the Anglo-Saxon colonial system to be a magnanimous and generous benefactor to such uncivilized and less enlightened races.

It was she, not King Edward VIII or Prime Minister Stanley Baldwin, who stood on the platform of Victoria Station on 3 June 1936 to greet the Emperor and his family when they arrived. Photographs in the newspapers show thousands of banner-waving people who had waited for hours lining the nearby streets to greet him, although the Foreign Office diverted his route in order to avoid them. The Dean of Winchester was there, with representatives of many African organizations in their exotic costumes, and Sylvia produced a commemorative edition of the *New Times and Ethiopia News* on yellow paper.

Haile Selassie went immediately to appear before the League of Nations to appeal for their support. 'What answer am I to take back?' he asked. 'God and history will remember your decision.' The League did nothing.

A month later, on a bright summer day in July, R.P. Zaphiro, Secretary of the Imperial Ethiopian Legation, unveiled an unusual monument on the land in front of Sylvia's Red Cottage. It was a stone bomb. Recalling the Zeppelin raids over the East End during World War I, the British bombing of rebels in Burma and North West India in 1932 and the recent mustard gas bombings of Ethiopian civilians by the Italians, the message on the plinth ironically proclaimed: 'To those who in 1932 upheld the right to use bombing aeroplanes this monument is raised as a protest against war in the air.' An article in the *New Times* explained: 'There are thousands of memorials in every town and village to the dead but not one as a reminder of the danger of future wars. The purpose of the monument was to create a lasting reproach to those whose morality was untouched, whose consciences were unmoved and whose emotions were unaffected.'

Sylvia's apparent obsession with matters foreign at this time has been questioned by some historians. Why, for instance, did she appear to abandon her East Enders during the terrible economic Depression? The Depression, which had struck so hard in the industrial areas of Britain, did not affect the south-east quite so badly. Desperate men went on hunger marches all over the country and there was stone throwing and despair. But around London the huge amount of building brought some increased employment. George Lansbury, active still, was the Minister of Works and made himself immensely popular amidst the gloom by building outdoor restaurants and introducing mixed bathing in Hyde Park and at 'Lansbury's Lido' on the river frontage of the Tower of London.

In Woodford the fields and pastureland through which Sylvia, Silvio and Richard had been so happy to wander were fast disappearing beneath smart estates of houses named 'Innisfree' and 'Dunroamin'. East Enders themselves were becoming 'plotholders', buying tiny parcels of land carved from the gardens of the wealthy and erecting shacks on them for weekending and holidays. The cinema had not long been built and there was a sharp contrast with the misery of the industrial north and mining communities.

Although Sylvia's attention may now have been focused on international events, she never lost touch with her past. Her artistic spirit may have been refreshed by the surroundings of Woodford, but her son recalls how through all his childhood West Dene was home to a continual stream of both foreign refugees pouring in from fascist-stricken Europe and elderly Suffragettes and East End women; some were friends ever ready to help, others were themselves in need. Many recorded their impressions later of this shabby, indomitable bulldog of a woman, ageing now but still battering her victims for hours on the telephone. Her post bag was enormous; there were letters from mothers whose husbands had left them, women seeking affiliation orders, widows with pension problems and always the unemployed. She was a willing agony aunt, a one-woman Citizens' Advice Bureau and an adoring mother herself. There was not a moment to spare.

As far back as 1920, the *Workers' Dreadnought* had also been one of the first to spotlight racial inequality in South Africa. Even then, Sylvia and Silvio ran a regular and widely respected column, 'Africa for the Africans', which was reprinted in some of the most influential African papers. The *New Times and Ethiopia News* carried reports of momentous happenings all round the world, although it was never intended as a vehicle for international news. Despite Foreign Office denials, its circulation was around 10,000 copies weekly and eventually achieved a peak of 40,000. The standard of its journalism was high and the focus was Ethiopia.

Haile Selassie was revered throughout Africa and the black world. In the British West Indies the Rastafarians even believe him to be God and that Jesus was Black. He was admittedly an autocrat but he was also a reformer who had introduced a constitution and a parliament and had established a criminal code for the first time. Ethiopia 'was, and is,' says Mary Davis, 'an expression of black pride and identity'. There was still a great deal to be achieved but Haile Selassie was supervising a remarkable renaissance.

Throughout his five-year exile in Britain, the Emperor maintained a lonely and, it was always agreed, dignified position. Occasional holidays would be spent in a small Sussex hotel on the Worthing seafront, where visitors spotted him from time to time gazing out to sea from his window. He was also given the use of a house in Kensington owned by Francis Beaufort-Palmer, Honorary Secretary of the Abyssinia Association, and his wife. But his presence in the country was, nevertheless, an embarrassment to the government, and he soon found himself tucked out of harm's way and living in the genteel elegance of Bath. The King had refused to invite him to Buckingham Palace, and when he took tea at the Palace of Westminster, the Prime Minister was nowhere to be seen. No wonder that Sylvia's prolonged propaganda on his behalf was unpopular with the government. She knew only too well that persistence was the only possible way to get what she wanted.

The newly formed Abyssinia Association, which flourishes today as the Anglo-Ethiopian Society, was chiefly a support and fund-raising body but was reluctant to become involved in anti-fascist politics. For a time Sylvia had been a member, until her customary impatience with all officials and her relentless energy ruffled the rather formal feathers of many members. When, inevitably, Sylvia and the Association parted company and Sylvia was 'on the road' reporting or lecturing, Francis Beaufort-Palmer occasionally helped Silvio to run the *New Times*. The two men got on well and the Beaufort-Palmers were full of admiration for him and his extraordinary devotion to Sylvia.

Once the Emperor was established in Britain and it appeared (not to Sylvia of course) that the military situation in Ethiopia had settled down, the British government was inclined to side with Italy, to abandon sanctions and, in 1938, even recognized the Italian 'conquest'. In Sylvia's view this was outrageous; she became even more active and her newspaper, now subtitled 'The National Anti-Fascist Weekly', became even more explicit. She was convinced, not without reason, that Ethiopia did not represent the limit of Mussolini's ambitions to build a new Roman Empire.

Sylvia made frequent visits to Bath. At first the Emperor and his retinue stayed at the Spa Hotel, from where he embarked on an indefatigable programme of sightseeing. He was a familiar figure in the town, striding in his knee-length cape (black in winter, white in summer) and his homburg or trilby hat. He even bought a cap. Local people responded to him because he liked dogs and children and raised his hat when greeted. According to Lutz Haber, who has written a study of Haile Selassie's time in the city, they loved his 'dignified affability and exotic charm'.

When Sylvia visited him she found him living in a six-bedroom Georgian mansion, 'Fairfield', with extensive servants' quarters and just over two acres of garden. The Foreign Office had persuaded the Italians to ship out the

Imperial Regalia, clothes and furniture from storage, and so the rather faded old house was strangely transformed into an Ethiopian palace. At that stage he had cash, plate and jewellery worth around £650,000 (in the values of 2003), but according to Lutz Haber, it 'just melted away' on opulent living and travel, although a great deal went on supporting other Ethiopian refugees. The Emperor was soon in severe financial trouble and he began, literally, to sell the family silver. The local authorities tried to ease his pain by waiving payment for rates and electricity. Even the coal merchant 'forgot' to charge. There seems to be no question, as has been suggested, that the Emperor was personally subsidizing the *New Times* or Sylvia herself. He needed every penny he could muster for himself.

The Emperor's command of English was passable but he spoke fluent French and Italian, and besides, there was always an interpreter on hand; communication was not difficult. As Sylvia and he strolled in the grounds, they discussed Sylvia's activities and future plans: on one occasion when Richard was with her, the little boy took pictures on his box Brownie camera. Sylvia and the Emperor were never as personally close as has been alleged, nor was he the 'father figure' that he certainly was to his subjects. He was sometimes critical of her lack of diplomacy, although always grateful for her determination. Mutual appreciation is, perhaps, a better description of their relationship.

The Emperor did not forget his debt to the people of Bath and later, when he had returned home, he asked to be kept in touch. On his return to Addis Ababa in 1941 he renamed one of his palaces at Harar 'Fairfield' and in 1958 he gave the villa to the people of Bath. It is now, appropriately, a thriving Multi-Ethnic Community Centre with a plaque by the door which says in English and in Amharic: 'During the years 1936–41 of exile from his beloved country Ethiopia, occupied by forces of aggression, His Imperial Majesty Haile Selassie I Emperor of Ethiopia resided in Bath in this villa. In memory of his residence and in appreciation of the warm and courteous hospitality of the people of Bath, his Imperial Majesty has donated Fairfield Villa to the Corporation of Bath to serve as a home for the aged. May 1958.'

Sylvia and Silvio had established an exceptional network of reliable correspondents in Ethiopia that was useful to the Ethiopian Legation, which had a weak information service. She also kept a close watch on the writings of British journalists sent to Ethiopia and commented on their reports in her paper. Silvio was writing, editing, dealing with the production and making regular fact-finding journeys to London. Sometimes he took young Richard to watch the paper rolling off the presses in Walthamstow where the Managing

Director, H.V. Wiles, was becoming increasingly anxious about the effect on his own reputation of this *enfant terrible*.

Sylvia became friendly with the Emperor's youngest daughter, the Princess Tsahai, who unlike her father spoke good English. She was a gregarious 18-year-old when Sylvia first met her, training as a nurse at Great Ormond Street Children's Hospital. There she often worked in conditions that were a far cry from the splendour of her Palace home in Addis Ababa, but she was very popular, swam with her colleagues, went dancing and spent much time helping her father. The Matron, Dorothy A. Lane, said that Haile Selassie inspected the hospital before his daughter's admission. 'We did not realize until afterwards what it must have cost him to give his consent, for his daughter was the first Ethiopian woman to take up nursing and she was a princess.' After qualifying, the Princess worked at Guy's Hospital.

Sylvia was also greatly helped by her friendship with Haile Selassie's Ambassador in Britain, Dr Ajaz Martin, who wrote a weekly article for the newspaper. She hung his portrait on the wall of her over-cluttered study in West Dene and he was soon writing enthusiastically to her 'you are very precious my darling'.

By 1936 the spread of fascism had become a major international issue. In July, General Francisco Franco instigated a right-wing revolt to overthrow the Republican Spanish government. Even so, the British public was more concerned over the death of George V in January and the drama of the new King Edward VIII's love affair and threatened abdication.

Churchill's warning 'We are entering a corridor of deepening and darkening danger' fell on deaf ears. Most people saw Hitler as a reformer who had abolished unemployment and built superb autobahns for travellers enjoying the growing pleasure of motoring. They did not know yet about the existence of concentration camps. It took the Spanish Civil War to awaken the public consciousness to what was really happening on their doorstep. Franco appealed to Germany and Italy for help but Britain stepped in to propose a Non-Intervention Pact. At first Hitler, Mussolini and Stalin accepted the pact, but then they ignored it and sent troops and weapons to Spain. Idealistic young men poured in from all over the world willing to give their lives to stop the spread of fascism. Five hundred Britons and 900 Americans died there.

Sylvia was once again, as in the Suffragette days, taking part in mass rallies, organizing fund-raising garden parties in Woodford and putting out anti-fascist propaganda. She was hit by a stone at the infamous Battle of Cable Street in Whitechapel on 4 October 1936 as 100,000 anti-fascists rallied and blocked the street entrance with an overturned lorry. They were determined to prevent a march by 2000 Blackshirts led by Mosley himself. They succeeded and Mosley was forced to abandon his demonstration.

Sylvia had become a national institution by now. But, also, just as they had always done, her overpowering manner and inability to play second fiddle caused considerable irritation, even amongst those she was trying to help. They were often embarrassed by her methods and her sensational exposures of Italian atrocities. Never one to hold back, Sylvia set about publishing lurid photographs in her newspaper – mutilated bodies, severed heads, anything to catch her readers' attention. If the stuffed shirts in authority were upset, so be it.

Meanwhile, the Ethiopian resistance movement fought on unaided, and yet all through the early part of 1939, the government continued to extend Anglo-Italian Trade Treaties along the East African Coast as though nothing was happening. Sylvia was angry that the Italians, as she claimed, were hijacking black Somali soldiers from the British Colony and recruiting them into their army. In July 1939 she asked the Foreign Office if the 300 Somalis who had been sent home from the Italian army in Ethiopia had been repatriated because they were ill or disaffected. Lord Halifax replied, 'categorically', no, they had volunteered for service originally and had been sent back when their true nationality was discovered. But that was not good enough for Sylvia, who produced a report from a new source claiming that recruitment by the Italians was actively in progress. A Parliamentary question was answered weakly by the statement that the drift of British nationals into the Italian army was natural due to the higher wages being paid.

Long ago, in the Keir Hardie days before World War I, Sylvia's pacifism had put her on a collision course with the government and with her mother and sister. She and Hardie had warned of the danger of war in Europe ten years before it materialized and she was vehemently against the reasons and motives for that war. But by the late 1930s, for the first time in her life she was on Churchill's side, feeling that the mistakes of the last twenty years had made war inevitable. She saw the tragedy ahead as one of ideology rather than economics.

In September 1938 Neville Chamberlain, who had already had two meetings with Hitler, returned from a third in Munich promising 'peace in our time'. The infamous 'scrap of paper' had handed half of Czechoslovakia to Germany in return for Hitler's signature on a document expressing 'the desire of our two peoples never to go to war with one another again'. Only the day before, Hitler and Mussolini had agreed that war with Britain was inevitable.

The public was near hysterical with relief, while Sylvia and Silvio condemned that journey with the headline 'The Basest Day in British History', and one of her contributors wrote, 'The flowers piled before 10 Downing Street are very fitting for the funeral of British honour.'

In 1939 events came to a head. First, the Spanish Civil War ended when General Franco took Madrid and clamped a dictatorship on his country. The way was then clear for Germany and Italy to move inexorably towards their goal of European domination, as forecast by Churchill's 'sinister and uncontrollable events'. Both Churchill and Sylvia had excellent services feeding them inside information and were again loud and united in their protests at what they judged to be not appeasement, but the inertia of the government.

On 1 September, Hitler invaded Poland. Everything Sylvia had forecast was coming to pass and, as Martin Pugh has said, she 'had grounds for believing she was working with the grain of history'. On 2 September the *New Times* headline protested 'Fascism is the Enemy. Absurd to Stay Neutral.' Sylvia's editorial lamented, 'We regret to find the old Manchester Guardian, which has often broken a lance for freedom, wooing the Italian dictator, with compliments, to what it describes as his "shrewdness and Italian fineness of perception". His is the fineness of the stiletto, in our opinion.' Mussolini now rated Sylvia's activities highly enough to encourage articles about her in the Italian press and her name was added to those on Hitler's list to be arrested when he occupied Britain.

On 3 September, Chamberlain told the nation over the radio that we were at war with Germany. But not, to Sylvia's dismay, with Italy. With her usual wide ranging view of the world scene, she added President Roosevelt to her mailing list. She advised him to start an economic boycott of Japan to put the brakes on fascist infiltration into China. Then, in a 3000-word flourish she resigned as Vice-President of the London Federation of Peace Councils, with a letter to Stalin denouncing the non-aggression truce he had just signed with Hitler and Mussolini.

In Wales, on a camping holiday with sixty boys from his son's school, the Emperor Haile Selassie was sleeping rough in a small tent. And in Woodford the children were already excitedly helping their parents to stuff sandbags.

25

The Lion Roars

'You will share my joy at re-entering my capital. Your unceasing efforts and support in the just cause of Ethiopia will never be forgotten by myself or my people.'

Cable from Emperor Haile Selassie to Sylvia Pankhurst, 17 May 1941

Like so many parents in 1939, Sylvia was suffering agonies of conscience about her child's welfare. In January 1936, at the age of nine, he had set off for 'big school'. Originally, Sylvia had selected the respected Chigwell School for Boys, a train ride away. But in 1938 Richard had transferred from there to Bancroft's School, on Woodford Green, in those days for boys only, too. At Bancroft's he became 'Pank', with his sleek dark hair, serious demeanour and horn-rimmed spectacles. This in itself would have set him slightly apart, and any additional 'eccentricities', such as the fact that he (quite sensibly) took a bottle of water to school for lunch, 'which he drank surreptitiously through a straw', would have been jumped on by the other boys as 'odd'.[1] Richard was the kind of boy who could well have been bullied but curiously enough he wasn't.

Emmeline Pethick-Lawrence had expressed surprise about his mathematical skill in a letter to Sylvia when he was only five years old: 'His craze for numbers is extraordinary. I do not count that among the Pankhursts' "many and great gifts".'

One of his fellow pupils at Bancroft's and later a friend at the London School of Economics was Basil Taylor, who after the war became a regular visitor to West Dene. Basil recalls that the boys at school were largely unaware of 'Pank's' mother's activities or the family notoriety. 'There was one occasion when he brought an excuse note to be let off rugger and the fact that it was signed simply "his father" did cause comment. But on the whole we didn't talk

---

1. For some reason pupils were not allowed drinking water at lunchtime.

about such things – he would only have been given a hard time if he had done something wrong himself.'

At first there was little land action in the war, almost a sense of paralysis – a time known as the 'phoney war'. The Germans, who were outnumbered, hoped that Britain and France would back out of the war; the French, who had bitter memories of the trenches in World War I, did nothing and prevented the British from bombing the Rhur for fear of reprisals. British ships were already being sunk by U-boats and Churchill was brought in as First Lord of the Admiralty.

In the spring of 1940 Hitler invaded Norway and Denmark. In May it was the turn of Holland, Belgium and Luxembourg, and Neville Chamberlain, who had clung to office despite growing unpopularity, was deposed. King George VI sent for Churchill to replace him as Prime Minister of a coalition government.

While keenly trying to prevent Italy from entering the war as well, Churchill wrote: 'Down all the ages, above all the calls, comes the cry that the joint heirs of Latin and Christian civilisation must not be ranged against each other in mortal strife.' It seems appropriate that today a fierce bronze statue of Churchill looms over the eastern edge of Woodford Green and that not far away to the west is Sylvia's Bomb, warning against the dangers of war in the air. Between them the Cricket Club still plays peacefully on a Saturday afternoon.

The first bomb fell on Woodford in August 1940. Over 3 million people escaped from London to safer areas, and many children were evacuated to the country or even abroad. Sylvia had an invitation for Richard from friends in Canada, but the idea of parting caused her enormous distress and at such times of turmoil she still turned for counsel to Emmeline Pethick-Lawrence. Emmeline wrote to her in July 1940:

Darling Sylvia,

Your letter brought you very close. What a darling boy and how clever to make those bunks so that you can both sleep at night and be ready for the next day's work! That is the spirit that is unconquerable. As for the question of letting Richard go to Canada or the United States, I not only would not give any opinion but I have no opinion. It is such a very personal question. I do not even know whether you and Richard could live in any happiness apart from each other. It is a very serious decision; if you come to any decisive resolution, make up your mind finally that whatever happens you will never reproach yourself or vainly regret having taken the course. One must consider once for all to act for the best and leave it at that.

You and Richard can never be parted in the inner and spiritual reality. Your two lives are mentally and morally and spiritually interwoven. My conviction adds 'for ever'. The veil of the senses wears thin . . . You, as an artist should understand that. The materials of paint and clay and print are not the vision, but only serve to express it.

You ask what I 'think of it all'. I think the unconquered mind is the citadel. If the people could indeed cast out fear, the forces against us could inflict great suffering but not defeat. Civilians should make the behaviour of the BEF waiting on the beaches of Dunkirk their standard.

I admit that where the safety of beloved children is concerned that attitude is almost superhuman.

Her letter, richly philosophical but hopeful for the long-term future, continues for several pages, concluding: 'My love to you and Richard. His garden on the verandah [sic] still thrives and grows. His calendar hangs on the wall, where I see it every day. Yours ever, darling . . .'.

Richard did not go to Canada. He stayed with his parents in Charteris Road. First came the building of the Anderson air raid shelters in the garden. 'We had two,' he recalls, 'one for my parents and one for me; it was very cold and damp. I hated it. I remember the cups clattering on the wall when the bombs began to fall and that we gave all our pots and pans to the war effort.'

Sylvia's immediate local response to the outbreak of war was to run regular jumble sales collecting clothes for evacuees and to abandon her vegetarianism on the grounds that it would be inconvenient. The doctor advised that Richard should eat fish instead of meat. She became Hon. Secretary of the War Emergency Council set up to protect the living standards of working-class families, and was gratified to find that the Ministry of Food in particular was to start a series of Cost-Price Restaurants based on her description of the East End during World War I in *The Home Front*.

Sylvia thundered on, flying the flag for the oppressed and particularly for Ethiopia. Due to many abusive letters and even Nazi and fascist death threats, she was under police protection – an extraordinary turn of events. Following a request from Mussolini, officials at the Foreign Office had actually discussed the possibility of banning the *New Times*, a move which, they decided, would probably rebound in Sylvia's favour.

Italy declared war on Britain on 10 June 1940. Sylvia's son Richard remembers the event clearly. 'That Sunday, several Italian anti-fascist refugees had come for dinner as they often did at weekends, "for a plate of macaroni" and we turned on the BBC evening news. The announcement was like an electric shock which then gave way to a feeling of hope.'

Sylvia was ready. Churchill made his 'Jackal of Europe' speech and Silvio proclaimed in the *New Times*: 'At Last! The long agonising vigil is over . . . We shall free the Italian name from the shame you have cast upon it . . . Hitler and Mussolini are now one: united in crime and dishonour they shall fall together.'

Sylvia was now largely pre-occupied with persuading the British government to accord Ethiopia the status of an ally and the BBC to play the Ethiopian National Anthem on Sundays when other Allied anthems were played. In this she was eventually successful but Parliament still refused to send arms to the Ethiopian guerilla resistance and was reluctant to allow the Emperor to return home to join his troops. She was also deeply involved with the Friends of Free Italy, trying to obtain the release of anti-fascist Italians interned on the Isle of Man following Italy's entry to the war in June.

A few hours spent at the Public Record Office at Kew, browsing through the Foreign Office papers of the war years, is revealing and entertaining. Inter-departmental memos, telegrams, letters to ministers and to various officials in Ethiopia still rustle with anger and irritation at the activities of 'this old lady' and her 'poisonous rag'. 'Sylvia Pankhurst is a blister,' they yelled. All her life, with reason, Sylvia had been an enemy of complacent authority and stuffed shirts. She interfered, got in their way, tripped them up and made them think. No wonder they were not happy.

Haile Selassie finally flew from Britain to Khartoum, in the Sudan, at the end of June 1940. He stayed for several months in a pleasant villa under the name of 'Mr Smith' and was treated with a respect not accorded to him in Britain. In January 1941 he re-entered his country at Omedla ready to rally his compatriots. The Allied Forces then launched a two-pronged attack on the Italian East African colonies from Kenya in the south and the Sudan in the west, and began to make their way towards the capital.

A tiny rebel Ethiopian army, 'Gideon Force', had been formed by the manic-depressive eccentric Lieutenant General Orde Wingate. He was an extraordinary genius with a habit of conducting strategy meetings in the nude, 'his spare bony figure with its crouching gait and the hang of an animal run down by hunting and yet hungry for the next night's prey'.[2] Despite his often wayward behaviour, he was a visionary, devoted to Ethiopian independence and consequently an invaluable source of information for Sylvia later. At his side was Brigadier Daniel Sandford, 'solid, bespectacled and benevolent', who

2. Christopher Sykes, *Orde Wingate*, Collins, 1959.

had longer experience and was better known in Ethiopia than any other European, having farmed there for many years.

Gideon Force, with Haile Selassie at its head, began the arduous and dangerous journey from the Sudanese coast. In overpowering heat and with even camels dying by the way, the journey involved everyone, including the Emperor, manhandling trucks down gorges and building roads as they went.

Addis Ababa was actually captured on 6 April 1941 by British forces, determined to claim the victory before Gideon Force, but the Emperor, to his anger and bitter disappointment, was then barred from re-entering his capital. Orde Wingate and Brigadier Sandford were both disgusted. Eventually the Emperor, taking matters into his own hands, drove with Brigadier Sandford and the tattered remnants of Gideon Force into Addis. Orde Wingate rode into the city on a white charger, wearing his famous sunhat and shorts.

The Times editorial of 5 May 1941 commented:

... the return of the Emperor had greater significance than that of a local victory. Those who knew this African leader during his long regency and brief reign ... and those who met him in exile ... bear witness to his unfailing dignity and his upright character ...

The liberation of Abyssinia has a special importance for the British war effort. Africa is peopled by many races of whom the majority share the condition of subjection to European rulers. They are far from passive subjects. Italian methods of conquest and rule, most of all the use of poison gas against women and children, filled Africa from north to south with horror. And now, when Britain has fought a victorious campaign to liberate an African race from Italian tyranny, have their faith restored in Great Britain.

But for Sylvia this was not enough.

Ethiopia was now classed as 'occupied' enemy territory and the Emperor given only limited power, so Sylvia's *New Times* campaign became that of the 'liberation of Ethiopia from its liberators'. Even then Sylvia could not relax. For when eventually, on 4 February 1942, an Anglo-Ethiopian agreement was reached, it was a far cry from full independence and approached the humiliating status of a British protectorate and so undermined the authority of Haile Selassie.

The Emperor, who was a devoted family man and considerable scholar, was anxious to ensure the best education for his second son and heir, Prince Makonnen, Duke of Harar. He invited John Gardner, then looking after the distinguished library of Addis Ababa, to become the young Prince's 'carer' – officially his 'Private Instructor and Personal Counsellor'. 'The Emperor was very kind to me and I came to know him very well,' he recalls. 'But he was very hands-on too and, without suggesting I was incompetent, drew up his own hour by hour programme for the Prince's tutorials. It was impossible and so I threw it away expecting to find myself in an unpleasant Ethiopian gaol. But no, he left us alone after that. I believe that, in the early years, he was indeed one of the world's great men. But later, as he was growing older, after the two terrible famines [1972 and 1973] there was much feuding behind the scenes and he lost his way.'

Between 10 January and 7 February 1942 the *New Times* carried a series of provocative articles entitled 'Ethiopian Mystery', which were based on material supplied to Sylvia by an angry Orde Wingate. They were in Sylvia's colourful prose but laced with what Christopher Sykes describes in his biography of Wingate as, 'the angry ring of his besetting ideas'. The charge was made that victory over the Italians had been achieved by Gideon Force rather than the British army and that there was a high level conspiracy in London to 'divide and rule' – giving various parts of Ethiopia to Kenya and the Sudan.

There were personal celebrations for the Emperor that year, for his daughter, Princess Tsahai, was married on 26 April, wearing a white velvet dress hand-painted with gold leaf. But tragedy followed all too soon. A few months later she suffered a haemorrhage following pneumonia and died on 17 August. She was only 22 years old. It had been Tsahai's dream to build a fully-equipped hospital in the capital. Silvio Corio, appreciating Sylvia's considerable fund-raising powers and sensing her need for a new cause, suggested that she should start a fund to build the hospital in memory of her friend. This was an inspired suggestion, for Sylvia undoubtedly had a special gift for extracting money from all and sundry.

Lord Amulree, the gentlemanly physician and Liberal peer, was one of those willingly captured by her earnest determination. He met her for lunch at a smart hotel expecting to find a 'flaming modern feminist' and was astonished to see a 'funny little creature' who refused his offers of a martini. 'If you were somebody Sylvia got hold of and were asked to build a hospital you simply helped to build a hospital,' he said.[3]

Emmeline Pethick-Lawrence agreed to become Vice-President of the Princess Tsahai Memorial Hospital Council. Sylvia was to be Honorary

3. Patricia Romero, *E. Sylvia Pankhurst. Portrait of a Radical*, Yale University Press, 1987.

Secretary and readers of the *New Times* were invited to send letters (but wisely no money) to her. Lord Amulree was given the unenviable task of controlling the profligate Sylvia, who was, it seems, liable to buy equipment when there was nowhere to put it and before the money had been found to pay for it. 'She was terrible to work with,' he admitted, but he found her dedication 'irresistible'.

Donations were sensibly to be looked after by another member of the committee and the target was set at a then astonishing £100,000. Committees were set up in London and in Addis. In fact, according to Sylvia, Queen Elizabeth II after her coronation in 1953 also agreed to contribute to the fund but only once it had reached £40,000. No one thought (apart from Sylvia) that the target was achievable in a lifetime, but not surprisingly, although it was ten years before the Princess Tsahai Memorial Hospital accepted its first patients, Sylvia proved them all wrong. During those years she attracted the active and enthusiastic support of Gordon Selfridge's daughter Rosalie, married to a Russian émigré, Prince Viazemsky, and the Woodford sculptress Elsa Fraenkel, both of whom became good friends.

In 1944 Sylvia, at the age of 62, found herself, as in a dream, the personal guest of Haile Selassie, taking her first aeroplane flight. She was greeted on arrival in Addis by the Emperor himself and invited to several private dinners with members of the Royal Family. She was welcomed by officials with arms full of flowers and given a personal car with chauffeur, and a villa equipped with servants was placed at her disposal. To her delight she also found that a street had been named after her.

The Foreign Office, uneasy about the presence of such an agitator in a volatile situation, was strongly opposed to her visit but unable to intervene in a private undertaking. They understood that Sylvia was officially going to Ethiopia to help locate a site for her hospital, but they also knew the Emperor was behind the invitation.

If the British authorities hoped that her journey would allow them a respite from her almost daily castigations, they were disappointed. She had developed close friendships with a number of Ethiopian officials while they were in exile, and two in particular were Eritrean and strongly in favour of Eritrean union with Ethiopia. From an economic and cultural point of view, they argued, union with the former Italian Colony would give Ethiopia access to the sea and greater security. The alternative was to return the country to Italy. It was a hugely complex and controversial subject that Sylvia immediately established as her next mission. She was angry at the way in which, as she saw it, the government was now treating Ethiopia as enemy-occupied territory and was still occupying the Ogaden. Consequently she alerted President and Mrs Roosevelt to what she saw as colonial ambition and lobbied Churchill for full independence.

When she travelled down to Asmara, in Eritrea, the fur began to fly. She addressed a meeting of English-speaking Eritrean chiefs and officials, at which she expressed the hope that the Horn of Africa would one day be united under African government. In Asmara she met for the first time Edward Ullendorff, who was then the young editor of the *Eritrean Weekly News*. Dr Ullendorff believes that 'Sylvia did a great deal of harm' while she was there and that she was not nearly critical enough of Ethiopia or Haile Selassie himself.

Certainly the Foreign Office was embarrassed. The newly established British Embassy in Addis sent a vituperative letter to Anthony Eden. It claimed, 'Miss Pankhurst clearly set out on her journey with her mind already made up; she was going to visit a citadel of freedom populated by brave, virtuous and wholly admirable defenders, beset by the machinations of European imperialists . . . Miss Pankhurst's sense of her own importance, which shelters inadequately behind an affectation of modesty, received great encouragement here when she was met by nearly all the leading political figures . . .'.

Addis itself was still hardly more than a shanty town, but for Sylvia, with flowers in her room and a log fire for the evening, it was an exotic Wonderland. She described it at length in the *New Times* and embarked on a punishing round of visits to schools, war orphanages, handcraft centres and factories; she would broadcast (at length), and wherever she went she spoke with her accustomed frankness and lack of diplomacy. At a British Embassy dinner she said of one die-hard official, 'he was born half dead and now his age is telling against him'. On 7 January 1945 she was present at a gathering of 3000 schoolchildren invited to sing before the Emperor and was distressed at the number of war cripples. The Embassy account of the visit is less than enthusiastic and often gleefully derisory. 'The car provided for Miss Pankhurst's visit broke down repeatedly. She met with the usual unpunctuality both in her chauffeur and the Ethiopians she called on. She received medical treatment and also tried various medical remedies recommended by friends for destroying some burrowing parasites . . .'.

While she was away the *New Times* continued its attacks on British policy, successfully riling Westminster. On 29 January 1945 officials at the British Embassy wrote to Anthony Eden asking: 'Has the latest issue of this horrid little paper come to your notice? . . . This confounded Pankhurst woman who has always been *plus fuzzy-wuzzy que les fuzzy-wuzzies* is making all kinds of disgusting allegations against the British administration and about supposed

British intentions. It may be that the paper has a circulation of five . . . on the other hand the chances are that this sort of stuff gets taken up by the Jacobins and the King's enemies at home and abroad in general . . .'.

Equally annoying from the British point of view was the Emperor's unannounced unilateral decision to honour the wayward Sylvia with two awards rarely given to foreigners: the Order of Sheba and also a Patriot's medal with five palms. For a skilled diplomatist such as Haile Selassie, such a breach of protocol was surprising and seems likely to have been an expression of irritation with the British. Immediately, there was a flurry of inter-departmental memos to London querying Sylvia's right to accept such a medal. Sensitive to the situation, she wrote to Anthony Eden on her return: 'The British Minister afterwards pointed out to me that no British subjects may accept such decorations without the permission of His Majesty The King.' She asked him to pass her request to the King and it seems to have been decided to let the matter rest. Sylvia kept her Orders.

No one disagrees that, as in the East End of London, Sylvia's hands-on, non-political work to improve conditions for the people of Ethiopia made her a folk heroine. In *The Fighting Pankhursts*, David Mitchell comments on her political activity: 'with ungaggable integrity (or busybody insolence according to one's interpretation) she had bitten the hand of the Government which had permitted her to go to Ethiopia, bitten it with a snarl so loud, that it echoed about the troubled Horn of Africa for years to come'.

Back in Woodford after her journey, Sylvia was delighted to find that Richard, now 17, was following in her footsteps. He had developed a real talent for historical research and had written a number of articles for the paper. It was gratifying for Sylvia, as a parent, to realize that her dream for his future might well come true. She now had the security of knowing that as Silvio was ageing and ailing, she would not be alone. There was another Pankhurst ready to join the family team.

26

'Oh Addis Ababa,
Oh Fair New Flower'

'Do you think my active life is over?'

Sylvia to Richard, 1957

In 1947 Richard Pankhurst presented himself at the London School of Economics for an interview with the greatly respected Professor Harold Laski and, to quote the old music hall song, 'mother came too'.

Professor Laski and his wife Frida had been close friends and supporters of Sylvia since her Chelsea days. Frida had also worked with her in the East End and later described that three-cornered meeting to David Mitchell: 'Sylvia was a demon mother. Richard was completely subjugated. When my husband asked him a question, she would answer. My husband got quite annoyed, sent them both away and told Richard to come back by himself.'

Richard was accepted by the LSE on his own merits and there he re-met fellow student and Old Bancroftian, Basil Taylor, who became a regular visitor to Charteris Road. Basil likened Sylvia at that time to Margaret Thatcher. 'She could be amiable one minute and then suddenly she was there, eyes flashing, tense and tight. She had tremendous presence and invited great respect – the sort of woman who made you feel you should stand up when she sat down.' Basil kept a diary of those student days and recalls Richard's arrival at the LSE to study politics and atheism. 'He was so worked up I thought he would collapse from exhaustion.'

9 July 1951

Richard Pankhurst came to tea (and a very pleasant tea mother arranged). He is the son of Sylvia Pankhurst the famous suffragette, . . . he seemed rather unhabituated to greetings and the formalities of hospitality in addition to his hesitant, quietly spoken manner – how different from his mother!

July 10 1951

. . . then to The Holme, Regent's Park for Sylvia Pankhurst's Garden party in aid of the Princess Tsahai Memorial Hospital, Ethiopia. I sold several copies of her recent book 'Ex-Italian Somaliland' and many baskets of strawberries.[1]

This was a full-scale artistic event attended by many high ranking dignitaries. Sylvia loaned her portrait of Keir Hardie, taken from its place in her study, and her friend from Woodford, Elsa Fraenkel, the well-known artist, sculpted a silver bust of the Princess. This was later donated to the hospital.

Elsa Fraenkel had very fond memories of Sylvia. 'Sylvia Pankhurst was a great artist . . . perhaps to compare with Augustus John . . . and a great lady. She was one of the greatest women England ever had', she wrote enthusiastically in a letter to David Mitchell in 1965. They had met early in 1951 when Elsa was organizing a Festival of Britain Exhibition in Loughton, Essex. Sylvia had allowed her Hardie portrait to leave its home again. 'This strong face with its sensitive feelings was a sensation,' said Elsa.

Wednesday 22nd August, Thursday 23rd August 1951

Met Pankhurst . . . went with him to see a new American technicolour film called Lorna Doone . . . Richard said when he met the directors of the 1947 film 'Fame is the Spur' he and his mother were impressed by their cultural vulgarity . . .

Red pepper sauce and boiled rice with grated cheese, rolls and butter and Russian tea. Also with us were Mr Corrio [sic] . . . who is/may be Richard's father if a hint of Tekle's is right. He does not speak English as well as he ought . . . and is rather 'an old dear' and very pleased to see us. He was dressed more as an odd job man in a fawn overall and with no collar on! Indeed Richard is the only tidy part of the household! in his buff gabardine suit.

Basil refers in his diary to two young Ethiopians, Heptab, a student at the LSE, 'a very intelligent, likeable fellow', and Afewerk Tekle, aged 17, who had spent some years at various public schools and was due to join the Slade School of Art in the Autumn. The students played four-handed chess together that evening.

1. She was at this time also busy raising funds to help Seretse Khama, the chieftain-designate of the Bamangato tribe, who had married a white typist, Ruth Williams. Eventually he led Bechuanaland to independence. Sylvia was also working with Jomo Kenyatta against British policy towards the Kikuyu tribe in Kenya, which led to Mau Mau terrorism and Kenyatta's imprisonment.

Since the end of the war, Sylvia had gathered numbers of young people under her wing – this time her charges were mostly Ethiopians. Her kind-heartedness was not without problems (two of the boys were accused of sexual misdemeanours and asked to leave their school). But Heptab and Tekle were among the many who turned West Dene into an Anglo-Ethiopian cultural centre and for whom it became a second home. Tekle was a particular protégé and they remained friends to the end of her life. He eventually became official Artist Laureate in Ethiopia.

Friday 24 August 1951

After lunch I cycled to Woodford. They live in a fairly large detached house . . . I should think last decorated inside and out in the 1920's.

  Most of the rooms had bookshelves packed with books from floor to ceiling on two walls or three . . . The furniture was all old fashioned . . . mostly from junk shops. The garden . . . was a tangled thicket of tall weeds . . . all about 2–3′ high! Sylvia Pankhurst was as usual very charming and quietly courteous . . . we had tea in the kitchen, off assorted crockery.

From 1945 throughout this period, Sylvia was in full literary flood, now focused on the unification of the former Italian colonies of Somalia and Eritrea with Ethiopia. She dismissed any suggestion that Ethiopia was not itself in a financial position to fund or prevent tribal war in these isolated and poverty stricken ex-Italian territories.

She has been criticized for allowing herself to become a tool for the Emperor's ambitions and being blinkered about his weaknesses and alleged resistance to the re-distribution of land to peasants. But Sylvia made her views on Eritrea known independently of the Emperor and before he had made a public statement on the issue. Besides, he was not alone in seeing the value of unification and especially the resultant access to the sea for Ethiopia. A number of Sylvia's Eritrean friends, from the days of their exile in London, were now in the government and supported the Emperor. Cynics might say that their judgement had been corrupted by the source of their pay packets and that many ordinary Eritreans might have preferred to be independent. But on balance her views appear to have been founded on thorough research and a deep conviction that she was right: that the majority of the people believed, as she did, that reunion with Ethiopia would be best for all concerned.

She saw the three territories as a natural geographic and economic unit, which in many ways they were not. She had been appalled to discover that the British had been stripping Eritrea of its assets and that Italian judges had been allowed to remain and preside over fascist-style trials and executions. The colour bar, as operated by the Italians, was also still effective. In her view the worst evils of fascism, which she had fought against for so long, were being allowed by the British to flourish in the Horn of Africa.

Professor Ullendorf called her intervention in Eritrea 'disastrous', whereas Geoffrey Last, Head of the Medhane Alem School in Addis, believes, 'What she wrote was true. The Brits *were* robbing the Eritreans. Of course they did not like what she was saying.'

Over the years, whatever her current campaign, Sylvia always developed a superb international network of diversely gifted, knowledgeable and reliable informants and she provided them with a voice. The Public Relations machine of the Ethiopian Embassy was ineffectual and so Sylvia perfected the art of 'well informed needling' on their behalf. If she was told that the British were misbehaving, she had no reason to doubt it and she would continue to harass and bombard them.

In 1949 the United Nations gave Italy trusteeship of Somalia for ten years. In 1950 a Federation was announced between Eritrea and Ethiopia, which met the Emperor halfway and Sylvia counted as a victory. On 11 September 1952 the Federation was ratified and Queen Elizabeth II sent 'cordial greetings'.

Sylvia also produced many pamphlets over this time on topics such as 'Italy's War Crimes in Ethiopia', which filled Foreign Office filing cabinets. There were also three books: *The Ethiopian People: their Rights and Progress* (1948), *Ex-Italian Somaliland* (1951) and *Eritrea on the Eve* (1952).

One of her main and most outspoken critics was the Oxford academic Margery Perham, who according to Martin Pugh, 'added a certain academic respectability to the Government's imperialism'. And although she did not have Sylvia's inside knowledge of the country, she had always been outspoken in her objection to Sylvia's 'distorted' representation of Ethiopia's situation. Basil Taylor once sat next to Miss Perham at a dinner in Nuffield College and heard her complain that Sylvia 'was at the back' of the Abyssinian authorities' refusal to allow Miss Perham into the country. 'A hysterical rag of a paper,' she said of the *New Times*.

For a brief moment, however, all that was put on hold when in September 1951 an invitation arrived at West Dene. It was from the Emperor and was to the grand opening, at last, of the Princess Tsahai Hospital on 1 November 1951. This time Richard was included, and accompanied by her son and Lord Amulree, Sylvia set off on her second journey to 'that entrancing wonderland'. She remained there by herself for six months, as Richard, under pressure to complete his thesis on William Thompson, who had played so important a part in the early nineteenth-century women's movement, had to return home. Basil Taylor says that Richard was depressed about England – it was smokey, the people miserable and sad-looking and he could not understand why anyone would choose to live there.

During October in England, there had been a general election and Winston Churchill, now aged 77, had ousted Sylvia's other former neighbour, Clement Attlee. On Sylvia's return, she set about completing her magnum opus, *Ethiopia and Eritrea*, an explanation of the Emperor's desire for unification. She finally sold Red Cottage in order to raise the necessary funds for publication. As usual, she was behind schedule for the printers and, as usual, in a rush when she set out to catch the post at the central Post Office overlooking Woodford Green. As she grew older, Sylvia had put on weight and the long upward slope to the Green proved too much for her. On her return she collapsed outside the house with her first heart attack.

Originally there was serious concern and she was not even allowed to feed herself; but her illness brought with it an unexpected and very welcome letter. It was dated 3 May 1953 and it came from Christabel in Santa Monica. After all those years, the sisters were again in touch with each other. Christabel wrote:

Sylvia dear,

This is your birthday and I am writing to wish you, with my love, many happy returns of the day.

I hear you are not as well as usual and I hope that you are improving and feeling stronger in this spring and your birthday month.

Your mind often goes back, I know, as mine does to those good years of our childhood, when we still had Father and Mother and the home they made for us . . .

We had wonderful parents for whom we can always be thankful, whose memory is as vivid with us now as it has ever been.

Your son must be a great joy and a comfort to you and I am sure there is a beautiful bond between you and him,

I view the things that are happening in the world with concern but with strong, with invincible hope in the final triumph of goodness and justice and of glory surpassing all human dreams. God is in his Heaven. All is and must be right with the world.

Sylvia replied by return sending a photograph of Richard, but that letter has been lost. The sisters continued reminiscing and sharing family memories through 1953 and from then until Christabel's death in 1958. The letters are warm but show little genuine emotion and no reference to or understanding of the events of 1913 when Sylvia and Adela were ejected so forcefully and ignominiously from the WSPU. There is no mention of Adela at all.

During that summer of 1953 Sylvia faced an uncertain future. She had always appeared to be indestructible, yet now so many of the threads that had strengthened her long life – Silvio, Emmeline Pethick-Lawrence and Christabel – were soon to be cut.

She made an apparently full recovery and, defying the odds, with Richard's increasingly knowledgeable research launched herself into yet another gargantuan book, the 735-page *Ethiopia: a Cultural History*. It was dedicated to the Emperor, 'Guardian of Education, Pioneer of Progress, Leader and Defender of his People in Peace and War', and was written with a genuine love for the country. The review in *The Times* Educational Supplement was appreciative, even enthusiastic, when it was finally published in 1955.

While Sylvia was writing, appearing on radio and television, attending anti-apartheid rallies and speaking on behalf of Jomo Kenyatta and Seretse Khama, as well as giving interviews to the press and putting up the usual stream of refugees, students and friends, Silvio was sickening. His doctor, Lord Amulree, attended him regularly, but he had developed asthma and was suffering from the English winter.

In January 1954 the *New Times* devoted almost its entire issue to lamenting his death at the age of 77 and describing him as 'a great comrade'. It was a fulsome, yet curiously detached and impersonal obituary for the man who had been her mainstay and loyal friend for so many years and the father of her beloved son. But in private there was undoubtedly grief. Richard remembers how she wept for days and, in view of her recent heart attack and inability to deal with distress, he persuaded her not to go to the funeral in Walthamstow.

In March 1954 came the second blow, the death of her dearest friend, Emmeline Pethick-Lawrence. She did not attend this funeral either, but wrote instead a deeply felt letter to Frederick Pethick-Lawrence:

Dear Fred

I feel you might perhaps think it churlish of me not to have been at the crematorium.

But I cannot help crying so much and getting upset when I care so poignantly that I felt I should only be a bother to other people . . . When Richard's father died, Richard asked me not to go to the crematorium with him because he knows I am like that and he told me he would be upset if I came and begged me not to go. I can't control my tears and all that. You know I am not very well now – sometimes I feel almost the same as before but anything upsets me. I never go out now unless someone will drive me in a car and very seldom at all.

I should have been ashamed to go and be a trouble . . . though I would have desired to manifest my love and admiration for beloved Emmeline . . .

I have lost one of the pillars of my world, the dearest of long loved friends . . .

Emmeline left Sylvia a small annuity of £50, and £100 to Richard.

The latter part of the year was brighter for Sylvia when, in October, the Emperor Haile Selassie returned, this time on a State Visit, the arrangements for which caused the usual anguish at the Foreign Office. The Emperor had just completed a State Visit to the United States as part of his world tour and was exhausted. On 23 July the Ethiopian ambassador requested that the government avoid anything approaching so strenuous or elaborate a timetable as was prepared for him in America. A Foreign Office memo on 20 August despaired (wrongly), 'his English is not good enough to stand up to even a brief interview'.[2]

It was agreed that the Emperor and Empress would arrive on 14 October and stay privately for two restful days before launching into official business. There was to be a State Banquet at Buckingham Palace, lunch at Windsor Castle and lunch at the Guildhall. These events would be followed by a government reception at the House of Lords. By 24 October, Haile Selassie planned to be staying in the Sussex countryside at Withyham with his friend Earl De La Warr, who had been head of the British delegation that negotiated the military agreement with Ethiopia in 1944 and was now Postmaster General. It was an exciting time for Sylvia, who was invited to several of these occasions, including the Guildhall lunch.

In 1954 there were even greater changes afoot and an almost poetic completion of historical circles. Basil Taylor recalls that, at about this time, 'Richard, who never usually mentioned the name of any woman from one month to the next, apart from his mother, began talking about "Rita" and I thought "aha, something's afoot".' 'Rita' was Rita Eldon, the daughter of a Romanian family of Jewish extraction who had emigrated to Britain many years before. She was teaching both in the extra-mural department of London University and at Toynbee Hall. This was where they met. Richard was also busy writing and acting as a research worker at the National Institute of Economic and Social Research. In appearance he was a blend of Sylvia and his

2. FO/371, Ethiopia.

grandfather, the first Richard, but was more self-effacing than either and had a crinkly smile all his own.

Rita remembers all too well the first time that her future mother-in-law came to dinner at her family home in Belsize Park. 'My parents thought I was an adventuress and couldn't understand how I could think of living in the same house as "that strident woman". They were very much against our marrying because they didn't think I could keep her in check.' Rita's first visit to Charteris Road is marked mainly by her memory of the food, 'which was pretty awful'.

Richard had completed his doctorate by now and about this time received an offer of a post in the University of Ethiopia from the Emperor himself. Sylvia, relying more and more on her son, replied that she could not spare him yet. She was, in fact, tidying up the ends of her life. She decided that, with Corio gone, the British having left the Ogaden and the hospital completed, her campaigning role was done.

On 14 February 1956 the National Portrait Gallery Heinz Archive received a letter from Sylvia asking if they would be interested in her two portraits of Keir Hardie. They were. So on 17 February the larger charcoal and chalk drawing was taken down and together with the watercolour were wrapped up and taken by Richard to London where they were gratefully accepted by the Trustees.

Sylvia was very shy about the quality of these works. She wrote: 'I am very conscious that this is only a sketch and was purely a preliminary study to assist me to do a painting which circumstances, subsequently rendered impossible.' And then she added modestly, 'I recognise the acceptance was not for any merit save its subject.'

Later, when there was a problem over deterioration, she wrote again: 'I am troubled by what you write about my chalk drawing of Keir Hardie, the more so as there is no portrait existing by an artist which could replace it. I reflect however that it is upward of forty years old and for many years was lying in a portfolio with no other protection than a bit of tissue paper and the portfolio was not always too carefully handled by my family and domestics . . . it was framed about three years ago . . .'.

She was asked for permission the following year for the picture to be exhibited by Winsor and Newton, manufacturers of artists' materials. They planned to include her among Britain's most 'distinguished amateur artists', to which she responded, 'the designation hardly applies to one who gave up her profession in the hope of becoming more useful and the idea does not appeal to me much . . .'.

When Winston Churchill finally retired in April 1955 at the age of 80, Sylvia reflected in the *New Times*, 'Ethiopia has reason to be thankful that Winston Churchill was Prime Minister and not some other more reactionary, die-hard imperialist British statesman, at the time of her final great struggle to expel the Italian invaders from her soil, for Winston Churchill had certain qualities of insight and prescience which enabled him on occasion to break away from the imperialist traditions in which he was reared.'

On Sylvia's birthday, 5 May 1956, she closed her newspaper. Its demise seems to have been genuinely regretted by many people. Already looking to the future, she published a lengthy eulogy in the last edition, 'O Addis Ababa, O Fair New Flower':

> O Addis, in thy beauty named New Flower,
> Flanked by the Entoto mountains and the plains
> Rendered so smiling by those tropic rains
> That bear to Egypt her perennial dower.
> Great Menelik did build thee for his bride,
> With fragrant eucalyptus set thy ways
> And here St George's silver dome did raise
> And there the Golden Lion, Judah's pride.

Sylvia had finally decided that if Richard still wanted to take the post in Addis Ababa, he should. She was emotionally ready to cut her ties with England and accept the Emperor's generous invitation of a home in his country.

27

Citizen of the World

'I would like to be remembered as a Citizen of the World.'

Sylvia Pankhurst, notes on 'How I
Would Like To Be Remembered'

According to the *Woodford Times*, in 1956 the developers were greedily eyeing chunks of old Woodford that were threatened with compulsory purchase for the creation of smart new apartment blocks and suburban villas. As early as 29 October 1954, Cllr J.M. Dandy was warning: 'There is none in this borough with a large garden or a large plot of land who can feel safe.'

Even so, when the 'Sold' board went up outside West Dene, Sylvia was under the impression that she was handing it over to a private purchaser. Instead, within months of her departure the bulldozers rumbled in and one of Woodford's most historically important houses, like its owner Sylvia Pankhurst, was gone.

The last few weeks in Woodford were too frantic for nostalgia, and much of the time was spent clearing out papers and catching up with correspondence. Richard recalls that it was a dirty business, as many of the bookshelves hadn't been dusted for years. The furniture was put up for auction, although there was little of serious value and most was bought by curious locals.

In May, TBG had re-emerged. She had approached Sylvia for help 'in a humble and complimentary manner', having been commissioned by the *Manchester Guardian* to write Sylvia's obituary. Sylvia agreed and the two women met for what must have been a difficult session, with Sylvia in her usual articulate form.

Even so, the interview was followed immediately by a 'scrawled' seven-page letter, in pencil because 'I have lost the only pen which suited me', and listing all the things she had forgotten to say. Sylvia's name is largely remembered today for her Suffragette heyday. But the conclusion of her letter to TBG paints a very different self-assessment of her life:

> On the whole the victory of Ethiopia has been the most satisfactory achievement I have seen – Votes for Women was marred for me by its partial character and the fact that there was not a sufficiently large, intelligent, progressive and active movement to make it as effective as one would desire. Granted, the vote has brought an all-round improvement in many directions – the improvement has been gradual rather than dramatic.
>
> The fall of fascism and the defeat of the Italians in Ethiopia was complete and dramatic. I have derived much satisfaction from the subsequent progress of Ethiopia and Eritrea since the Federal re-union. I think I told you the 1955 Constitution gives the Parliamentary vote to every man and woman over 21 years . . .

Sylvia was to regret that interview with TBG. During this period the Liberal MP Roger Fulford was researching for his book *Votes for Women* and Sylvia was incensed that he did not call or make contact personally with any of the remaining sisters. Instead, he seems to have relied on TBG for information and, taking into account TBG's bitter split with the WSPU all those years before, the results were, not surprisingly, less flattering than she would have liked and rankled with Sylvia for the rest of her life.

On 1 May 1956 Sylvia wrote to Frederick Pethick-Lawrence: 'Dear Fred, I am going away to Ethiopia for a long time and shall have to say good-bye to you and everyone. Probably I shall never return . . . In many ways I am sad to go – to part with dear friends – and packing and disposing of house and goods is a terrible toil.' In the twenty-six years since Sylvia had first taken baby Richard to the house called West Dene, her life had been largely focused on the country that was to be her new home.

As a girl it had been her one-world vision, her refusal to differentiate on grounds of sex, class or colour that placed her so far ahead of her time. In Woodford in her later years, she had continued to welcome and work with an impressive succession of leaders both black and white.

As a campaigner in the East End she had been inspired by the 'bonnets rouges' of the French revolutionaries and designed her own symbolic red caps to be carried high on demonstration marches. Now, as an ageing revolutionary, she had no need of a red hat – she had worn one and run her stick along the railings of convention all her life.

On the international stage she had played a prominent role in a series of cataclysmic events. On communism, fascism, colonialism, colour prejudice and women's rights she had bombarded the authorities with words. By now the Union Jack had been lowered over most of the Empire. The young Queen Elizabeth II was no longer ruler of India.

On the day of her departure a crisis with Egypt threatened the Suez Canal. It was to prove the final, anguished death throe of British Imperialism and signal the 'wind of change' that was about the blow through Africa.

Hoping that she might, at last, find time to revive the art she had abandoned so long ago, she tucked a secret supply of paints and a palette into her luggage. Then Richard and his mother, with the cat in a basket and the inevitably bursting brown paper parcel tucked under her arm, left for Heathrow in a taxi. Rita was to follow in the autumn. Not surprisingly, on the plane she appeared to sleep but her relentlessly untiring brain was already hard at work. The last issue of the *New Times* may have been put to bed, but Sylvia was already hard at work planning a monthly journal to be called the *Ethiopia Observer*, which was to be a record of the life of the country and its people.

Addis Ababa now had many modern buildings fronting wide, tree-lined avenues, but behind the façade there was still terrible hardship and suffering, and the standard of living and welfare provisions for the poor were unacceptable. Sylvia could see there was work to do.

The Emperor had had to move slowly with the new constitution at first, restricted within the power structures of the time. He had introduced the franchise for all men and women over 21 and was gradually reforming the old system; two years after Sylvia's arrival the first women were elected to Parliament.

She went at first to a state guesthouse for temporary visitors. It had formed part of the Italian legation, high above the city, among her favourite eucalyptus trees. She was welcomed there by two maids, a gardener, a cook and a chauffeur, who were all there at the Emperor's command. Her eventual home was an Italian-built bungalow that she shared with Richard and then, in November, with Rita, who had been appointed librarian at the National Library of Ethiopia. She described it all in a letter to Frederick Pethick-Lawrence in November:

Dear Fred. We at last have a charming house surrounded by eucalyptus trees. We reach it up an avenue of eucalyptus . . . we have some geraniums some of which grow to 8 feet high and mean to have more as well as other flowers.

> There is a room in front . . . which has windows the entire length. This is where
> I work. There is a little veranda where we have lunch and a round summer
> house with a thatched roof with a window on two sides. I believe that will be
> a good place for writing on chilly days (of which there are many at present). It
> is used by a man who does odd jobs and gardening. Later there will be a house
> for him built in Ethiopian style . . .
>
> The earth is very light here. Much of it is red. It is volcanic.

She goes on to describe the countryside and then in a postscript refers to Suez:

> What awful news about Suez! . . . The stopping of the Suez Canal is ruinous to
> this country. Coffee is their greatest export, after that hides, skins, oilseeds,
> honey, beeswax and various agricultural products. Coffee is far and away the
> greatest source of revenue. It goes in largest quantity to the USA after that
> Britain and Europe . . . the East does not take it. The Emperor's visit to India
> is opportune and some trade will result but not to compare, I fear, with coffee.
> Transport problems in this mountainous land make cereals a costly export and
> cereals can be obtained more cheaply from the great farms, highly mechanised
> elsewhere . . .

Rita's parents' fears about the problems their daughter might face, living with
so dominant a mother-in-law, seem to have been unfounded. Rita, being
efficient and practical, took charge and Sylvia was happy to leave domesticity
to her and pursue her own new and rapidly burgeoning enthusiasms. For most
of the day Richard and Rita were out at the National Library or the University
and Sylvia was alone and unchallenged in her own brave new world. The
familiar Pankhurst pattern of work, work and yet more work continued as it
always had. Evenings and weekends were a concept that none of them
recognized, especially as Richard was also helping his mother with the
newspaper, which she wrote in longhand and sent to Manchester for
publication.

In Addis her ramshackle old Fiat became a familiar sight, and as it bumped
around the capital in search of news, she became a national institution. She
brushed aside Richard's justifiable anxiety when she undertook several longer
journeys into the remote and comparatively unexplored countryside.

In 1957 Richard and Rita were married in a simple ceremony at the British
Embassy, followed by a reception in the evening, to which some of the young
Royals came.

*

The three sisters had had very little contact since the parting of the ways all those years before.

In 1957 Roger Fulford's book *Votes for Women* finally appeared and resulted in further correspondence between Sylvia and Christabel, each in her own, very different way eager to protect the family name.

Adela, a happily married devoted mother of seven and a rather jolly chain-smoker of hand-rolled cigarettes, had battered her way, Pankhurst style, into the newspapers time and again, side by side with her beloved husband. They had flirted, like Sylvia, with communism and, like Sylvia, been disillusioned. Adela's good-humoured life was carried on with a chuckle, and in most of her photographs she is smiling. She lived, as did Sylvia, in a disorderly whirl. Clothes and food were not a priority. Tom Walsh, who was apparently equally absent-minded, did most of the cooking, but her children adored her and the feeling was mutual.

Adela was saddened by the way in which women had, as she saw it, abused the privileges of having been given the franchise. She was loud in her assertion of family values and believed that nursery schools and crêches, such as Sylvia believed in, were an abrogation of parental responsibility. Driving around the countryside, she became a vigorous flag-waver for Britain and in 1937 was awarded the George VI Coronation medal.

But Adela and Tom saw developments in Europe during the 1930s from the far side of the world and their position could not have been more opposed to Sylvia's. They believed the rise of fascism to be the timely end of communism. Significantly, and sadly as it turned out, Japan was to become Adela's Ethiopia. It was a decision that was to bring her downfall. She championed its ancient culture and promoted the hugely provocative thesis that Britain, Germany and Italy could overcome the threat of Russia.

In December 1939 Tom and Adela (now 53 years old) left Australia on a lavish tour, paid for by the Japanese government. Adela, being a Pankhurst, wrote a starry-eyed book, *Japan as Viewed by Foreigners*. Sadly, and to the distress of her loving children, her dalliance with the Empire of the Sun was, once again, to lead to imprisonment in 1942 and the end of a rumbustious political career.

In 1936 Christabel had been created a Dame Commander of the British Empire (DBE). She had long ago mastered the art of self-protection and on the outbreak of war immigrated to Hollywood. There she became a star, if not of the screen, then at least of the party circuit, and there she remained for the rest of her life, with occasional evangelical forays to England. Her mission – and she was good at it – was to re-invent Christianity.

Elegantly Edwardian as ever, she won converts to her cause of 'heavenly politics' and the second coming of Christ. Even David Lloyd George, the former damp squib on the Pankhurst fire, grunted approval, and she was invited to Chartwell by Winston Churchill. Christabel was indignant that in Fulford's book she had been given very little credit for her role in the WSPU Campaign. Sylvia was more concerned about what she saw as Fulford's historical inaccuracies and, what she judged, were slurs on her parents. In 2001 Dr Richard Pankhurst commented in *Women's History Review* on these recently discovered 'frank and personal' letters that 'renewed contact did not lead to any real meeting of minds'. Sylvia, writing on *Ethiopia Observer* notepaper, explodes:

> I am horrified . . . by the manner in which he [Fulford] expresses his 'deep obligation' to me while distorting everything I have ever written. This is of course odious . . .
>
> I am most wounded and horrified by the belittling of dear father . . .
>
> I consider it your duty to act. I have done my best to defend the WSPU on previous occasions which means defending mother and you. It is your turn to come forward in the interests of historic truth . . . This letter may appear peremptory to you but it is not intended in that way. It is because I find myself handicapped here . . .
>
> For my part all that sort of atmosphere – I mean the old rivalries of the WSPU the Women's Freedom League etc is utterly distasteful. I never cared to have a position in the WSPU or anything like that. In the East End I felt I was helping people just as I have done . . . in Ethiopia. I would rather shut ears and eyes and have nothing to do with Fulford and all the rest.

Christabel's reply is a multi-page tirade defending, in retrospect, every action of the WSPU and, in particular, those of herself and her mother. She accuses Fulford, who she describes as a failed Liberal party parliamentary candidate, of using his book for political purposes.

Sylvia's reply 'hurrying to catch up time' was, as far as is known, the last exchange between the sisters. 'I have tried in my life to follow and learn what I imbibed from Father and not to desert the cause to which he dedicated his life and energy – human welfare and progress in its many aspects. Often I have been mistaken . . . I was probably mistaken in giving up my art but what I conceived to be duty impelled me to courses which made the achievement of good and successful work in art impossible . . .'. The letter is signed, quite formally, 'As ever, Sylvia P.'

Six months later, on 13 February 1958, in Santa Monica, Christabel was found sitting bolt upright in a chair overlooking the ocean. She had died alone and the local paper reported that no cause had been found for her death; there is no record of Sylvia's reaction. Her death was reported in the *News Chronicle* and read by Norah Smyth, who wrote to Sylvia in 1959 from Ireland, having received a letter from her old friend. 'I was astonished and delighted to get your letters and know you were still in the land of the living . . .'. She had read in the British press that Sylvia had died. Far from it.

There was not much time for social life in Addis, although in the course of her professional activities, Sylvia met many of those in positions of influence and they were curious to invite her to official functions and private dinner parties. Rita was amused that in this new circle the sartorially challenged Sylvia became tied in knots over what to wear for such functions. 'We weren't on any official guest lists,' says Rita, 'so we were never quite sure what was expected and Sylvia, in old age, became terribly anxious not to put a foot wrong by ignorance of the dress code!'

She went also occasionally to the palace to see the Emperor – always by appointment – and having become close to the young princes and princesses, they in turn dropped in for tea at the bungalow. 'The Emperor was well aware of her positive influence on the young Royals,' says Geoffrey Last, who was one of those who got on well with Sylvia. He had been by chance an unknown neighbour of Sylvia's when she was in Charteris Road and he moved to Woodford after his marriage.

Something of a rebel himself, Mr Last was by this time Headmaster of the showcase Medhane Alem School. Many of Mr Last's pupils at the school were the sons of chieftains, from Ethiopia and Somalia, scooped up by Haile Selassie, in order to give them a broad education and lessons in practical politics. Many were amputees, the victims of hand grenade accidents. 'Sylvia wasted absolutely no time at all when she arrived before she was involved in all kinds of charities and social work,' he recalls.

'She came to see me often and we worked together on her many projects. She shared the Emperor's concern that since Ethiopia was a strongly Christian country, too many people were leaving their money to the church; she wanted to encourage them to remember the hospitals and the schools instead when they died.

'It is arguable that, being the Emperor's unofficial mouthpiece, she closed her mind to the fact that some of her idealism was misplaced. There were, for instance, many Somalis who did not want to be united with Ethiopia. They had too much fun with the Italians and wanted their freedom,' he claims.

One of her particular concerns was – as it had been in the East End – for the babies. UNICEF was operating a scheme at the time whereby mothers were issued an allowance of dried milk for under-nourished children. But having had no instruction in child care and no understanding of the value of milk, they would take it away and sell it in the market. Sylvia and Mr Last got together and persuaded UNICEF to let them have the necessary equipment; they then collected beakers, made up the dried milk and boiled it, while the boys and girls lined up eagerly for the treat. 'Health was demonstrably improved,' he said.

'On another occasion we had decided that since my parents didn't understand what the school was all about I would defy the authorities, close it for two days and open instead on Saturday and Sunday. That way parents could come and watch what we were up to. We also twisted the Americans' arms to build us a demonstration house and we held Home Economics classes there in practical surroundings. Sylvia was also involved in setting up a leprosy centre. She was quite capable of picking up a crippled child from the streets and persuading the Emperor to arrange hospital treatment, paying for it herself.'

Afewerk Tekle had been one of her 'charges' when she was in Woodford, and now in Addis she continued to encourage and care for him. She wrote to Elsa Fraenkel with nostalgia for her own abandoned talent: 'I have persuaded him to get a model and do life drawing regularly: models here are so inexpensive and so beautiful! The scenery here is magnificent but one can hardly ever persuade him to leave the studio. I deeply regret being too old and too busy for it . . . Such wonderful colour. Such wonderful costumes and people.'

Miss Fraenkel approached Sylvia for permission to organize another exhibition of her work in London; 'The ashes of fifty years ago,' wrote Sylvia when she replied to say thank you. The exhibition, which was held at the French Institute, was organized by the Woman's Freedom League, the Suffragette Fellowship and the Royal India, Pakistan and Ceylon Society and was opened by the Indian High Commissioner, Mrs Vijaya Laksmi Pandit.

About the same time, Sylvia received a letter from the Townswomens' Guild in Woodford, who were staging a pageant, 'Women Through the Ages', in which they hoped to include Sylvia. She responded: 'Dear Mrs Bird, I am delighted at your enterprise . . . I should of course be honoured by inclusion in your pageant and hereby formally give you my permission . . .'. She had not been forgotten at home.

During the evening of 26 September 1960 Geoffrey Last had one of his frequent lengthy telephone chats with Sylvia. She was in fine form. They discussed her determination to establish some much needed blood banks and her proposal that his school be used as a base. 'She was incensed that only the educated and the wealthy were getting benefits from governments reforms and felt that they should give something back to the community.'

Next day Dr Catherine Hamlin, co-founder of the Fistula Hospital in Addis Ababa, took an urgent call from one of Sylvia's distressed staff. She and her husband Reg, a surgeon, were friends of Sylvia through their mutual concern for the terrible suffering of Ethiopian women during and after labour, where the female mortality rate is the highest in the world. Dr Hamlin had herself trained in Sylvia's Princess Tsahai Hospital. Not only has she written a book, *The Hospital by the River*, describing her fight to fund and build the Fistula Hospital, but in 1999 Dr Hamlin was also nominated for a Nobel Peace Prize.

On a recent journey to London she described what happened when she arrived at Sylvia's home. 'My husband and I were on duty that weekend,' she recalls, 'and went immediately to the bungalow where we found Sylvia in great pain. We realized she had had a coronary. We gave her morphine and oxygen, and knowing what a great friend of the Emperor she was, we phoned the palace and two of the princesses came straight away. Soon Sylvia became unconscious and as I sat beside her, now and then she squeezed my hand until, after about two hours, she died.'

But by the time Rita and Richard returned from a camping trip in the country later that day, to be greeted by their tearful cook, Sylvia, the indestructible, was dead. She was 78 years old. Dr Hamlin said, 'She was an inspiration to us all. I felt privileged to know her.'

Sylvia's passing was marked with dignified respect and regret in England, with a memorial service at Caxton Hall, tributes from leading figures such as Lord Amulree and, of course, her old friend Frederick Pethick-Lawrence. In Ethiopia it was a different matter. The Emperor was one and a half hours away by air in Dire Dawa, in the east of the country. He returned immediately to Addis Ababa and ordered a State funeral the following day, during which he stood to attention for two hours. It was a masterpiece of instant theatre and pageantry, conducted in Ge'ez, a language used only for religious occasions and unintelligible to most of the congregation.

Geoffrey Last was among the 3000 mourners who lined the streets and gathered at Holy Trinity Cathedral. 'It was unique,' he recalls, 'there had been nothing like it for a foreigner, before or since. The entire Royal family, including weeping princesses, the entire cabinet and the diplomatic corps turned out. The Emperor himself stayed to the end of the service and led the mourners as the coffin, draped in gold cloth, was taken for burial surrounded by the Imperial Guard and elaborately robed Coptic priests bearing sunshades.'

The Ethiopian Church did not recognize the name 'Sylvia' and so they gave her a new one. It reflected the affection and the reverence in which she was held by her adopted country. Maybe she would not have minded too badly that, ironically, at the end the life-long devotion of the atheist daughter to the principles of her atheist father were side-stepped. Sylvia Pankhurst was buried in a splendid tomb as 'Walata Cristos' (daughter of Christ).

In one sense it could have been described as Sylvia's last gift to the Emperor. In life she had always been his most active and effective propagandist. There is no doubt he felt sincere affection for her. But he was also doing a great deal for the continent of Africa as a whole at that time. Geoffrey Last offers his own explanation for such a high profile funeral: 'Sylvia was in cahoots with all the early African rebels. The Emperor needed a spectacular unifying event and her death offered such an opportunity.'

The eulogies flooded in from all over the world – from India, Israel, America, Mexico, Japan, Germany – people humble and great who had known her at all stages of her life.

Henry Harben: 'She was a great woman and there are very few persons of whom I would say that.'

Beine Sellassie, her chauffeur: 'Kind Miss Pankhurst, helper of the poor and mother of the orphans, worked night and day without rest, used all her energy and her brilliant mind to help the people. What makes me sad is that there were so many things she wished to complete.'

Lidj Endalkatchew Makonnen, Ethiopian Ambassador in Britain: 'She was a true and loyal citizen of her country and an equally devoted daughter of humanity.'

Princess Rosalie Viazemsky: 'She was wonderful and devoted. She must have had many happy thoughts . . . She will never be forgotten and her name will live for ever.'

Brigadier Philip Banks, who re-organized the Ethiopian police after the liberation: 'I was honoured to call her my friend . . . One who lived for her ideals and never, under any circumstances, anywhere, flagged in her determination to achieve them. She leaves behind her shining name and a brave example.'

From Corio's children, Roxanne and Percy, then sharing a house in Westerham in Kent, came the touching message to Richard, 'wherever we are is your home'.

And from Adela? A telegram: 'Deepest sympathy.'

'Which ever way you turn her memory is there in Ethiopia,' says Geoffrey Last. 'She was like Queen Victoria on her most delightful, non-traumatic days. Unique.'

For many years after her death Sylvia was remembered in Britain and other parts of the world mainly as a Suffragette, but largely eclipsed by her mother and charismatic sister. The fact that her work for the Suffragettes occupied only ten years of her long life, most of which was devoted to the world's oppressed and underprivileged, is barely recognized.

The fact that she was, according to Elsa Fraenkel, 'a great artist' was not appreciated. How thrilled she would have been that in 2002 a number of her paintings, mostly from her journeys through industrial England, fetched around £15,000 apiece at a London sale organized by the auctioneers Bonhams. The paintings had been rescued from a skip by descendants of an East Ender, Ernie O'Brien, who knew Sylvia during World War I. According to family tradition, when Sylvia owed money she would sometimes offer a painting in lieu of cash. For years the pictures were unframed until they were rescued and hung on the walls of the Milton Keynes home of Ernie O'Brien's granddaughter, Molly Cook.

When the paintings were sent to the auction, it was realized that Sylvia herself had written on the back of one, in particular, painted in the potteries: 'to M.G. O'Brien in remembrance of some of the holes you had us out of. E. Sylvia P.' Minnie is mentioned several times in *The Suffragette Movement* and *The Home Front* as a keen supporter of the ELFS and described as 'Little Minnie O'Brien with her bent little legs and pinched face showing childhood's rickets'. This, and a painting of the pottery workers, were bought by the House of Commons at the auction to hang in the library.

In 1962, two years to the day after Sylvia's death, Rita gave birth to a son, Alula, and in 1964 Helen was born. The family lived, much as Richard had as a child, in a whirl of dedicated commitment to causes amidst books and surrounded by fellow activists. Richard continued to edit his mother's journal, the *Ethiopia Observer*.

Like Helen, Alula remembers their growing up with affection. 'We were given a great deal of freedom and friends came to play. Possibly remembering his own rather lonely childhood with a very powerful mother, Dad tried not to over-influence us, but books were everywhere; from the beginning he always encouraged us to read widely and that in turn stimulated our natural curiosity about the world around us.

'My father has inherited my grandmother's drive, determination and love of Ethiopia and he also inherited her ability to use the media as a focus for his many campaigns. Because he appears frequently on the only Ethiopian channel and broadcasts too, he is very widely respected. Through him my grandmother and the Pankhurst name is still well known in Ethiopia.

'It is important to see my grandmother and the Emperor in the context of their historical period. In particular, the issue of Eritrean nationalism was limited in those days. Sylvia was outraged by the way in which the British dismantled the infrastructure of the country when the Italians left and urged reunification. This was what most people wanted. The question of Eritrean independence only became a real issue long after her death. Like the Emperor, she was working towards Pan-Africanism. Haile Selassie was enlightened for his time and Sylvia's wish to reunite Eritrea with Ethiopia echoed his and was reasonable in the 1950s.

'The Emperor had integrity and vision but he did also make mistakes. After her death, as he grew older, he didn't manage the balance between those wanting to keep the status quo and those urging reforms very well. His views eventually became marginalized. He had not declared who would succeed him and so there was no natural heir.'

Alula is aware – and objective – about Sylvia's historical status today. 'There is a growing romanticism among young Ethiopians,' he says. 'They have no personal experience of the Imperial period. They tend to look back on Haile Selassie's reign as a time of peace and contentment when the country was prospering and everyone was happy. My grandmother, by her association with the Emperor and the huge amount she achieved, is a part of that nostalgia for a Golden Age.'

The Emperor died, almost certainly assassinated, in 1975 at the age of 81. The man, worshipped by many as God, was buried beneath a Palace toilet and was not discovered until 1992. His remains were then safeguarded in Holy Trinity Cathedral, where Sylvia was interred, until 2002, when he was given a lavish, but not a state, funeral. In December 1960 the Emperor had returned from a visit to South America to find his entire Cabinet murdered and the Royal family held hostage.

Earthquakes also threatened at the time. The situation was dangerous and Richard and Rita decided they must parcel up Sylvia's papers and send them out of the country for safe-keeping. The Dutch Embassy was situated at the end of their road, and since speed was important, this is how all the boxes from Charteris Road found a new home and were flown to Holland.

Richard has never visited the International Institute of Social History, whose windows look out over the now peaceful waterfront of the entrepot harbour in Amsterdam. In the nineteenth century this was a busy bonded warehouse servicing the huge cacao trade between Holland and the Indies; today it has been transformed into a remarkable repository for rare, social, political and historical books and manuscripts from around the world.

Among them are stored the 5 metres of his mother's original, deeply moving, often pencil-written and illegible, corrected, smudged love letters, poems on lined and scrappy paper, documents, photographs and a torrent of essays, reports and writings. They are the jigsaw of an extraordinary life, each page folded carefully between sheets of brown paper, just as Sylvia was once taught to fold her clothes in America. They are labelled simply 'The Pankhurst Papers'.

They may well have remained Sylvia's most poignant memorial had it not been for the enthusiasm of a number of people dedicated to establishing her justifiable place in history. First, in Woodford itself came Sylvia Ayling, whose house in Monkhams Drive is round the corner from Charteris Road and was once Winston Churchill's Committee Room. Sylvia lectures and broadcasts and has become a one-woman fount of knowledge on all things Pankhurst, in particular Sylvia. In the 1980s she managed to obtain a Grade II listing for the stone bomb, which was by then almost forgotten and overgrown. Soon after, the moss covered bomb was stolen, pitched into Epping Forest, recovered, sandblasted and replaced on its plinth, and today is an object of curiosity rather than veneration.

In 1991 four women who had been friends for many years met to launch the Sylvia Pankhurst Memorial Committee. The founder members of the Committee were trades unionists Megan Dobney and Philippa Clarke, together with Barbara Switzer, President of the National Assembly of Women, and Mary Davis, lecturer at North London University. Former actress turned MP Glenda Jackson is a patron. Their aim was to find and commission a statue to be placed on College Green near the Houses of Parliament.

The Sylvia Pankhurst Memorial Committee website names the proposed sculptor as Ian Walters, winner of the Millennium Prize for portraiture. His previous sitters have included Nelson Mandela, Harold Wilson and Trevor Huddlestone. It is a remarkable statue, a living portrayal of the real Sylvia as she is remembered – eyes ahead, and on the run.

The Committee has met with parliamentary enthusiasm but also some red-tape obstruction from those who would prefer Lloyd George to grace the empty plinth and others who think Rodin's masterpiece of the *Burghers of Calais* is a better idea.

In 2002 a trades union hall in Sheffield was renamed in Sylvia's honour after the picture of Keir Hardie that had hung on the wall was tactfully removed. In its place there is now a maquette of the proposed statue. Her old school, the Manchester School for Girls, has also bought two maquettes to boost the memorial funds.

Tucked among the Pankhurst Papers in Amsterdam lies a long hand-written and unpublished letter. To Sylvia from herself, it is written from the heart and headed 'How I would like to be remembered': 'Let me be counted among the citizens of the world who own no barriers of race or nation, whose hopes are set on the golden age of universal fraternity we believe to come.'

Sylvia would have been very happy to know that her son Richard, in addition to his literary work which focuses largely on the history of Ethiopia, is also agitating for the return from Rome of the Aksum obelisk, 'looted' by the Italians in 1937. He and Rita are also fundraising for a new library for the Institute of Ethiopian Studies.

Sylvia's grand-daughter, Dr Helen Sylvia Pankhurst, is a social anthropologist and head of international programmes for Womenkind Worldwide, an organization concentrating on gender development and the empowerment of women. Helen is passionate about the name Pankhurst, much more so than her father who says he doesn't attach much importance to names. She says she has learned much from him that he learned from Sylvia. 'I think he is very happy that I have stayed so close to his values and to those of his mother.' At 16 Helen travelled widely, alone, went first to a Lycée and then to an international school in Wales and now speaks French, Amharic and Russian. As her father says, with some pride, 'she was an internationalist from an early age'. She is married to David Loakes but has kept the Pankhurst name, They have two children, Laura Pankhurst and Alex Loakes.

Alula married an Ethiopian girl, Konjit Seyoum, and lives in Addis Ababa, where he is one of the country's most respected academics. His children are registered as Hennoq Alula and Heleena Alula. Their surname is Pankhurst.[1] Hennoq and Heleena will grow up equal in a multicultural community with family and friends in many countries. Their challenges will be different but no less great than those that faced their great-grandmother, but, like Laura and Alex, they will inherit the legacy of everything to which she devoted her life. They will be Sylvia Pankhurst's citizens of a future world – though perhaps not yet her Golden Age.

---

1. It is customary in Ethiopia for children to take the first name of their father as their second name.

Bibliography

Asquith, Margot (ed), *Myself When Young*, Frederick Muller, 1938

Atkinson, Diane, *Purple White and Green*, Museum of London, 1992

——*The Suffragettes in Pictures*, Sutton Publishing/Museum of London, 1996

Beasley, John, *The Story of Peckham and Nunhead*, London Borough of Southwark, 1983

Beetham, Margaret, *A Magazine of her Own*, Routledge, 1996

Benn, Caroline, *Keir Hardie*, Random House, 1992

Benning, Keith, *Edwardian Britain*, Blackie, 1956

Blackburn, Helen, *Women's Suffrage*, Williams and Norgate, 1902

Booth, Charles, *Life and Labour of the People of London 1895–7*

Boyle, Josephine, *Builders of Repute, the Story of Reader Bros*, The Suitable Press, 2002

Brakeman, Lyn (ed), *Chronology of Women Worldwide*, Eastwood Publications, Ohio 1997

Brazil, Angela, *The School by the Sea*, Blackie, 1914

Brockway, Fenner, *Towards Tomorrow*, Hart Davies, 1977

Cardillo, Joseph, *Haile Selassie, King of Kings, Conquering Lion of the Tribe of Judah*, The Dread Library, 1998

Castle, Barbara, *Sylvia and Christabel Pankhurst*, Penguin, 1987

Chronicle of the 20th Century, Longman, 1990

Cole, G.D.H., *The British Working Class Movement 1789–1927*, Allen and Unwin, 1932

Cooper, W., *The Passion of Claude McKay*, Shoeken, New York, 1973

Crawford, Elizabeth *The Womens Suffrage Movement*, UCL, 1999

Croom, Helen, *The Labour Party's Political Thought. A Study*, 1985

Cunningham, Antonia, *Essential British History*, Usborne, 1991

Dangerfield, George, *The Strange Death of Liberal England*, 1936

Davis, Mary, *Sylvia Pankhurst a Life in Radical Politics*, Pluto Press, 1999

Dunham, Joanna, *Amy K. Browning, an Impressionist in the Women's Movement*, Boudicca Books, 1995

Europa Biographical Dictionary of British Women, 1983

Fishman, W. *East End 1888*, Duckworth, 1988

Fowkes, Reginald L., *Woodford Then and Now*, University of London, 1973

Fulford, Roger, *Votes for Women*, Faber, 1957

Haber, Lutz, *The Emperor Haile Selassie in Bath*, from Bath History, Vol.III, 1990

Halsey, A.H. (ed), *Trends in British Society Since 1900*, Macmillan, 1972

Hamlin, Dr Catherine, *The Hospital by the River*, Pan Macmillan Australia, 2002

Haward, Ian, *Manchester and the Ship Canal Movement*, Keele University Press, 1994

Holman, Bob, *Good Old George*, Lion Books, 1990

Houfe, Simon, *Sir Albert Richardson. The Professor*, White Crescent Press, 1980

Kendall, Walter, *The Revolutionary Movement in Britain 1900–21*, Weidenfeld and Nicolson, 1969

Kenney, Annie, *Memories of a Militant*, Edward Arnold, 1924

Kenyon, J.P. (ed), *Dictionary of British History*, Wordsworth Editions, 1994

Lansbury, George, *My Life*, Constable, 1928

Last, Geoffrey and Pankhurst, Richard, *A History of Ethiopia in Pictures*, OUP, 1969

Lenin, V.I., *On Britain*, Lawrence and Wishart, 1934

London, Jack, *Beyond the Abyss*, 1903

Marins, Jane (ed), *Suffrage and the Pankhursts*, Routledge and Keegan Paul, 1987

Marlow, Joyce, *Votes for Women*, Virago, 2000

McClean, Iain, *Keir Hardie*, Allen Lane, 1975

McFee, Carol and Fitzgerald, Ann, *The Non-Violent Militant*, Routledge and Kegan Paul, 1987

McKay, Claude, *A Long Way from Home*, Pluto, 1985

Mitchell, David, *Women on the Warpath*, Jonathan Cape, 1966

——*The Fighting Pankhursts*, Jonathan Cape, 1967

——*Queen Christabel*, Macdonald and Janes, 1977

Moekler, Anthony, *Haile Selassie's War*, OUP, 1984

Morgan, Kenneth, *Keir Hardie*, Weidenfeld and Nicolson, 1975

Morgan, Kevin, *Harry Pollitt*, Manchester University Press, 1993

Palmer, Alan, *Four Centuries of London Life*, John Murray, 2000

Pankhurst, Christabel, *Unshackled*, edited by Lord Pethick-Lawrence and published posthumously

Pankhurst, Emmeline, *My Own Story*, Eveleigh Nash, 1914

Pankhurst, Estelle Sylvia, *Writ on a Cold slate*, Dreadnought Publishers, 1922

——*The Suffragette*, Sturgis and Walton, 1911

——*The Suffragette Movement*, Longmans, 1931

——*The Life of Emmeline Pankhurst*, T. Werner Laurie, 1935

——*Soviet Russia as I Saw It*, Soviet Workers' Dreadnought Publisher, 1921

——*India and the Earthly Paradise*, Sunshine Publishing House Bombay, 1926

——*Delphos, or the Future of International Language*, Kegan Paul, 1928

——*The Translated Poems of Mihail Eminescu*, Kegan Paul, Trench, Trubner & Co., 1930

——*The Home Front*, Hutchinson, Longman 1931, reprinted Virago 1977

——*Ethiopia and Eritrea* (with Richard Pankhurst), Lalibela Press, 1952

——*Ethiopia: A Cultural History*, Lalibela Press, 1955

Pankhurst, Richard, *William Thompson*, Watts and Co., 1954

——*Sylvia Pankhurst. Artist and Crusader*, Paddington Press, 1979

——'Sylvia Pankhurst and the Matteotti Committee', *Socialist Review*, Vol.19 Sherborne Publishing Company

——'Suffragette Sisters in Old Age', *Women's History Review*, Vol.10, 2001

Pankhurst, Richard and Last, Geoffrey, *A History of Ethiopia in Pix*, Oxford University Press, 1969

Pankhurst, Rita, *Women's Studies International Forum*, Vol.11, No.3, 1988

Pethick-Lawrence, Emmeline, *My Part in a Changing World*, Gollancz, 1938

Pethick-Lawrence, Frederick, *Fate Has Been Kind*, Hutchinson, 1943

Pollitt, Harry, *Serving My Time*, Lawrence and Wishart, 1940

Pugh, Martin, *The Pankhursts*, Penguin Press, 2001

Raeburn, Antonia, *The Militant Suffragettes*, Michael Joseph, 1973

——*The Suffragette View*, David and Charles, 1976

Ramelson, Marian, *The Petticoat Rebellion*, Lawrence and Wishart, 1976

Robertson Scott, J.W., *The Story of Womens Institutes*, The Village Press, 1925

Robson, John M., *John Stuart Mill*, Macmillan, 1968

Romero, Patricia, *E. Sylvia Pankhurst*, Yale University Press, 1987

Rosen, A., *Rise Up Women!: The Militant Campaign of the Women's Social and Political Union 1903–1914*, Routledge, 1974

Rowbotham, Sheila, *Hidden from History*, Pluto Press, 1973

Smyth, Ethel, *Female Pipings in Eden*, Peter Davies, 1933

Soames, Mary, *Speaking for Themselves, the Personal Letters of Winston and Clementine Churchill*, Doubleday, 1998

Sykes, Christopher, *Orde Wingate*, Collins, 1959

Taylor, Rosemary, *In Letters of Gold: The Story of Sylvia Pankhurst and the East London Federation of Suffragettes in Bow*, Stepney Books, 1993

Thomas, David A., *Churchill, The Member for Woodford*, 1995

Thompson, Laurence, *Robert Blatchford*, Gollancz, 1951

Trease, Geoffrey, *This is Your Century*, Heinemann, 1965

Ullendorff, Edward, (translated), *My Life and Ethiopia's Progress 1892–1937*, 1975

Webster's Dictionary of Biography

West, Rebecca, *The Post Victorians. Mrs Pankhurst*, Nicholson and Watson, 1933

Williams, Val, *Women Photographers*, Virago, 1986

Winslow, Barbara, *Sylvia Panhurst. Sexual Politics and Political Activism*, UCL Press, 1996

Archival Sources

The Anglo-Ethiopian Society

The Bancroft Library, Stepney, for the thesis by Elaine Ellen, 'Women's Suffrage and the Labour Party in Stepney'

Barbara Winslow thesis, University of Warwick

Bath Local Studies Library

The Society of Authors: correspondence between George Bernard Shaw and Sylvia Pankhurst

Carolyn Stevens, thesis, 'A Suffragette and a Man', Rochester University, USA, 1978

City of Westminster Archives

The Glasier Papers, British Library

The Harben Papers, British Library

Heinz Archive and Library, National Portrait Gallery, London

The Historic Manuscripts Commission

The House of Lords Archives

Jackson Library, Michigan

Keele University Archives

The Keir Hardie Museum

London and Essex *Guardian* newspapers

The London School of Economics

Lucia Jones MA thesis 'Sylvia Pankhurst and the Workers' Socialist Federation – the Red Twilight 1918–1924', 1973

The Manchester Central Library, Local Studies Unit

The Marx Memorial Library, Clerkenwell Green, London

Museum of Labour History

The Museum of London, Suffragette Collection, London Wall

The National Federation of Women's Institutes

New York Public Library, the Berg Collection, Isaac Gewirtz

The Newspaper Library, Colindale

Nuneham Park Global Retreat

St Bartholomew's Hospital Archives

The Pankhurst Centre, Manchester

The Pankhurst Papers at the IISG Amsterdam

The Pankhurst/Walsh Papers in the Australian National Library, Canberra

The Papers of the Society of Authors, British Library

The Press Association

The Public Record Office. In particular Source sheet 16 gives useful pointers to relevant files in the sections HO (Home Office) FO (Foreign Office) and MEPO (Metropolitan Police) and PCOM

The Redbridge Library, Ilford

Theresa Lucas, thesis, 'The Pankhurst Sisters after 1914', Warwick University Press, 1987

The Royal Archives, Windsor

The Suffragette Collection and the David Mitchell Papers and recorded interviews at the Women's Library, Old Castle Street, Stepney

The Sylvia Pankhurst Memorial Committee

The Townswomen's Guild

The Working Class Movement Library, Salford

Trinity Kings College Library, Cambridge University, for the Pethick-Lawrence Papers

W.H. Smith Press Office

Index